THE PROTESTANT
TRADITION

THE PROTESTANT TRADITION

AN ESSAY IN INTERPRETATION

BY

J. S. WHALE, D.D.

CAMBRIDGE
AT THE UNIVERSITY PRESS
1955

PUBLISHED BY
THE SYNDICS OF THE CAMBRIDGE UNIVERSITY PRESS
London Office: Bentley House, N.W.1
American Branch: New York
Agents for Canada, India, and Pakistan: Macmillan

Printed in Great Britain at the University Press, Cambridge
(Brooke Crutchley, University Printer)

UXORI

DILECTISSIMAE ET AMANTISSIMAE

ADIUTRICI PER XXX ANNOS PATIENTISSIMAE

AUCTOR

HOC OPUSCULUM

D. D. D.

MCMLIV

FOREWORD

The Thomas White Currie Bible Class of the Highland Park Presbyterian Church, Dallas, Texas, in 1950 established a lectureship at the Austin Presbyterian Theological Seminary in memory of the late Dr Thomas White Currie, founder of the class and president of the Seminary from 1921 until 1943. According to the terms of the lectureship a distinguished scholar is invited each year to address a midwinter convocation of ministers and students on some phase of Christian thought.

The series of Lectures on this foundation for the year 1953 is included in this volume.

DAVID L. STITT
President

AUSTIN PRESBYTERIAN
THEOLOGICAL SEMINARY
AUSTIN, TEXAS

CONTENTS

ix

PART IV. MODERN ISSUES

ABBREVIATIONS

Abbreviations recur in the footnotes as follows:

WA   *Weimar Ausgabe* of Luther's Works.

DG   Reinhold Seeberg's *Lehrbuch der Dogmengeschichte*: third edition of volumes I, II and IV, ii (Leipzig, 1922, 1923 and 1920); fourth edition of volumes III and IV, i (Leipzig, 1930 and 1933).

Ges. Aufs. Karl Holl's *Gesammelte Aufsätze zur Kirchengeschichte*: volume I on Luther (fourth and fifth editions, Tübingen, 1927); volume III on *Der Westen* (Tübingen, 1928).

PREFACE

THIS essay has a threefold origin. As the Foreword indicates, it includes five lectures on *Classic Protestantism and Modern Issues* which I delivered at the Presbyterian Theological Seminary, Austin, Texas, in February 1953. A week in Texas is unforgettable, even for an Englishman who has long known at first hand the great friendliness and hospitality of Americans all over the United States. I take this opportunity of recording my special gratitude to Dean James I. McCord, who made it possible for me to share so much of the Protestant tradition in all its Texan vitality.

It also contains the substance of six lectures which I delivered during February and March 1954 at St Olaf College, Northfield, Minnesota, under the generous auspices of the Louis W. and Maud Hill Family Foundation, and entitled *Our Protestant Heritage in the Modern World.* Living for six weeks on the campus of a famous Liberal Arts college of the upper Mid-West enabled me to appreciate the Protestant tradition in ways which were new to me. It was my first sustained contact with Lutheranism outside Germany; also my first experience of a Lutheran piety and liturgy which had originated in Scandinavia. Further, my sojourn at St Olaf with fifteen hundred students of all faculties was absorbingly interesting, not only because of the warmth of their cooperation, but also because their fine natural loyalty to their Lutheran heritage gives to their university life a notable homogeneity. To them; to the President of the College, Dr Clemens M. Granskou; to Faculty members in

xiii

all departments, and particularly to Professor Harlan F. Foss, I can only say: May the 'Oles' ever flourish!

I am also indebted to the proprietors of *The Expository Times* for permission to make use of paragraphs from an article which I contributed to that journal in 1934; to *The Independent Press* for permission to reproduce parts of my address to the Dissenting Deputies in 1934; and to Longmans, Green and Co. for allowing me to quote the opening paragraph in my William Ainslie Memorial Lecture (1949), which is now out of print.

The original material in these lectures and addresses has been much supplemented however, and the whole entirely recast and rewritten. I now regret that I have not included a discussion of the Protestant doctrine of the Sacraments; but perhaps I may refer the reader to my chapter on 'The Eucharistic Theology of the Reformers', written for the projected composite volume entitled *Eucharistica* which is to be published by the S.P.C.K.

The following publishers and others have graciously allowed me to make certain quotations, details of which are given in the text: George Allen and Unwin (Edwyn Bevan's *Symbolism and Belief*); Hodder and Stoughton (John Burnaby's *Amor Dei*, and *A History of the Doctrine of the Work of Christ* by R. S. Franks); James Clarke (F. J. Powicke's *Henry Barrow*); The Student Christian Movement Press (Karl Barth's *Dogmatics in Outline*, and Otto Piper's *Recent Developments in German Protestantism*); the Beacon Press, Boston, Mass. (Roland Bainton's *The Reformation of the Sixteenth Century*); Mrs Patrick and the Lutterworth Press (Denzil Patrick's *Pascal and Kierkegaard*); the Confraternity of Christian Doctrine Office, Washington, D.C. (*A Catechism of Christian Doctrine*).

If there are other acknowledgements which I should have made I offer my apologies.

All translations from other languages are mine, unless otherwise stated.

J. S. WHALE

WILD GOOSE
POUNDSGATE
DARTMOOR

30 August 1954

PART I

LUTHER

CHAPTER I

THE HISTORICAL PROBLEM

ONCE a year, at the end of October, many Protestant congregations throughout the world celebrate the Reformation. They reaffirm their evangelical faith and churchmanship at that particular time because it was on the last day of October 1517 that Martin Luther nailed ninety-five theses to a church door in Wittenberg. He used this formal scholastic procedure to draw attention to the current doctrine of Indulgences, and to ask that it should be debated in the light of the Gospel as proclaimed in Holy Scripture. His action, as such, was neither unprecedented nor revolutionary; but, coming when it did, it raised ultimate and unavoidable questions as to the character and meaning of the Christian religion, and so led to that crisis which released the pent-up forces of reform. His theses, therefore, are now remembered as a most momentous turning-point in the history of Christendom; indeed, as the beginning of the Reformation.

But history knows no absolute beginnings; and the choice of such convenient anniversary dates to commemorate movements of the human spirit originating in the classic past is always somewhat arbitrary. The dramatic event which seems to precipitate momentous and enduring changes in human affairs is itself bound up with other, earlier events, and is in some sense their outcome. Even the creative genius who dominates his age is himself inexplicable apart from it;[1] and the work of even the most

[1] 'Les plus grands génies sont eux-mêmes entrainés par leur siècle' (Turgot).

I-2

revolutionary innovator is no abrupt knot but a prolonged splice, in the long line of historic continuity.

This inescapable complexity of history is nowhere more formidable than in the sixteenth century, when three figures of gigantic personal stature emerge. In what sense are Luther, Calvin and Loyola the product of revolutionary forces which are bringing a new age to birth? Can men of such creative originality be so 'explained'? The standard histories of the period make us aware that here our facile and partisan generalizations are likely to be wrong; but they also make us familiar with certain formative ideas which were abroad in Western society, and with certain changes which were taking place in its pattern. Historians of all confessions seem to agree that the creative forces of the time may be roughly summarized under at least six heads.

One such force may be described simply as moral; the moral reform of society seems to have been a general aspiration of Western Christendom as the medieval system visibly waned before men's eyes. Indeed, it is part of Janssen's vast and learned apologia for late medieval Catholicism that the Counter-Reformation itself is adequately explained on this basis. The Catholic historian depicts the Church as struggling energetically against the decadence of the age and realizing a salutary reform in her own way at the council of Trent; Luther and Calvin, so far from quickening and hastening a belated activity, were mere destroyers of a moral urgency prior to and independent of both. That Janssen's thesis is disputable is here irrelevant; what is indisputable is the essential fact on which it is based—Christendom's cry for moral renewal at the close of the Middle Ages.

Again, there were new intellectual forces abroad, some

4

of them soundly critical and healthy, some 'precious' and poisonous.[1] The critical temper of the new humanism had a disintegrating effect on the ecclesiastical and doctrinal presuppositions of the medieval world, and tended to weaken the hold of an infallible and indispensable church on the 'intelligentsia' of court and university, and on the rising 'bourgeoisie' of city and town.

Again, forces which can only be described as anti-clerical were the complement to the foregoing. Dislike of monk and priest seems to have been so intense and widespread that the emergence of consciously lay movements throughout Western Europe became its most intelligible expression. The bitter statement of Erasmus that monks were almost universally hated (*orbi fere invisos*) must have meant something more serious than the robust anti-clericalism which characterizes the natural man in every age; it goes far— along with the familiar fact of greed—to account for the widespread dissolution of monasteries.

Again, mystical and pietistic movements in their wide variety, quietly indifferent rather than actively hostile to the outward forms and institutions of historic Christianity, were a similar solvent of traditional religious loyalties in the Rhineland and the Low Countries. Religious quietism of the sect-type became one of the distinctive phenomena of the age.

Again, new political forces were already dominant. Indeed, some historians contend that the new nationalism, profoundly modifying the traditional relation of Church and State, is the supreme fact of the sixteenth century and the real beginning of modern history. They add that what became explicit in the age of Machiavelli's *Prince* had been implicit since the age of Dante; and that with the

[1] See p. 124 below.

5

gradual dissolution of the medieval ideal of a *respublica christiana*—a Holy Roman Empire of two conterminous spheres ruled respectively by Pope and Emperor—nationalism had come to be an established fact a hundred years before Luther addressed his appeal to the Christian nobility of the German nation.

Finally, along with the new political and intellectual energies of the new age there went new economic energies. The agrarian economy of a feudal order of society was now giving place to the money economy of industrialists and bankers; the rise of capitalism in its distinctively modern form is already discernible.

So much for the historian's broad survey of the sixteenth century landscape. Our problem is the relation of a Luther or a Calvin to the complex religious situation disclosed by this sixfold analysis. Popular accounts of the Reformation, consciously or unconsciously influenced by a theological liberalism which reached its zenith at the beginning of this century, have sometimes been blandly content to represent the Reformers as heroic personifications of these forces of modernity. Was not Calvin's Geneva, for example, an active expression of the moral demands of the Gospel and of a fully Christian ethic? Again, Luther's vindication of the Liberty of the Christian Man was surely akin to that intellectual emancipation from scholastic dogma which is the main mark of the Renaissance. Again, Luther's assertion of the priesthood of all believers is surely the positive truth behind the negations of anti-clericalism. Again, were not the Spirituals and Pietists of the Reformation era early witnesses to the principle of liberty of conscience, and to the conviction that true religion is indefeasibly personal and inward, and that the true differentia of churchmanship is not a hierarchy of priests but a fellowship of believers. Again, though the new nationalism is ugly enough in a modern world ravaged by the wars of sovereign states, need we be ashamed that Protestantism took the form of established or state churches wherever it first triumphed? May not this state control of religion, admittedly very dangerous, be interpreted with equal justice as the religious control of the state; the permeation of the community with the values of Christianity? Ideally considered, the state itself is always more than a secular convenience; as a God-given institution it can and should be even a means of grace; 'the powers that be are ordained of God'. Lastly there is the economic individualism of the modern era which few would now defend. But though it is fashionable to make Calvinism the whipping-boy for the worst excesses of capitalism and industrialism, may we not fairly argue that the private enterprise of free men *need* not work out as the enslavement of the Economic Man; and that, ultimately, such enterprise is preferable to feudal servitude? Are not Protestantism and progress virtually synonymous, then?

The modernism and theological liberalism of forty years ago is here somewhat caricatured rather than fairly delineated, admittedly; but, even so, truly modern research on the Reformers and their work has something different and surprising to say. For, surprising and even shocking though it may be to many, Luther was not at all like the average modern Protestant. Essentially conservative by nature, he spent his life in active opposition to four of those six tendencies of his age which we have been examining. So far from being one with the moralists, humanists, spirituals and bankers, he was ranged against them all his life. This very reluctant rebel was no mere iconoclast; and

7

the fact that he helped to bring about a huge breakaway from medieval catholicism does not exhaust the meaning of what he was and did. In its high sacramentalism and its classic credal orthodoxy his understanding of religion was ancient rather than modern. He was far more of a high churchman and probably far less of an Erastian than is generally supposed. In short, the primary and essential significance of his reforming work was religious. Its root is to be sought not in social utopianism, Renaissance libertinism, a new political situation or a new economic situation, but in his rediscovery of biblical religion, and in his evangelical experience of the saved soul. The *Lutherforschung* of the past eighty years leaves no doubt that his positive achievement has to be expressed theologically. He was not only the greatest of the Reformers but also one of the most important figures in the history of religion itself. Though he was not, of course, the sole source of the evangelical faith and churchmanship of the modern world, he was its principal source; and in thinking of our Protestant heritage we think primarily and rightly of him. Even those of us who inherit the tradition of Geneva rather than of Wittenberg have to confess that a greater than Calvin is here. Here is something of enormous significance and importance which seriously changed, both for good and for ill, the character of our Western civilization. When Luther confronted, alone, the majesty and power of half the world at Worms, something very old was recovered, and something constitutive of the modern era was born. What was it?

8

CHAPTER II

LUTHER'S CONTEMPORARY RELEVANCE

THE first thing to be noticed about all serious answers to this question is their astonishing contrariety. They range from extravagant hero-worship to passionate hatred; from an enthusiastic gratitude to a horrified disgust. Three examples of these polar differences of opinion about Luther, during the last hundred years, may illustrate this.

First, in the nineteenth century. To Johannes Janssen, the Catholic historian whose special field was fifteenth-century Germany, Luther was an unambiguously evil man, the modern Judas. To Janssen's contemporary Robert Browning—poet, lover of the immemorial tradition of Italy, and not unaware of the enduring greatness of Catholicism—the Reformer is 'grand old Martin Luther'.

Again in the nineteenth century there is Döllinger, theologian and learned Church historian, friend of Lord Acton and Gladstone, the Catholic who broke with Rome in 1870 over the new dogma of papal infallibility, was excommunicated, and became the virtual leader of the so-called Old Catholics. But even for him Luther was a godless criminal lusting to destroy; one who had forfeited the right be to considered even as a Christian, and whose 'reformation' was not (as Protestants vainly suppose) a return to the simplicity and purity of primitive Christianity, but the second Fall of Man. Yet Döllinger's contemporary Thomas Carlyle—who was brooding over the human scene throughout the same period and writing

9

history with the stark insight of a prophet—could say of the tower-room where Luther had his decisive and momentous experience: 'When I was standing in that room I felt that it was the holiest spot I had ever seen in this world; and I think so still.' Döllinger and Carlyle. Could the extremes of informed judgement be more astonishing?

The third contrast comes from our own century and from its new and thoroughgoing Luther-research which has been so remarkable. Here, on the one hand, is the Dominican, Father Denifle; a very able, though hardly impartial, scholar for whom Luther was the pretentious degenerate, whose real trouble was ignorance and sensuality, and whose case against the scholastic tradition in theology rested on malicious falsehood.[1] On the other hand the massive critical scholarship of Reinhold Seeberg's great *Dogmengeschichte*, and the even more remarkable erudition of Karl Holl's work on Luther in the same field, have effectively discredited this impressive onslaught, refuting Denifle point by point and, in places, very properly 'wiping the floor' with him. Nevertheless, here on the highest level of learned research we meet this same cleavage between serious men's considered judgement about Luther.

The second thing to be noticed here is the special significance of this recurring diversity of judgement. Luther is of such a stature that each generation has to reckon with him. Part of the meaning of his giant stature is this recurring contemporary relevance. In Germany he seems to mirror contemporary issues in successive centuries. In the seventeenth century, the era of Protestant scholastic orthodoxy, he is the theologian, the great Doctor. To

---

[1] The Jesuit Fr. Grisar presents much the same thesis of disparagement; more credibly, however, because less extravagantly.

Schiller in the eighteenth century, and to not a few Catholics of the early Romantic era, he is the great Liberal, championing the freedom of the human mind from priestly tutelage. In the early nineteenth century, just after the Napoleonic era, he is the great German, prototype of German piety, virility and independence, the national hero; and therefore coupled with Marshal Blücher on wayside inn signs and other forms of popular art. This, too, is the meaning of Goethe's verdict in 1827. Goethe had no great sympathy with Luther or Lutheranism,[1] but he did recognize and say that Luther's genius was no passing phenomenon but enduringly provocative and creative, and long destined to be so.

Indeed, rather to our surprise, we have come to realize this for ourselves during the past thirty years. For us, too, Luther has become a contemporary. Before the First World War, in the heyday of modernism and theological liberalism, we thought that we might politely ignore Luther as a theologian. After all, did he not believe in the devil, and original sin; and even the wrath of God? It was faintly embarrassing. Further, Ernst Troeltsch had been telling us that the real break between the medieval and the modern worlds was not the sixteenth century (with its 'Renaissance' and 'Reformation') but the eighteenth, the so-called Age of Enlightenment; and that much of Luther's distinctive theology, therefore, had now no more than an antiquarian interest. In spite, said

---

[1] His attitude to the French Revolution is that of Erasmus to the Reformation. Hence his famous lines coupling the two 'disturbances':

'Franztum drängt in diesen verworrenen Tagen, wie einstmals
Luthertum es getan, ruhige Bildung zurück.'

(In these days of disturbance the French are putting back the clock of civilization just as the Lutherans did.)

Troeltsch, of Luther's wonderful originality in rediscovering the evangelical heart of the New Testament and in asserting the liberty of the Christian man, he was essentially medieval in the content and the categories of his thought; and his achievement consisted in no more than a rearrangement of ideas still intrinsically medieval.[1] That was just over forty years ago; and much has happened since 1911, in the field of theology as elsewhere. Much confident liberalism has become discredited as naïve. Much modernism, so called, is out of date because it is no longer modern. If the modern generation wishes to hear the distinctively modern note in theology, it has to listen to a Barth, a Niebuhr or a Nygren (to name only these three); and it then realizes that these modern theologians have in their turn been listening intently to Kierkegaard, Pascal and Luther. In short, truly modern theology is rediscovering some of the riches of its ancient past, and it may be said to have three notable characteristics.

First, it is realist. Two world wars in one generation have taught us half-forgotten truths about man and sin, and brought back an older realism into theology. The Reformers are not so far away after all. The famous debate about the human will, which took place in 1525 between the 'once-born' Erasmus and the 'twice-born' Luther, may serve as a yardstick for measuring our new sense of proximity to the Reformers, for it points the contrast between the self-confidence of the nineteenth century and the moral disillusionment of the twentieth.

Luther, like Augustine a thousand years before him, had insisted doggedly that as the natural man is the bondslave of sin, his will is 'free', not to choose the good, but only to

[1] 'Eine Umformung der mittelalterlichen Idee.'

express its own enslavement to evil. This seemed extravagantly pessimistic and even unwholesome to the plain man of the nineteenth century, for whom the humanism of Erasmus was saner, and more in line with the sturdy moralism and evolutionary optimism of the Age of Progress. For Erasmus, virtually content with a Pelagian psychology of volition, had insisted that man's will is unambiguously free, and that he can fulfil the demands of the moral law if he will. Erasmus had too little experimental understanding of the profound psychology of Rom. vii ('the evil that I would not, that I do') to appreciate the insight of Luther's dictum: 'a debere ad posse non valet consequentia' ('*can* is no necessary result of *ought*').[1] And in spite of Evangelical Revival and Oxford Movement, which met the rationalism of the age with the witness of supernatural and sacramental religion, the average modern Protestant from the generation of Benjamin Franklin to the generation of H. G. Wells shared the theological presuppositions of Erasmus rather than those of the Reformers.

Doubtless, very many still do so. Yet serious people in the twentieth century have found themselves forced to reckon with the paradox, so offensive to their predecessors, that man is evil as well as good, contemptible as well as

[1] Cf. Augustine, *de Gratia Christi*, xxxiii, 36: non est autem consequens ut qui habet donum scientiae, quo noverit quid agere debeat, habeat etiam charitatis ut agat (a man may be gifted with the knowledge which tells him what he ought to do; it doesn't follow that he will also be gifted with the grace enabling him to do it). Of his debate with Erasmus in 1524 (Is the will free or enslaved?) Luther writes: 'I cannot praise you enough that you alone have attacked the essential thing, the real knotty problem; instead of pestering me with tiresome trifles about the papacy, purgatory, indulgences and other futilities of the same order. You have truly seized me by the throat.' And Calvin says in one of his sermons on Job (*Opera*, xxxiii, 526): 'Here is the greatest difference which we have with the papists.'

admirable: that he is not only the soaring idealist capable of heroism, self-sacrifice and even sainthood; there is also something mysteriously, radically and permanently wrong with him; he is capable of pride, envy and all uncharitableness, of appalling brutality and degradation. The pilgrim making his way to the celestial city (*homo viator*) is also a wolf to his brother man (*homo homini lupus*), and at no time in human history was it more true than now that man's inhumanity to man makes countless thousands mourn. The experience of the twentieth century leaves little room for the sentimental optimism which supposes that sinful man can discover within the actual system of his civilization the saving power which he needs. As we look back to its opening decade we see that we were claiming most confidently to save ourselves just when there was least evidence of our ability to do so.

In short, this disharmony in man is fundamental; it is his abiding predicament. And if it be argued that the unimaginable marvels of applied science may yet transform man's world and so deliver him, the answer is that he is not good enough for science; his bigger and better bombs make nonsense of his blue-prints for Utopia.[1] Modern man is discovering the truth of Nietzsche's dictum that his culture is ever in danger of destruction by the very instruments of culture.

But what, it may be asked, of the fundamental, simple goodness of ordinary, decent people? May we not fall back on that? Would it not be sophistry to deny that there is much nobility and moral beauty in human life everywhere? Yes, of course. And the Reformers did not deny it. But their incontrovertible point is that even this human good-

---

[1] And, anyhow, salvation is not synonymous with a social Utopia, but is concerned with the eternal God and his eternal kingdom.

ness is tainted with man's proud and fatal egocentricity; and that it is far less disinterested, wholehearted, deep-rooted and stable than good and cultivated people suppose. The modern generation was at first a little affronted, and then increasingly interested, to discover that though it may dislike this from Augustine and Luther, it has to take it from Freud.[1] Nauseated by a terminology which included 'original sin' and 'total corruption' it has had nevertheless to rediscover the reality for which such terms stood; namely that every child of Adam is strangely corrupted—no weaker word will do—at the centre of his moral being: that is, in his will. This is the submerged rock on which utopian idealism in its many forms is always being shipwrecked. To take a trivial example: a popular versifier of a generation ago dismissed man's innumerable gods and faiths, and pronounced that

> Just the art of being kind
> Is all the sad world needs.

An unexceptionable sentiment, yet not very profound. For 'just the art of being kind' is just the problem which has been with man from the beginning and, like the tares in the wheat-field, will be with him to the end. To take another, less trivial, example: Thomas Carlyle, the 'Great Impatient' of the Victorian age, repudiated much of the Christian orthodoxy of his day and had some hard things to say of the Church and its preachers, even though the essential

---

[1] Freud has shown that even when we suppose our thinking to be open, honest and free from all alien influence, it is nevertheless largely influenced and even controlled by subconscious desire. The cool temper of the cultivated observer is less impressive than it was, therefore. 'Il se flattait d'être sans préjugés et cette prétention était à elle un gros préjugé' (he complacently assumed that he was a man without prejudices, not realizing that this very assumption was blatant prejudice). (Anatole France, *Le Crime de Sylvestre Bonnard*.)

stuff of Scotland's Calvinism never ceased to smoulder, and sometimes to blaze, in his deepest being. Seated once with his ageing mother by her fireside at Ecclefechan, and inveighing against the preachers of his day, he exclaimed: 'If I had to preach, I would go into the pulpit and say no more than this: "All you people know what you ought to do; well, go and do it."' His mother continued knitting in silence, and then replied: 'Aye Tammas; and will ye tell them how?' All that matters of the issue between Pelagius and Augustine, or between Erasmus and Luther, is there summed up. Man needs redeeming grace if he is to be lifted to a new level of moral freedom; nothing else will meet his case. It is part of the realism of modern theology, therefore, that it has again become concerned with what the Reformers knew as the Fall and Original Sin.

In the second place, modern theology has become increasingly 'existential'. Here this mouth-filling word means that if there be a God, concern with him is necessarily a life-and-death matter, involving not so much one's intellect as one's whole existence. The aesthetic attitude of the mere observer is impossible. A purely philosophical theology, seated in its Aristotelian armchair and presenting arguments for the existence of God, may give us theism— an Ultimate beyond phenomena,[1] a regulative concept for unifying the data of experience; what William Temple once called 'the logical glue which holds multiplicity together'. But theism is very different from belief in God. Necessary Being—the *ens necessarium* of scholastic philosophy—is not the God and Father of our Lord Jesus

---

[1] For a fine example of this appeal to the *philosophia perennis*, see A. E. Taylor's remarkable chapter in *Essays Catholic and Critical* (S.P.C.K. 1926), pp. 31–81.

Christ. Indeed, the knowledge of God is not a theological blueprint which we may scrutinize when in the mood, and file for reference. It is not one topic among the many offered for our consideration in a university lecture-list. The eternal Ground of all being cannot be an object of study as, say, feudalism or Homer or the stratosphere are objects of study. A god whom we could discuss in a leisurely way, with our feet up, would not be the living God with whom we have to do, but an idol fashioned out of our aesthetic speculation.

This is in part what Luther meant when he said: 'To believe in God is to go down on your knees' (*habere deum est colere deum*).[1] From the outset he had had the suspicion that all philosophical investigation of theological issues involves something very different from the God of Christian revelation; it involves what Luther's modern compatriots call a *Grenzbegriff*; that is, a boundary-concept which expresses the very boundary or limit of thought, and beyond which further thought is impossible; an ultimate like the *ne plus ultra* which the old cartographers printed at the edges of their maps. That there *is* an Ultimate, the *deus absconditus*, Luther does not doubt. But what this Hidden God is in the mysterious depths of his unknowableness is his own secret. 'Das hat er für sich', says Luther. The only God whom Luther knows or will know is the *deus revelatus*, God in the flesh (John i. 14). And when he says that the only way of discovering God is to experience and adore him in Christ, he means that God is real only when I leave the Aristotelian world of scholastic speculation and enter the biblical, Hebraic world of decision and active obedience. There God confronts me, in person, as it were;

---

[1] Cf. the profound and searching remark of Julius Wellhausen: 'Prayer is the only adequate confession of faith.'

in the person of the Son, our Saviour. And I no longer speak *of* him but *to* him. Or, rather, he speaks to me. I hear his word, and I have to answer; I have to say yes or no.

In short only secondarily is real faith intellectual assent to authoritative teaching; primarily it is what Karl Barth has called *Entscheidung* (decision); it involves one's whole being and existence. This is what Luther meant when he insisted that faith, in the biblical and Pauline sense, is not so much *assensus* as *fiducia*. Primarily and essentially it is personal commitment; it is confident trust in the amazing, irrational wonder of forgiveness, God's redeeming love in Christ. It is the risk, the self-abandonment, the leap—the agonized, despairing, joyous leap—across the abyss of sin and guilt, despair and death.

It is not surprising that in much contemporary theology this biblical existentialism coincides with a rediscovery of Pascal. For Pascal's *Amulet* or *Memorial*, one of the most remarkable autobiographical fragments in the history of religion, is nothing less than a wonderful expression of faith as *fiducia*: total commitment. Further, it contains the famous and much quoted phrase: 'Dieu...non des philosophes et des savants', which might have been Luther's own summary of his mistrust of metaphysic, and of his biblical attitude to the philosophical theology of the Schools. It is some indication, too, of the changed viewpoint of our time that Professor George Saintsbury's brilliant and sympathetic article on Pascal in the eleventh edition of the *Encyclopaedia Britannica* (1911), refers to this document as 'some lines of incoherent and strongly mystical devotion'. Modern theology does not find them incoherent. They are entirely and coherently biblical, and they might well serve as a commentary on Luther's attitude to the whole Bible as 'the crib wherein Christ is laid'.

The bare facts about the *Memorial* are that on the evening of Monday, 23 November 1654, after a period of intense and agonizing prayer, Pascal had an ineffable experience of the 'extraordinary assistance' of God's grace. He recorded it on a scrap of paper, which is still extant; and then copied it on parchment which he carried to the day of his death, sewn into the lining of his coat. It speaks for itself.[1]

The year of grace 1654
Monday, 23rd November, day of St Clement, Pope and martyr, and others in the martyrology.
Eve of St Chrysogon, martyr, and others.
From about half-past ten in the evening
until about half-past twelve.

FIRE

God of Abraham, Isaac and Jacob; not of the philosophers and scientists.
Certainty, certainty. Feeling. Joy. Peace.
God of Jesus Christ.
Deum meum et Deum vestrum.
Thy God shall be my God.
Forgetfulness of the world and of all, except God.
He is to be found only by the ways taught in the Gospel.
Greatness of the human soul.
O righteous Father the world hath not known Thee
but I have known Thee.
Joy, joy, joy, tears of joy.

---

[1] I take the translation of the *Memorial* from Dr Denzil Patrick's *Pascal and Kierkegaard*, vol. I, p. 76 (Lutterworth Press, 1947). The Scripture references, after the word 'FIRE,' are in the following order: Exod. iii. 6; Matt. xxii. 32; John xx. 17; Ruth i. 16; John xvii. 25; Jerem. ii. 13; Matt. xxvii. 46; John xvii. 3. Pascal's FIRE seems comparable with the light of which the mystics speak. Cf. St Augustine's 'unchanging light' (*lux incommutabilis, Conf.* VII, 10, 17) and Vaughan's 'great Ring of pure and endless light'; also his 'deep and dazzling darkness' in the poem entitled *The Night.*

2-2

I separated myself from Him.
Dereliquerunt me fontem aquae vivae.
My God, wilt Thou forsake me?
May I never be separated from Him eternally.
This is life eternal that they might know Thee, the only
true God, and Jesus Christ Whom Thou hast sent.
Jesus Christ
Jesus Christ
I separated myself from Him. I fled Him, renounced
Him, crucified Him.
May I never be separated from Him.
He is to be kept only by the ways taught in the Gospel.
Renunciation, entire and sweet.

In the third place, much modern theology is not only realist and existential; it is paradoxical. This is not just a fashionable fad; the current cult of Kierkegaard. Nor is it a woolly-minded evasion of the demands of logic. Some of the profoundest insights of religion may only be stated paradoxically: that is, in terms of logical contradiction. It is understandably fashionable in these days, therefore, to make much of Kierkegaard, that Scandinavian prophet of a hundred years ago, who was the great adversary of Hegel, and of all philosophical distortions of Christianity. Kierkegaard was a voice crying in the wilderness, for he was almost the only Christian thinker in the nineteenth century to understand the paradoxical character of the Christian faith.[1] It is this which makes us newly aware to-day of his kinship with Pascal in the seventeenth century, and with Luther.

For Luther abounds in paradox. His exuberant variety of statement, his truculent irrationalism, his self-contradic-

---

[1] So Otto Piper, *Recent Developments in German Protestantism* (S.C.M. 1936), p. 112. See below, p. 71, n. 2.

tions, are notorious.[1] He is too close to experience and to the Semitic genius of the Bible to endure the strait waistcoat of a strictly systematic theology. Whereas his successors, beginning with Melanchthon, do aim at logical sequence, formal structure, the closely articulated system (and reach it, alas), Luther's mind is agile, inexhaustibly creative, bold to the point of recklessness. Often his most distinctive insights are expressed in paradoxes; in the daring synthesis of logical opposites. There are five in particular which must concern us here.

[1] On the other hand modern scholars such as Adolf Köberle, Holl, and Pelikan insist that Luther's lack of theological system has been much exaggerated.

CHAPTER III

THE PARADOX OF LAW AND GOSPEL

T HE first of these paradoxes is that of Law and Gospel. Every informed Christian knows what the heart of the Christian revelation is, and why it is called εὐαγγέλιον, Gospel, good news. Though we are sinners who deserve κακαγγέλιον, the bad news of God's just wrath, God loves us with an everlasting love. The Gospel is the amazing declaration of forgiveness. Yes. But at once a notorious problem emerges, inevitably: all theologies of atonement—Greek and Latin, Catholic and Protestant, ancient and modern—have had to grapple with it. It is this: how are we to proclaim this forgiving love of God without making light of sin? Surely sin *is* sin, with its damning guilt upon it for ever. Stopford Brooke[1] put the point in crude but telling rhyme:

> Three men went out one summer night;
>   No care had they, or aim;
> They dined and drank; ere we go home
>   We'll have, they said, a game.
>
> Three girls began that summer night
>   A life of endless shame,
> And went through drink, disease and death
>   As swift as racing flame.
>
> Lawless and homeless, foul, they died;
>   Rich, loved and praised the men;
> But when they all shall meet with God
>   And justice speaks—what then?

[1] I owe the reference to the late Dr Sidney Cave.

Exactly. The tension between justice and forgiveness, between wrath and love, between law and gospel, is here inescapable.

Now it is Luther's fundamental experience that sinful man is saved by grace and by faith alone; but though this is the unalterable basis of his theology, he takes the divine law, the moral law, very seriously. No churchman before his time had taken it more seriously. Indeed, his great evangelical emphasis on justification by faith cannot be understood except in its relation to law. Suppose a man had suddenly to give a comprehensive summary of the Gospel, which could go into a telegram of a dozen words or be spoken to a dying man in a sentence: what should he say? Luther says it in five words: 'Christus Gottessöhn ist unser Heiland.' That is: Christ the Son of God is our Saviour. In so succinct and pregnant a sentence every word matters, especially that last word 'Heiland', or 'Saviour'; and it meant for Luther just what it must mean if language means anything, namely that apart from the Saviour we sinners are lost. He went on to say that it is the primary function of the law to tell us so. He took the law of God with an urgent and agonizing seriousness, and did not soft-pedal its moral demands.[1] As he once put it: 'God hates sin and the sinner; and necessarily; otherwise he would be unrighteous, and a lover of sin.' That is, the holy law of God has a holy and consistent wrath as its inevitable correlative. 'Depart from me, ye that work iniquity.' Luther brought again to a place of honour in theology that Pauline doctrine of

[1] Indeed, his explicit and thoroughgoing interpretation of the death of Christ as penal and vicarious satisfaction for man's sin, cannot be understood on any other basis. His doctrine of the Work of Christ *as a whole* contains much more than this, however; and as it is of central importance (see the *Schmalkald Articles*, part ii, quoted on pp. 43–4 below) an additional note is added as an appendix (pp. 74 ff.).

'Wrath' as a reality in God, which had been pushed into the background, chiefly by Augustine. And this new emphasis on the Pauline ὀργή θεοῦ meant a new turn of thought, not only about God, but also about his world. The thought of the Christian centuries had constantly been influenced, and sometimes menaced, by the Platonist mysticism which would see the world and its history as no more than a copy or shadow of the Real—time itself being but the moving image of the Eternal. But in saying that God is wrathful, Luther was again vindicating the reality and independence of God's creation. The world of men is real, and responsible to God its maker and judge. The moral law, which demands absolute realization, once again becomes the only valid norm of thought about the world.[1]

But for Luther this thought is always twofold. It is as terrifying as it is sublime. He sees that only the perfect may stand before him 'who is of purer eyes than to behold iniquity'. He sees, too, that no one can; for 'there is none righteous, no not one'. And if someone of less sensitive and scrupulous conscience than Luther should say at this point that this estimate of our abiding human predicament is too extreme in its pessimism, and that it is surely possible to keep the Ten Commandments, Luther would reply that the Commandments of the law do more than say: Thou shalt not kill; thou shalt not commit adultery; thou shalt not covet. The teaching of Christ in the Sermon on the Mount makes it terrifyingly clear that obedience to this law is much more than outward observance and overt act;

[1] It should be added that Luther was fully aware that the concept of 'wrath' as used of God, cannot escape the dangers of anthropomorphism. By *ira*, however, he did not understand human anger in its fitfulness and caprice, but that holiness and immutability of God's judgement on sin, of which our word 'wrath' is an obviously imperfect analogue.

it is concerned, rather, with inward disposition and covert inclination—the thoughts and intents of the heart. To give but one devastating example from that Sermon: looking on a woman to lust after her has the same meaning as actual adultery in the eyes of God (Matt. v. 28). But who then can be saved? For what man is there who has not so lusted? Who has not coveted? Empirically speaking, the law can never be fulfilled by fallen man.

> Not the labours of my hands
> Can fulfil Thy law's demands.

Is there more hope for us if we turn from the particularities and negations of the ancient law to the twofold commandment which sums up its positive meaning? 'Thou shalt love the Lord thy God with all thy heart, and with all thy soul, and with all thy mind, and with all thy strength: this is the first commandment. And the second is like, namely this, Thou shalt love thy neighbour as thyself. There is none other commandment greater than these.'[1] But here too, though the minatory 'Thou shalt not...' is absent, the Law is still concerned with the thoughts and intents of the heart, and at the highest conceivable level. Indeed, this pure, disinterested and wholehearted love towards God which is man's greatest obligation and his supreme good, is man's supreme difficulty. How is he to be set free from the fiercely strong impulse to love himself? For the saints and doctors of the Christian centuries this is the central religious issue. Can human love ever be completely disinterested? If not, how can self-love (*amor sui*) be compatible and reconcilable with pure love towards God (*amor Dei*)? And if such love alone be the fulfilling of

[1] Mark xii. 30–1; cf. Deut. vi. 4.

25

the Law, can the Law ever be fulfilled? Thus we come back to the original dilemma: what man, as man, must do is what man, as sinner, cannot do.

Will the horns of the dilemma be less sharp if we look for help to the great mystical tradition of the Middle Ages; to Plotinus, St Augustine, St Bernard and Eckhart, for whom, in spite of their obvious differences in method, thought and language, *amor Dei* is a common theological theme, since it is the way of redemption and therefore the chief end of man? To put this difficult question in another way: Why did Luther say No to mysticism, in spite of his acknow-ledged debt to St Augustine and St Bernard—the one a prince among mystical theologians, and the other a prince among Christian mystics?

Almost any generalization about mysticism will be erroneous in some respect, but our answer must begin with one. The medieval mystic was the residuary legatee of Platonism, and the pattern of his thought was therefore dualist: he conceived of man in terms of an outward and an inward element, a lower and a higher self; and of redemp-tion as an 'ascent' (ἀναγωγή) from the one to the other. Indeed, redemption is sometimes described as an 'inward' ἀναγωγή because the mystic seeks God at the very centre of the individuality, the deep heart's core. Several synony-mous images or metaphors common to the mystical tradi-tion are used to describe this precious and all-important 'inner' or 'higher' reality, the final 'ground' or 'needle-point' of man's being—which is not only akin to but is also a fragmentary part of the eternal 'substance' of the Divine. It is the ground of the soul (*Seelengrund*); it is the peak or topmost ridge (*apex mentis, acies mentis*) to which man must climb if he is to come to the ultimate ecstasy of union, to oneness with the One; it is the uncreated divine spark, the essential divinity of the soul (*Fünkelein, scintilla animae*); it is the spirit's ivory tower (*Seelenburg, Hütte des Geistes*), and though it be shut up in the prison-house of the body,[1] its ultimate release therefrom for union and fusion with the Divine is the great possibility and meaning of redemption. Thus, man has power to effect his redemption by following the *ordo salutis* with its specific technique of bodily and spiritual exercises—the three stages of purification, illumination and final union. He may deliver the divine nucleus of the soul from the baneful influence of the world ('this muddy vesture of decay') as he climbs to the peak of mystic vision, to the final consummation of ἕνωσις. In short, speaking very generally, mysticism's answer to the human predicament was that, in spite of sin and guilt, man has at the ground of his being an uncreated and indestructible link with God; a bridge for his ultimate deliverance.[2]

Few words in the vocabulary of religion are used more loosely and inexactly than the word 'mysticism'. Strictly understood, it should describe a distinctive and relatively rare phenomenon, which could only be identified with the warmth and intensity of normal Christian experience if its special and proper characteristics were ignored—namely a distinctive technique of spiritual discipline, a corresponding terminology, and that final loss of conscious personality in the ecstasy of the mystic vision which is its supreme differentia. Yet it can hardly be denied that there have been orthodox Christian mystics; and if the essential meaning of mysticism may be seen in its operation and

---

[1] τὸ μὲν σῶμα ἐστιν ἡμῖν σῆμα (Plato, *Gorgias* 493 A).

[2] See R. Seeberg *DG*[4], III, 136–7; E. Gilson, *The Spirit of Medieval Philosophy*, Appendix to ch. 14; J. Burnaby, *Amor Dei*, 260–1; A. Nygren, *Agape and Eros* (E.T.), III, 415–19.

outcome—the personal knowledge and love of the living God—Luther himself was a Christian mystic, as were St Paul and Pascal, St Francis Xavier and Charles Wesley, George Fox and Zinzendorf. Luther's faith was inward, personal and of lyrical fervour; that he was a new man in Christ is the indisputable evidence of his *Postille*, his letters, hymns, prayers, sermons; his prefaces to the several books of the newly translated Bible, his many expositions of the Lord's Prayer; it is impossible to read the glowing exposition of the second article of the Creed in his *Greater Catechism* and to doubt it. But Luther broke with the Platonist-mystical tradition of medieval Christianity, nevertheless; and for three main reasons.

In the first place he had learned from the later Schoolmen, notably Duns Scotus, to think of God in terms of personal will rather than of 'substance'. For centuries religious thought had used the ancient Stoic category of *substantia* to describe the things of the spirit. God was 'absolute substance'. Sin, as defect of being (*defectus, deprivatio*) was lack of 'substance'. Grace was the heavenly 'substance' which makes good this lack through the channel of the sacraments. Justification was the process of this rehabilitation whereby the soul makes substantial progress (so to speak) along the road of sanctification. In short, though 'substance', as a technical term of Stoic and Christian philosophy, did not mean what the word has come to mean in modern popular usage, the use of such terminology by Christian thinkers from Tertullian[1] onwards perpetuated the mental associations of an older naturalistic pantheism. From the beginning of the fourteenth century, however, when a school of Catholic

[1] See *An Introduction to the Early History of Christian Doctrine* by J. F. Bethune-Baker (Methuen, 1920), pp. 231–3, on *substantia*.

theology[1] began to follow a *via moderna*, and to seek relief from these ancient fetters, Duns Scotus, followed by William of Occam, laid increasing emphasis on God as personal will, and on sin as the expression and result of rebellious will in man.[2] Now Luther had been educated in this modern school of Scotist and, more particularly, Occamist theology; and though it was his life's work to attack its virtually Pelagian doctrine of the *sufficiency* of the will,[3] he remained a Scotist all his life in his attitude to ancient and medieval mysticism. He broke definitely with the idea that there is in the human soul a fragment of the eternal Substance, and that it is possible for man to bring his divine endowment into union, fusion and oneness with the eternal Godhead by means of a technique of *exercitia spiritualia*. To all this Luther said No. For him, as for Scotus, God is in no sense 'Substance' but personal will. Between this holy Will and the rebellious will of fallen and sinful man there does not and cannot exist a natural relationship or substantial kinship, as the mystics contend. From man's side, at any rate, there is an insuperable gulf, a contrast which is absolute; there is an 'infinite and quali-

[1] William of Occam, Pierre d'Ailly, Jean Gerson and Gabriel Biel were its most eminent representatives.

[2] His distinction between the grace of justification and sacramental grace was a similar attempt to describe spiritual entities in more appropriate terms; what Seeberg (*DG*, III, 667) describes as the reinterpretation and refinement (*Umdeutung und Verfeinerung*) of traditional concepts. 'For Duns Scotus God is no longer the absolute Substance but free, living Spirit' (*op. cit.* p. 670).

[3] I.e. man can do everything which he wills to do; he can fulfil the Law to the last detail, compel his reason to regard what is black as white, love God with his whole heart, mind and strength—*if he only will*. The will is the all-determining force of the soul's life, and it is itself determined by nothing: no deed or omission can weaken or strengthen it; it remains unchanged in quality and magnitude. Luther knew from experience that in spite of the lofty and ascetic idealism of the *via moderna* its psychology of volition was false.

tative difference' between God and man, Creator and creature, holiness and sin. To become one with the Divine is impossible. What is alone possible is a communion or fellowship between Person and person, the gracious initiative for it being and remaining ever with God, never with man—whose very response to it by faith is itself God's act and gift: all is of God. This, then, was the first main reason for Luther's repudiation of medieval mysticism: he learnt it during his novitiate from the masters of the *via moderna*.

In the second place, his teacher was his own sensitive conscience, which told him that his deepest ego, the soul's ground—so far from being free from the empirical ego, and reaching out beyond individuality to the infinite— was itself identical with and inseparable from the responsible, answerable and sinful ego. The ego was an indivisible whole. He could not go beyond the *Ich schadhaft*, the 'shameful Me', in this way. Whereas mysticism and scholastic philosophy assumed that the part of the soul known as its ground or depth shares in the divine changelessness and is 'still', Luther found it to be ceaselessly alive and active. The soul's ground is no neutral territory.[1] And behind this ceaseless activity stands the indivisible 'I', full of desire to assert a tough and narrow self-interest. 'For man cannot but put self-seeking first, loving himself above everything else: this is the root of his sinning.'[2] Delivering this starkly realistic judgement upon himself, as he stood trembling before the holiness and wrath of God, Luther

[1] res enim viva et quotidie movens est peccatum sicut et ipsa anima in qua habitat....Non enim quiescere potest anima, quia vel amet vel odiat ea quae dei sunt (i.e. sin, like the soul itself in which it lives, is alive and in daily movement....For the soul cannot be at rest; it either loves or hates the things that be of God). *WA*, VII, 110, 33 f., as quoted by Holl, *Ges. Aufs.* I, 61.

[2] quia homo non potest nisi quae sua sunt quaerere et se super omnia diligere, quae est summa omnium vitiorum. *Lectures on Romans* II, 75, 8, as quoted by Holl, *op. cit.* p. 61. Cf. Seeberg *DG*⁴, I, 89.

was not unaware, of course, that there is in man what he can only analyse as a 'higher' element, which recognizes that its true good is in God, and desires it. He knew that the very recognition of self-seeking as sinful presupposes this something higher within us, which even sin does not destroy.[1] Yet he refused to analyse man into parts. Ultimately man is a living unity; he is present as a whole in all his activities.

This brings us to the third main reason for Luther's break with the mystical tradition: the evidence of the Bible. He saw what the insight of modern theologians, notably Reinhold Niebuhr, has made newly relevant and alive, namely that the Christian doctrine of sin is bound up with the biblical doctrine of Man; a doctrine which is obviously Hebraic rather than Greek. Details apart, the Hebrew psychology of the Bible finds the secret of man's nature in his twofold status: he is both 'flesh' and 'spirit': that is, he is at once a finite creature biologically involved in the processes of nature, and one who transcends his finitude since he is made in God's image. This is the basic paradox of human existence; man's transcendence of the finiteness in which he is immersed. But the essential truth about this duality is that it is nevertheless a unity. And it is the witness of scripture that these two aspects of human nature may not be separated from one another or set over against one another to constitute a dualism, as in the Greek dualism of body and soul. Man is not eternal spirit imprisoned in a material body, nor is he an animal evolving

[1] 'The fact that the obligation to love can be felt as an obligation is a refutation of all unduly rigorous conceptions of total human depravity' (R. Niebuhr in *Christian Faith and the Common Life* (Allen and Unwin, 1938), p. 71). The prodigal in the far country of his alienation from the Father, comes 'to himself' (cf. Luke xv. 16–17). Luther's point, repeated by Emil Brunner in our day, is that if we deal seriously with the problem of moral evil, the deepest ego is not identical with, but in contradiction to, its idea of itself.

towards pure spirituality. The Bible speaks of him as a wholly unitary being: which means that his transcendence of nature intimately affects every aspect of his natural life, and that his natural life intimately affects every aspect of his transcendence. It means, for example, that his capacity for the eternal bears on and penetrates his experience and use of sex, differentiating this from that of the animals, to which it is in other aspects similar: and that the constitutive necessities and impulses of his physical being effectively penetrate and condition his philosophy, art and religion. In short, just where Greek psychology sees an ultimate dualism of higher and lower, outward and inward, material and spiritual, the Bible witnesses to a duality in unity where the traffic is, so to speak, two-way.[1]

It is not surprising that Luther's repudiation of much medieval scholasticism finds its main explanation in his rediscovery of biblical theology; and that his doctrine of man is correspondingly biblical and Hebraic. Here, then, is the fundamental reason for his break with the dualist psychology of the Gnostic-Neoplatonist-Mystical tradition. The Bible represents man as a unity: what Luther often describes as *totus homo*, man as an indivisible whole. Man is, at one and the same moment, both 'flesh' and 'spirit'; these two elements are separable only in thought, as a convenient device of analysis; so far from living alongside one another within him, they interpenetrate. As Luther put it in his early lectures on the Psalms:

The mistake arises when people distinguish flesh and spirit philosophically, as though there were two different substances,

[1] This bears on the contrast between the Greek and Hebrew concepts of human destiny beyond death: for the one the final meaning of human life is the immortality of the soul; for the other it is the resurrection of the 'body' (σῶμα).

whereas it is man as a whole who is spirit and flesh; spirit inasmuch as he loves God's law and flesh inasmuch as he hates it.[1]...I make no rash and precise distinction between flesh, soul and spirit...the flesh does not lust save through the soul and spirit...we are not to imagine two distinct men here, therefore...it is the one indivisible man who loves chastity, and the same man who is inflamed with lustful desire.[2]...My flesh does not do anything which I myself may not be said to do.[3]...The Paul who confesses each of these two facts about himself [i.e. in Rom. vii. 14 f.] is one man.[4]

Luther's doctrine of man is confessedly biblical therefore, rather than Platonist or mystical. Scripture teaches him that although man enjoys this uniquely dual status, he is nevertheless always one man and not two; he is not a schizophrenic monstrosity—now Jekyll, now Hyde; the duality is always a unity.

What bearing, then, has this biblical understanding of the nature of man on the immemorial problem of man's sin? The biblical answer seems to be that man sins, not because of his dual status, but because of his proud unwillingness to accept it. His dual status is at once his uniqueness and his fatal temptation. He wants the self-transcendence[5] which is the mark of the divine image in

[1] causa erroris est quod...carnem et spiritum distinguunt metaphysice tanquam duas substantias, cum totus homo sit spiritus et caro, tantum spiritus quantum diligit legem dei, tantum caro quantum odit legem dei (*WA*, II, 415, 6 f. as quoted by Holl, *op. cit.* p. 62 n. 1).

[2] ego mea temeritate carnem, animam, spiritum prorsus non separo, non enim caro concupiscit nisi per animam et spiritum...non ergo duo isti homines diversi imaginandi sunt...totus homo est qui castitatem amat, idem totus homo illecebris libidinis titillatur (*ibid.* II, 585, 32).

[3] non enim caro mea aliquid facit quod non ipse facere dicar (*ibid.* 587, 2).

[4] unus est homo Paulus qui utrumque de se confitetur (*ibid. WA*, VIII, 119, 14).

[5] By 'self-transcendence'—a phrase which is fully expounded in Reinhold Niebuhr's Gifford Lectures, vol. I—is meant that though man is a finite creature, immersed in the vital processes of nature and the relativities of history, he is nevertheless able to transcend nature in his free self-consciousness.

him, but not the finiteness and mortality with which the Creator has bounded and determined it. He seeks to resolve the mysterious paradox of his created being by repudiating and destroying its unity. Thus sin, according to the witness of Scripture,[1] is always more than error due to ignorance, or the missing of the mark because of incompetence; it is man's wilful rebellion against the finite and determinate character of his existence as God has made it. Everyman (Adam) interprets the transcendent dimension of his being not as freedom *for* God but as freedom *from* God. In the life of every child of Adam there is a fundamental, 'original' self-assertion or self-seeking (Luther uses the traditional term *concupiscentia*) which affects and corrupts all his particular activities.[2] This self-love or self-sufficiency is not only rebellion against God; it is a form of idolatry; it is man's proud attempt to destroy God in whose image he is made, and to be his own God. The divinely intended unity of man's dual status splits and breaks, and the notorious struggle between 'spirit' and 'flesh' in him is the result. Indeed, the important point to notice is that sin is not the result of this struggle between 'spirit' and 'flesh', but its cause. The prime fact and mystery is our universal rebellion; Paradise is lost because man is first disobedient.

Of all the expressive, traditional imagery which Luther uses to describe the sinner's rebellion and his resulting predicament—unbelief, pride, idolatry, self-love, con-

---

[1] See Kittel's *Theol. Wörterbuch zum N.T.* s.v. Sünde.

[2] It is, as Luther put it, '*summa omnium vitiorum*'; that is, it is Sin, of which particular sins are the manifest expression. Cf. Archbishop William Temple's Gifford Lectures, p. 367: 'The centre of trouble is the personality as a whole, which is self-centred.... The whole personality in action is the will; and it is the will which is perverted.' 'It is the spirit that is evil; it is reason which is perverted; it is aspiration itself which is corrupt' (*ibid.* p. 368).

cupiscence—none is more apt than the phrase *incurvatus in se*, 'curved inwards upon himself'. This metaphor of curvature or declination, to express our stooping, crippled, muck-raking condition, is a common one. For St Augustine the sinner is *curvatus*, bent down to earth. In his profound analysis of the soul's vitiation in his eightieth sermon on the *Song of Songs*, St Bernard contrasts the soul standing upright (*recta*), obeying no other law than the divine love, with the soul as *curva, quo appetens terestrium*; that is, stooping down to earthly things and losing its intended rectitude.[1] But for Luther, as Nygren[2] points out, the sinful soul is bent down *upon itself*. And the difference becomes clear as soon as we recall how medieval piety thought of salvation, the righting of the predicament. For St Augustine, the situation changes when the soul directs its desire upwards towards God and the heavenly world. But Luther had found that even the soul *appetens supernorum* (striving to heaven) can still be bent inwards upon itself, governed as it is by the yearning desire for blessedness. St Augustine had recognized this element of self-seeking even in the desire for blessedness; in the tenth book of his *Confessions* (c. 20) he wrote: 'When I seek Thee, my God, I seek for happiness.'[3] Luther pursued this thought in the light of his own quest for a gracious God; it had become the special and profound concern of medieval mysticism, and Luther thought it through to its ultimate issue with an earnestness and penetration which none of the great masters before him had exceeded.[4] He contended

---

[1] So, Etienne Gilson, *The Spirit of Medieval Philosophy*, pp. 249–55.

[2] *Agape and Eros*, III, 267 f., 482 f.

[3] cum enim te, Deum meum, quaero, vitam beatam quaero.

[4] Holl, *op. cit.* p. 138: 'schärfer als irgendeiner vor ihm hat er den Zusammenhang von Glückstreben und Selbstsucht und damit auch den Gegensatz zwischen Seligkeitsverlangen und wirklichen Gottesdienst erkannt.'

3-2

that sinful man's desire to love and serve God is never disinterested; it is never free from the fatal corruption of egocentricity. Just because self-love pervades the whole man (*homo* being *totus homo*), all his activities are tainted thereby, even at the highest religious level. There is no unspoiled divine nucleus at the deep centre of man's individuality—a saving bridgehead, as it were, reaching out beyond individuality to the Infinite; the individuality itself is corrupted. 'Total' corruption means just that. Man's impulse of self-love and self-seeking is sin, even where his quest is for salvation therefrom;[1] and it is sin in the full, rigorous sense, since here too is that secret motive of self-regarding desire which, according to the Saviour's Sermon on the Mount, is already a deed; sinful, guilty and judged as such. 'Concupiscence', in short, pervades the whole man, and is sleepless even in the religious man.[2] The badness of 'goodness', as illustrated by Christ in the parable of the Pharisee and the Publican, may be sin at its most subtle, deceiving and deadly.

Once again, we are back with the original dilemma. 'Thou shalt love.' But how may the sinner obey this first and great commandment? How may I attain to full redemption from the corruption of self-love? 'Wie krieg ich

[1] *incurvatus in se* is not a metaphor peculiar to Luther. Its independent recurrence in Thomas Carlyle is an interesting confirmation of the Reformer's insight. Castigating self-centred religiosity (in his essay on Abbot Samson, *Past and Present*, ch. 15) he adds: '*Methodism with its eye forever turned on its own navel*; asking itself with torturing anxiety of Hope and Fear: "Am I right, am I wrong? Shall I be saved, shall I not be damned?" What is this, at bottom, but *a new phasis of Egoism*, stretched out into the Infinite; not always the heavenlier for its infinitude!' (My italics.) Cf. Percy Lubbock's story of the woman who went to Assisi for six weeks every year, 'to be alone with my emotions'.

[2] Luther understood more clearly than St Augustine that 'concupiscence' is spiritual, and not exclusively sensual.

einen gnädigen Gott?'[1] How is the paradox of Law and Gospel to be resolved?

Luther answers by saying three things about the Law. He uses the three metaphors of the mirror, the hammer and the mask, to describe its successive functions.

First, the Law is a mirror. It shows us ourselves, and the mysterious nature and operation of our sin. It reveals our impotence and our secret unwillingness to do the will of God. For this clear mirror of the Law, as interpreted by Christ in the Sermon, manifests our self-love, the idolatry of our self-worship, the self-regarding taint in all our activities; even our moral and religious activities which we like to think are disinterested. In short, the Law discloses our self-centred alienation from God even in our very quest for God. And the result, among other things, is despair.

For, in the second place, the Law is a hammer. It breaks us down, at last reducing us to despair. Just as grace may be defined as love in action, so wrath is law in action; the Law is more than mirror; it is the hammer of God actively at work upon us, that wrath of God which is revealed against all unrighteousness.[2]

God's nature is to exalt the humble, to feed the hungry, to enlighten the blind, to console the wretched and afflicted, to justify sinners, to quicken the dead, and to save the desperate and the damned. For He is an almighty Creator, making all things out of nothing. But that most pernicious plague, man's opinion of his own righteousness, which will not be a sinner,

[1] 'How do I get a gracious God?' This famous sentence had already been anticipated by an older member of Luther's order, Johann von Paltz: *quomodo inveniam deum placatum?* (how shall I find a forgiving God?). It is one of many indications that Luther was not a complete innovator.

[2] Rom. i. 18.

unclean, miserable and damned, but just and holy etc.—
prevents God from coming to His own natural and proper
work. Therefore God must use that hammer, to wit, the Law,
to break, beat, pound and, in a word, reduce to nothing
that beast with its vain confidence, wisdom, righteousness,
and power, that at length it may learn that it is lost and
damned.[1]

And we cannot mitigate its severity by earning our salvation, bringing something meritorious to God, and bartering
our achievements (or the vicarious achievements of the
saints) for the desired status of sonship with Him. Sin
cannot thus be 'made good'. God cannot be bought or
obligated. Nothing which man can do can put the Holy
One in his debt. Indeed it is the evangelical function of the
Law to bring us to this despair of self: *de profundis clamavi ad
te, Domine*.[2]

Thus, the Law has a third function; and here Luther
begins to expound its evangelical import. The Law is a
mask, since the sinner's despair is part of God's beneficent
intention. For it is only when we despair that he does his
'proper work' of redemption in us; only when we say
'Nothing in my hand I bring', can he come to us as sheer
grace. Luther learns from St Paul—and it is the turning-
point of his life—that God gives to man freely and utterly
what man can never earn and so 'compel' from God.
From St Paul he learns that salvation comes, not because
he seeks God through the works of the Law, but because
God seeks him through Christ crucified. Under the
imagery of a mask, then, Luther faces the old paradoxical
problem of wrath and love, of law and gospel—in God

---

[1] *Commentary on Galatians*, II, 70, quoted by R. S. Franks, *A History of the
Doctrine of the Work of Christ* (Hodder, 1918), I, 385.
[2] Ps. cxxx. 1; cf. Pss. cxx. 1, vi. 1, xii. 1, cxliii. 2.

himself. Each element in the paradox has to be maintained in its entirety, and yet there is a unity behind their contrast. Luther found it in Isaiah:

Wherefore hear the word of the Lord, ye scornful men, that rule this people which is in Jerusalem. Because ye have said, We have made a covenant with death, and with hell are we at agreement; when the overflowing scourge shall pass through, it shall not come unto us: for we have made lies our refuge, and under falsehood have we hid ourselves: Therefore thus saith the Lord God, Behold, I lay in Zion for a foundation, a stone, a tried stone, a precious corner stone, a sure foundation.... Judgment also will I lay to the line, and righteousness to the plummet: and the hail shall sweep away the refuge of lies, and the waters shall overflow the hiding place. And your covenant with death shall be disannulled and your agreement with hell shall not stand; when the overflowing scourge shall pass through, then ye shall be trodden down by it....For the Lord shall rise up as in mount Perazim, He shall be wroth as in the valley of Gibeon, *that he may do his work, his strange work; and bring to pass his act, his strange act.*[1]

Here the prophet speaks to the proud, self-confident men of Jerusalem of God's wrath as his *opus alienum* (Vulgate): that is, an activity alien—as it were—to his eternal purpose of redeeming love, yet used by him nevertheless for the ultimate fulfilment of that purpose. Love is his proper work since his nature and his name is Love for ever; yet wrath is also his work, albeit alien. It is the mask behind which God hides. Through his alien activity he works his proper activity.[2] His wrath, says

[1] Is. xxviii. 14–18, 21.
[2] alienum est opus eius ut operetur opus suum; quia perdit ut salvet... sic aeternam suam clementiam et misericordiam abscondit sub aeterna ira. *WA*, III, 246, 19 and *WA*, XVIII, 633, 9 as quoted by Holl (*op. cit.* p. 41, nn.)— who gives references to several similar statements. On p. 29 n. 1 he quotes several passages, including a profound exegesis of Ezek. xvi. 42, to illustrate

Luther, is a wrath of compassion.[1] 'Thus we see that real love is at once Enemy and Friend, since its punishment is severe but its succour sweet; it has a hard shell but a sweet kernel; it is bitter to the old man, but sweet to the new man.'[2] We understand the comfortable words, 'Come unto me,' only because we have heard in the very depths, 'Depart from me': which is what Kierkegaard meant when he observed that no man can know God as his friend who has not known him as his enemy. The same paradox is found in St Augustine: 'In a manner wondrous and divine He loved even when He hated us.'[3] In short, we might say that rightly to look into the terrible mirror of the Law is to find it, in the end, a dissolving mirror; it is to find heaven in the very depth of hell, grace in the very operation of judgement, joy and peace in believing where there was nothing but crushing despair.[4] Or, as Luther put it in a paradox of wonderful vividness: 'unter und über

Luther's lifelong conviction that when man supposes himself to be farthest away from God in his alienation, he is in fact most nigh unto him. Recalling epigrams of St Bernard he says that the greatest temptation is to have no temptation; the greatest adversity of all is to know no adversity; and God is most wrathful when he is not (tunc maxime Deus irascitur, quando non irascitur). Which is only another way of saying that whom the Lord loveth he chasteneth. 'Woe unto them that are at ease in Zion.'

[1] This paradox did not mean that Luther knew nothing of a wrath of perdition. He distinguishes between the *ira severitatis* which only punishes and destroys, and is to be manifest at the Last Judgement, and the *ira misericordiae* which refines, purifies and redeems.

[2] *WA*, x, i, 266, 6. [3] *Tract. in Jo.* 110.

[4] Yield to me now, for I am weak,
But confident in self-despair;

Charles Wesley's great hymn *Come O Thou Traveller unknown* based on Jacob's encounter at Jabbok (Gen. xxxii. 24 f.), well illustrates the Lutheran doctrine of the *opus alienum*. Who was the mysterious opponent who wrestled with Jacob in the darkness, in order to bless him? Luther answers: 'This man was not an angel but our Lord Jesus Christ, who is the eternal God, and yet was to become a man and was crucified.'

dem Nein das tiefe, heimliche Ja' (deeper than the No, and above it, the deep, mysterious Yes).[1]

Luther discovered the Gospel just here where its revelation of God's love is heightened to an incredible wonder against the dark background of God's Law.[2] He discovered the astonishing paradox in the biblical meaning of the word 'righteousness'; that it does not mean what it necessarily means for the moralist and the philosopher— namely, the distributive justice which rewards the good and punishes the evil. Ultimately the righteousness of God in Christ is not punitive but redemptive. Luther at last came to see for himself that the δικαιοσύνη θεοῦ of Rom. i. 17 is not a judge's merciless verdict against us but a father's costly gift to us. Here there is no calculus of rewards and penalties. God's pardoning grace is not a recognition of the goodness of its objects; it creates that goodness; while we were sinners Christ died for us; we love because he first loved us. It cannot be said too confidently that just as Luther took Law, so he took God's love more seriously than any of his predecessors had done. He 'developed far beyond anything in Augustine or Abelard the thought of the revelation of God's love in Christ. The point where he transcends these predecessors is the thoroughness with which he carries out this thought, in opposition to the view of God as revealed in nature and the moral law....For Luther the Incarnation, with the

---

[1] *EA*, 11, 120.

[2] 'We should understand why Luther makes a definite distinction between the Law and the Gospel. He resists those who think that they can be saved by fulfilling laws and doing good works....But Luther also attacks his friend Agricola and others who wished to abolish the Law and replace it by the Gospel. Both are vital. Only men terrified by the Law can grasp the Gospel; only a man saved by the Gospel is released from the tyranny of the Law' (H. H. Kramm, *The Theology of Martin Luther* (Jas. Clarke, 1947), p. 66).

consequent life, death and resurrection of Christ, is above all a revelation of God's love, in which he is manifested as he is not manifested in nature and reason, through which He appears as a lawgiver.'[1]

Law and Gospel. Luther understands each in its relation to and distinction from the other. Apart from this fundamental paradox his religion and theology would hardly be intelligible.

[1] Franks, *op. cit.* I, 385.

CHAPTER IV

THE PARADOX OF JUSTIFICATION BY FAITH ALONE

THE second and most famous of the paradoxes affirmed by Luther is that of Justification by God's grace alone; which is, from man's side, justification by faith alone.[1] The most daring form of this paradox occurs in the Epistle to the Romans where St Paul actually writes that God justifies the ungodly (τὸν δικαιοῦντα τὸν ἀσεβῆ Rom. iv. 5). Stated less provocatively, justification by faith means that God freely pardons the sinful and puts them right with himself if they will but trust his love in Christ. For Luther this is central, fundamental and final. In colloquies or formal debates with opponents, when some concession on points of doctrine was the obvious condition of any working agreement, this was the one point on which he would make no concession. Before the proposed colloquy at Schmalkald, he wrote:

The first article here is the most important; namely that Jesus Christ our Lord and God died for our sins and rose again for our righteousness; that he alone is the Lamb of God that taketh away the sins of the world; that God hath laid on him the iniquity of us all; that all have sinned, but that they are justified freely, without works or merits of their own, by his

---

[1] Eph. ii. 8 and Rom. iii. 28. In his open letter on the art of translating (*WA*, xxx, ii, 627) Luther defends his translation of Rom. iii. 28 where he has introduced the word 'alone', though it does not occur in the original Greek text. See below, pp. 73-4, for an abridged translation.

grace....Since it is necessary to believe this, and since it cannot be apprehended and acquired by any work, law or merit, it is certain and clear as St Paul says that faith alone justifies us. We cannot in any wise depart from this article or yield it up, though heaven and earth and all perishable things should fall....On this article stands firm and secure all that we hold in doctrine or in life against Pope, Devil or World.[1]

What is at once noticeable here is that the import of 'justification by faith alone' for Luther is easily misapprehended. It was not a new doctrine, but a new standpoint. *Sola fide* became a fighting slogan admittedly, but it was not regarded by the Reformers as a separate article of belief. Indeed it was not once mentioned—as a doctrine or even as a useful formula—in either of Luther's famous catechisms. As the foregoing quotation shows, the primary article of belief—unquestionable for Protestants and Catholics alike—was the atoning death and the redeeming victory of the incarnate Son of God. Luther insisted that it be taken seriously by being *believed*. He did not regard the work of Christ as one doctrine and justification by faith as another: they were the objective and subjective aspects of one and the same truth. Luther was in fundamental agreement with the medieval schoolmen in their doctrine of the Work of Christ and the Person of Christ; like all the Reformers he was unflinchingly orthodox, accepting without reserve the great creeds and definitions of the ancient Church. But, to quote R. S. Franks, 'what he found especially amiss in Catholicism was that it did not, in his view, take the Work of Christ in sufficient earnest as the sole ground of man's salvation, but endeavoured to supple-

---

[1] *Schmalk. Art.* part II. See special note on Luther's concept of the Work of Christ, appended to this chapter, pp. 74–80 below.

ment it with a further ground of salvation in human merit'.[1]
Justification by faith was not an additional article of belief,
therefore, but Luther's way of insisting on the one article
which mattered supremely, namely that 'Christus Gottessöhn ist unser Heiland';[2] and therefore, as he put it in the
document prepared for the Schmalkald Colloquy, 'Christ
alone, and not men's works, saves souls'.[3]

Was this evangelical principle of justification by faith
denied, then, in the centuries before the Reformation?
Certainly not. It was often qualified, in one way or another,
and almost always with the best of intentions;[4] but it was
not denied. Justification was central to the catholic system
and its vocabulary, as were the great concepts of grace and
faith. To choose a pertinent example: St Bernard of
Clairvaux (1090–1153), though a zealous advocate of
monastic asceticism and of the meritorious value of good
works, occasionally declared the forgiveness of sins to be
the excellence of all excellences and justification by faith
to be the only basis for the sinner's new life in God.[5]
'Grace freely justifies me and sets me free from slavery to
sin.'[6] The great abbot strongly asserts the freedom of the
will and makes constant use of the concept of merit; but,
however inconsistently, he also makes man's salvation
depend entirely and exclusively on God's grace. 'You must
believe, first of all that you cannot have forgiveness of sins
save through the merciful forbearance of God; secondly,
that no moral achievement at all can be yours except as

---

[1] *A History of the Doctrine of the Work of Christ*, I, 363.
[2] P. 23 above.   [3] *Schmalk. Art.* II, 12.
[4] Luther himself once described it as *praedicatio periculosissima*, i.e. 'a mighty
dangerous thing to preach'.
[5] See Seeberg *DG*[4], III, 136 and Loofs *Leitfaden*[4], pp. 524–5.
[6] gratia reddit me mihi justificatum gratis et sic liberatum a servitute
peccati (*in Cant. Canticorum*, serm. 67. 10).

God's gift; lastly, that by no moral effort can you merit eternal life unless it too be freely given to you.'[1] In short, though this medieval mystic and crusader preaches that good works must and will be the fruit of such faith, he insists unambiguously on the insufficiency of human merit. 'All that you need know of merits is that they cannot meet your need.'[2] 'The mercy of the Lord is my merit.'[3] Indeed, the preacher's appeal here is for responsive faith. 'It is not enough', he says, 'to believe in general that God forgives sins; thou must also believe that he forgives thee.'[4] The qualified assertion of such evangelical principles throughout the Middle Ages finds specially pertinent illustration in St Bernard because the words just quoted had a noteworthy influence on Luther. These were the very words with which the Master of the Novices at Erfurt sought to relieve the anguish of the young Magister in 1506. Luther never forgot them. He felt them to be the first words of comfort to reach him, in his lonely struggle to find a 'gracious God'. His own distinction between *da* and *dir da*[5] seems to resemble them too closely to be independent.

But how far was this evangelical note in St Bernard typical, either of his own piety and thought considered as a whole, or of the long tradition of medieval Christianity itself? In giving so explicit an emphasis to these evangelical

[1] necesse est enim primo omnium credere quod remissionem peccatorum habere non possis nisi per indulgentiam dei; deinde quod nihil prorsus habere queas operis boni nisi et hoc dederit ipse; postremo quod aeternam vitam nullis potes operibus promereri nisi gratis tibi detur et illa (*in annunt. Mar.* 5. 1, 1). This is entirely Augustinian. Cf. *Enchiridion*, c. 107.

[2] sufficit ad meritum scire quod non sufficiant merita (*in Cant. s.* 68, 6).

[3] meum meritum miseratio domini (*in Cant. s.* 61, 5).

[4] This well illustrates the distinction between *fides quae creditur* and *fides qua creditur*. See p. 70 below.

[5] 'That God is there (*da*) and that he is there for thee (*dir da*) are two different things: he is there for thee when he adds his word thereto and says, here thou must find me.' *WA*, XXIII, 141; cf. XIX, 442.

elements which were, admittedly, a common heritage of medieval theologians, was he not exceptional? To some degree he was, though to what degree is less easy to say than Protestant apologists have sometimes assumed; for there can be no doubt that though the Middle Ages were in one sense strongly legalistic in temper, assuming that men must earn their immortal salvation by their merits, they were also in another, and no merely nominal, sense steadily evangelical. Their uncrowned king for a thousand years (though his monarchy is never absolute!) is St Augustine, the great *doctor gratiae*, for whom the Christian life is nothing else than grace.[1] It seems true that medieval Catholicism, though giving nominal allegiance to this Augustinian doctrine of grace, was careful to neutralize it, in fact, by the semi-Pelagianism implicit in its cultus. But it is possible and legitimate to reverse this judgement and to say that though the theologians of the West were always prone to blunt the cutting edge of St Augustine's distinctive doctrine, it was an instrument which they never ceased to use: along with 'Ambrosiaster', the great name of Augustine dominates the entire medieval exegesis and interpretation of the Epistle to the Romans.[2] 'Ambrosiaster' actually uses the very phrase 'sola fide',[3] as the most famous Schoolman of all, St Thomas Aquinas, was to do six centuries later.[4] And even the Council of Trent (1545–63), truculently anathematizing Protestant 'inanities' at almost every session, decrees that 'faith is the

[1] vita nostra nihil aliud est quam gratia.

[2] See Denifle, *Die abendländischen Schriftausleger bis Luther über Justitia Dei* (*Luther und Luthertum* I, ii) and Holl's reply: '*Die Justitia Dei in den vorlutherische Bibelauslegung*' (*Gesammelte Aufsätze*, III, 171–88). The controversial methods of the great Dominican scholar show up unfavourably under Holl's detailed analysis, but the basic evidence is not in dispute.

[3] Migne, *PL*, vol. XVII, cols. 79D, 83A, 154C.

[4] *Opera omnia* (Paris, 1876), XX, 425.

beginning of man's salvation, the basis and root of all justification; to please God is impossible without it'.[1] It should be added, of course, that the word 'faith' as used here does not mean what it meant for St Paul or the Reformers; it means *assensus* rather than *fiducia*.[2] Indeed, the fathers of Trent go on at once to attack 'the vain *fiducia* of the heretics'.[3] But in spite of this piece of polemical extravagance, grace was as much the very ground and environment of medieval religion as was merit; and St Bernard may fairly be called as witness to the fact.

Denifle is not unjustified, therefore, in claiming that the Augustinian doctrine of justifying grace played a decisive role in the West for a thousand years before Luther appeared. But Protestantism has something more to say. It contends that, though the evangelical principle was thus asserted, it was nevertheless largely neutralized by the two facts which were and are distinctive of the whole Catholic system: the powerfully active ideas of sacramental grace and saving merit. If we are to understand Luther and the Reformation we have to consider these two ideas here in turn.

First, then, the medieval Church did not mean by 'grace' just what the Bible means. Its presuppositions were those of Stoic philosophy[4] rather than of Hebraic religion. Under the influence of the Stoic philosophy of 'substance' the grace of the Gospel in medieval Christen-

---

[1] fides humana salutis initium, fundamentum et radix omnis justificationis, sine qua impossibile est placere deo (*Conc. Trid.* sess. VI, c. 8).

[2] See p. 69 below.

[3] contra inanem haereticorum fiduciam (*ibid.* ch. 9).

[4] Not to mention strong survivals of primitive religion. Consciously or unconsciously, the Roman Church made large concessions to the folk-piety of the Mediterranean world. This temper of accommodation (coming to terms with primitive cultures and religious patterns) is part of its genius.

dom was not so much the personal attitude of God in Christ to sinners, as a quasi-material 'stuff' dispensed through the sacramental praxis of the Church in all its growing elaboration and variety. It was a supernatural medicine, the Western equivalent of the Greek φάρμακον ἀθανασίας;[1] a kind of heavenly 'vitamin' or energy-giving 'virtue', infused into the soul through the sacraments; notably the sacraments of baptism and penance; and through *sacramentalia*[2] in various forms. Indeed, it was formally defined as *gratia infusa*, infused grace; a divinely communicated quality or 'habit' of the soul. 'The administering and receiving of the sacrament automatically[3] mediates the divine grace which...is thought of as a mysterious material force (*geheimnisvolle dingliche Potenz*).... The mysterious "force", the wonderful "power" with which Catholics come into contact in sacrament and *sacramentalia* is constantly thought of as material (*stofflich*) or, rather, as impersonal.'[4] Heiler is here describing the unchanging Catholic concept of grace as *vis* or *virtus spiritualis*[5] placed miraculously within the sacraments by the ordinance and power of God, and working effectively in the souls of those who receive them. In baptism, for example, God has implanted a spiritual *virtus* in the water, that—as an integral part of the rite as a whole—it may wash away sin. Again, to the power (*potestas*) conveyed to

[1] Ignatius, *Eph.* xx, 2, though this 'medicine of immortality' meant something less physical than the words would suggest to modern ears. Cf. Irenaeus, iv, 18, 5.   [2] Friedrich Heiler, *Der Katholizismus*, p. 177.
[3] 'von selbst', i.e. ex opere operato.
[4] Heiler, *op. cit.* pp. 177, 181. The whole section on sacred powers, forces and actions, on consecrated objects and persons—is valuable as coming from a great *Religionshistoriker* and a sympathetic critic, who deeply respects the Catholic piety in which he was nurtured from infancy, and which he knows 'experimentally' from within.
[5] So Aquinas, *Summa Theol.* iii, q. 62, n. 4.

49

the priest through the sacrament of ordination, there belongs the power to consecrate;[1] thus equipped, not only by divine authority but also with divine power, the word of the priest brings about (*conficit*) the miraculous change in the eucharistic elements during the Mass. There is only a difference of degree between the sacramental realism here defined in terms of a scholastic philosophy of substance and the crudities of popular belief about transubstantiation. The vital issue here lies in the Catholic claim that this is that grace of the Gospel by which alone men are justified. It is sacramental grace. Indeed, the Council of Trent, consciously replying to the Reformers, declared that through the sacraments 'all true righteousness either begins; or, having begun, is increased; or, having been lost, is replenished'.[2] In short, Catholicism here interprets the grace of the Gospel, not as the attitude of God in Christ to sinners, but as 'topping up the battery' of the soul. Catholicism has always tended to think of grace in terms of things rather than of persons: as though redeeming love were a quasi-material entity or quality, communicated through a channel, as water is brought to a city, or as electrical energy is dispensed from a power station.

But is this familiar criticism sound? In his stimulating but somewhat wayward book, *Agape and Eros*,[3] the Lutheran professor (now Bishop) Anders Nygren dissociates himself from this Protestant criticism of the medieval conception of grace, because he feels it is the wrong ground on which to stand. The main issue, he contends, is not really here; the contrast between the 'evangelical' and

---

[1] *virtus consecrativa* (*Summa Theol.* III, q. 82, n. 1).

[2] de sanctissimis ecclesiae sacramentis...per quae omnis vera justitia vel incipit, vel coepta augetur, vel amissa reparatur (sess. vii, proem.).

[3] Vol. III (E.T.), p. 406.

'medieval' conceptions of grace is real and deep, but it may not be expressed as a contrast between an impersonal-magical and a personal-psychological conception; the medieval Church, so far from thinking of infused grace as quasi-physical, followed St Augustine in taking the concept directly from Rom. v. 5, and in thinking of its transforming power within human lives in the true personal and psychological sense.[1]

Professor John Burnaby of Cambridge is warm in his agreement. In his *Amor Dei*, the Hulsean Lectures for 1938, he brings his careful scholarship to bear on the Either-Or of Nygren's own theory—the clear-cut contrast between Agape and Eros—and subjects some its of generalizations to serious criticism. But he sees 'conspicuous merit' in the Scandinavian theologian's

decisive rejection of the superficial criticism which alleges that the Catholic doctrine of grace—as distinct from perversions of practice—is 'magical' or 'mechanical'. What St Thomas calls the 'infusion' of charity is that same working of the Holy Spirit for which Augustine found his *locus classicus* in the Epistle to the Romans. It is no thing-like substance

---

[1] Nygren is certainly right about St Augustine's own understanding of grace as the divine love itself in effective action; see *de Spiritu et Littera*, 56: 'the love of God which is said to be shed abroad in our hearts is not that love whereby he loves us but that whereby he makes us to become his lovers, just as the righteousness of God is that whereby through his gift we are made righteous, and the salvation of the Law is that whereby He causes us to be saved, and (the) faith of Jesus Christ is that whereby he makes us faithful.' So, *ibid.* 15 and Sermo 131, 9. [Incidentally, these passages illustrate Augustine's steady assumption that *fides Christi, caritas Dei, salus Domini* and *justitia Dei* are all objective genitives rather than possessive genitives. As exegesis of Rom. v. 5 and viii. 35 this is plainly a mistake, but it profoundly vindicates the paradox of grace, whereby even faith—our response to grace—is itself the gift of God.]

The question at issue is whether Nygren does justice to the complexity of the medieval tradition when he says *simpliciter* that it followed St Augustine. It diverged from him too.

4-2

introduced from without, but the purely spiritual influence of the divine Person whose dwelling is within the believer's heart. The testimony of the mystics is that the life of prayer *can* be lifted by God's grace into a perception of his loving presence that has an immediacy comparable to that of our own consciousness of self.[1]

But Professor Burnaby is not altogether convincing here, and for three reasons. In the first place, the word 'magical' is something of a red herring. Heiler himself, discussing the sacramental principle in the popular piety of the Middle Ages (see his chapter entitled 'Heilige Kräfte, Gegenstände und Handlungen'), begins by explicitly disavowing the facile criticism of rationalists and certain liberal Protestants, who make great play with melanesian *mana* and polynesian *tabu*, and dismiss the mediation of the sacred through material things or ritual acts, as 'magical'. Heiler deals severely with the confusion and error which result from so improper a use of a technical term.[2] The criticisms which James Denney, Karl Heim, John Oman or Paul Tillich bring to bear on sacramental grace, do not rest on so crude and dubious a basis; they are concerned with what Professor Burnaby merely glances at in passing, namely, 'perversions of practice'; or rather, with the unavoidable issue of principle which such perversions raise.

For, in the second place, Professor Burnaby's distinction between doctrine and perversions of practice is too relevant and important a distinction to be merely mentioned in a parenthesis. The Reformers were as much concerned with the day-to-day religious life and the varied sacramental practice of the medieval Church, as with the formal doctrine of its theologians and schoolmen. And

[1] *Amor Dei* (Hodder, 1938), p. 313.
[2] *Katholizismus*, pp. 167 f., 221 f., 366.

whereas the Cambridge professor, standing in the serene tradition of the Cambridge Platonists, contemplates the meaning of love in the *beata vita* in the company of St Augustine, St Bernard, St Francis de Sales and Fénelon, Luther faced a system which produced and defended Tetzel, and which can still produce a pastoral letter such as that of Archbishop Johannes Katschtaler (1905), a translation of which is given in a later chapter of this book.[1] Karl Holl's comment on it may be fitly added here: 'Catholic theologians always have great difficulty in finding expressions to veil the magical element in this whole system of ideas.'[2] This does not seem to be a superficial criticism; if it were, it would be more easily answerable than it is.

In the third place, therefore, Professor Burnaby's appeal to the testimony of the mystics, though altogether true and beyond question in itself, is hardly relevant here. For the Catholic doctrine of grace is indisputably bound up with the Catholic doctrine of the sacraments. And, apart from the familiar fact that the testimony of the mystics to the life of prayer is not necessarily concerned with sacraments—mysticism being notoriously able to dispense with outward forms of mediation altogether—the crucial issue here is with the Catholic doctrine of sacramental grace. That doctrine was worked out in systematic form by the great medieval schoolmen of the Franciscan and Dominican traditions: notably by Alexander of Hales and Thomas Aquinas, who gathered up and ordered the thought of the past in terms of precedent and developing practice. It is this doctrine which has become definitive and authoritative for Catholicism; and, variations of detail apart, three main affirmations stand out from its elaborate apparatus of technical definitions and distinctions.

[1] P. 259.　　　　　[2] *Ges. Aufs.* I, 8 n. (my translation).

The first is that sacraments contain grace (*continent gratiam*). Though symbols, they are more than symbols; these outward and visible signs cause and convey what they signify—inward and spiritual grace. *Significando causant*. As in the ancient world, so throughout the Christian centuries, the symbol has always been understood as, in some sense, the thing symbolized. As St Thomas put it, *sacramenta efficiunt quod figurant* (sacraments effect what they signify).[1] And Protestantism is here in close agreement. All its standard confessions insist that the two Gospel sacraments are never *nuda signa* (bare signs). Presupposing the personal faith of the worshipper—a vital condition— the presence of the Lord is real, and his supper is 'a means of grace'. The pregnant phrase means precisely what it says.

The second Catholic affirmation is that sacraments are so vitally necessary as to be indispensable for salvation. Justifying grace is 'apprehended' by sinful man in no other way. Only thus may original sin be 'remedied', and the threat of its eternal punishment removed. This, indeed, is the supreme significance of baptism. Only through the forgiveness of sins which it proclaims and makes possible are good works possible; and only through the further grace of penance and the eucharist may good works be so 'assisted' that eternal life may be won as a reward (*merces*). Sufficient and inescapable evidence that without the sacramental grace of baptism man cannot be saved, is provided by the fate of infants dying unbaptized. They are shut out for ever from the Kingdom of Heaven.

This appalling doctrine already illustrates the third main Catholic affirmation about sacramental grace. It is unambiguously objective in its operation. Indeed, it can be unambiguously impersonal. All the Christian sacra-

[1] *Summa Theol.* III, q. 60 n. 2.

ments cause the supernatural infusion of charity into the soul, and so enable salvation to be merited by the responsible and responsive 'subject'; but this subjective reference, though obviously important, is not the primary fact: primary and fundamental is the objectivity of an *opus operatum*. That is, sacraments are, *in actu primo*, effective *of themselves*, because of a divinely given power which inheres in them; they work *ex opere operato*—in virtue simply of their having been performed. Only *in actu secundo* (secondarily) does the subjective disposition of the recipient become a relevant consideration. The Catholic doctrine of the sacrament of baptism strictly illustrates this. A new-born child who lives just long enough to be baptized attains thereby to the vision of God and eternal blessedness.[1] A similar child who dies unbaptized for whatever reason, is excluded from salvation for ever. This is not only the ruthless doctrine of Tertullian.[2] St Augustine defends it on more than one occasion; though, by an arbitrary use of his own logic, he decides that such innocents will throughout eternity endure no more than the lightest punishment (*mitissima sane omnium poena*).[3] The logic of the Council of Florence (1439) is stricter; those who die in actual mortal sin or in original sin only (*vel solo originali*) descend to hell, though the severity of punishments there will be appropriately unequal (*poenis tamen disparibus puniendas*).[4] Heiler observes that when the Catholic theologian Herman

[1] Cf. *Exultate Deo*, Bull of Eugenius IV, November 1439: Huius sacramenti effectus est remissio omnis culpae originalis et actualis, omnis quoque poenae quae pro ipsa culpa debetur. Propterea baptizatis nulla pro peccatis praeteritis injungenda est satisfactio: sed morientes antequam culpam aliquam committant, statim ad regnum coelorum et Dei visionem perveniunt (Article 10).

[2] *de Baptismo*, XII, 13.

[3] *Enchirid.* 93; *Ep.* 215, 1; cf. *Ep.* 166, 5; 186, 27; 217, 22; *Serm.* 294, 3.

[4] *Laetantur coeli*, Bull of Eugenius IV, July 1439, art. 7.

Schell dared to dissent from the primitive crudity of this hateful doctrine in his *Katholische Dogmatik* (1893), and to hope that heaven's portals stand open at least to unbaptized babes, a storm of orthodox indignation was aroused which contributed materially to the placing of his book on the Index.[1] Moreover, as though anticipating the suggestion that this impersonal and mechanical conception of the grace of the Gospel is exceptional and relatively unimportant, Heiler goes on to describe its typical effects on authoritative liturgical practice. Grotesque and barbarous though it is, the practice of intra-uterine baptism can hardly be dismissed as a perversion by a Catholic, since it is formally authorized in the Corpus Juris Canonici, Article 746. Baptism here takes place by means of a special medical instrument, that the soul of the yet unborn child, who is in danger of being still-born, may be saved for eternal bliss. There is abundant evidence that the mentality here exemplified is no exceptional survival from primitive religion: it fairly illustrates the corruption which ever threatens the sacramental principle.

For these three reasons, then, Professor Burnaby's criticism itself appears superficial. But his whole paragraph raises a familiar and abiding issue of fundamental importance—nothing less than the true meaning of the sacramental principle in the Christian religion. Now it is notorious that Luther held a very high doctrine of the two Gospel sacraments. His doctrine of the mode of the Real Presence is almost a return to medieval ways of thinking. No informed person, therefore, could intelligibly accuse him of belittling the sacraments. He never doubts their necessity or their efficacy for the fullness of our redeemed

---

[1] Herman Schell, Professor of Apologetics in Würzburg, Catholic Modernist; he died in May 1906. See Mirbt's *Quellen*, no. 738.

life in Christ. But Luther broke nevertheless with the
medieval sacramentalism which has been discussed in the
foregoing pages. For him the common content of all the
Christian sacraments is not grace in the Catholic sense of
an infused *habitus*, administered in appropriate quantities
and qualities; but grace in the biblical, evangelical sense of
forgiveness and reconciliation—the attitude of the Father
to sinners as exhibited in Christ crucified. The sacraments
are *signa efficacia* in that they verily convey the Word of
Christ's redeeming Passion and Victory; that is, a Word
which is to be personally received and believed; a divine
Saviour who is personally present to be trusted and loved
and adored. Luther knew, as his close friend and disciple
Melanchthon put it, that 'grace is not medicine but good
will'. He had discovered through Christ that grace is
God's free, unmerited favour to the sinner, bringing that
sinner into fellowship with himself. God's love in action
is not an impersonal process or spiritual 'innoculation',
but a mutual confronting in terms of 'I and Thou', where
I am both judged as a sinner and received as a son.

To repeat what was said at the beginning about the
paradox of justification by faith alone: the Reformation
was not here pretending to substitute some new nostrum or
shibboleth for the central doctrine of the Gospel. It
looked at that unchanging doctrine with the new eye of
personal faith. 'What it did in principle', said James
Denney, 'was to expel *things* from religion and to exhibit
all its realities as persons, and the relations of persons'.[1]
The Lutheran branch of the Reformation Church went far
in the old direction, using late-medieval categories of
thought in defence of its unyielding sacramental realism.
But the earliest statement of its faith in the first edition of

[1] *The Christian Doctrine of Reconciliation* (Hodder, 1917), p. 91.

Melanchthon's *Loci* is regarded by many as the truer expression of its proper insight:

> Sacraments do not justify. The Apostle says that circumcision is nothing. So, baptism is nothing—and partaking at the Lord's Table is nothing—save sign and seal of the divine goodwill towards thee, whereby thy conscience may be assured when it doubts the good will and grace of God.... Thou mayest be justified, therefore, even without the sacrament; only believe.[1]

The best commentary, perhaps, on what these downright words mean, and do not mean, may be taken from Calvin, whose high doctrine of the sacraments speaks for itself and needs no defence here. The Genevan Reformer, whose sense of the necessity of the Eucharist led him to demand a celebration at least once a week (*semel ad minimum*) could also write: 'the thief on the cross became the brother of believers though he never partook of the Lord's supper.' Denney is not out of line with Calvin in saying that to emphasize the necessity of the sacrament for justification is to magnify the thing at the expense of the person, to subject the higher category to the lower. 'To make justification independent of the sacraments it to give the personal its true place in religion, and is alone consistent with the principle of the Reformation.'[2] This is the language of the early twentieth century, however, rather than of the sixteenth, and neither Luther nor Calvin would endorse it without qualification. But it may fittingly close our discussion of the first great fact dominating medieval Christendom; namely, the powerfully active concept of sacramental grace. Justification by faith, though always acknowledged in principle, was too often invalidated in fact by a conception of the grace of the Gospel which failed to be sacramental in the true evangelical sense.

[1] *Loci* (Plitt-Kolde), p. 235.   [2] *Op. cit.* p. 91; also pp. 320–2.

The second great fact dominating medieval Christianity in the West, and neutralizing, so to speak, the Pauline gospel of grace, was the powerful and pervasive idea of human merit. Throughout the Middle Ages and earlier, merit is the indispensable supplement which sacramental grace requires and makes possible.

The desire to earn rather than to receive one's salvation is, as Ruskin observed, the oldest of heresies. It appears within Christianity as early as the second century, when the evangelical language of the New Testament tends to be used without being understood. In the vigorously legal mind of Tertullian it becomes nakedly explicit, and through his disciple St Cyprian—that transitional figure of the third century whom Harnack rightly described as the father of the Roman doctrine of good works—it passes into the very blood-stream of Western Christianity.

Nor may any system of theology claiming to be fully Christian condemn it outright. If the legalism of *do ut des* and *do ut abeas*[1] be the oldest of heresies, law is the oldest of truths. Modern New Testament scholarship is increasingly aware that the concept of law is integral to the gospel of redemption itself. 'Stoic morals are woven into the fabric of New Testament ethics...in Christ man is confronted with the Word, Wisdom or Law which is the law of his creation.'[2] The greatest and most memorable statements of the evangelical theology of grace in St Paul's epistles are all 'prolegomena to ethics.' Indeed, the common-sense concepts of merit and reward need no apology and little exposition: not only do they express part, at least, of the

---

[1] I.e. 'I give that Thou mayest give'; and its apotropaic counterpart, 'I give that Thou mayest be off!'

C. H. Dodd, *Natural Law in the New Testament*, pp. 132 and 142 (*New Testament Studies*, Scribners, 1952).

implicit logic of moral training and endeavour in the everyday world; St Matthew's Gospel (x. 42 *et al.*) represents them as having some validity, on the authority of Christ himself, in the eternal world.

But the law of Christ (Gal. vi. 2) is not legalism (Gal. ii. 16; Col. ii. 16, 20–1). It was Tertullian who first formulated the gospel of salvation legalistically, and gave currency to the juristic concepts of satisfaction and merit as the way to secure its benefits. The faith is not only represented as divine law; asceticism, alms-giving, penance, restitution and all that is rightly summarized as good works, are here represented as having *potestas reconciliandi iratum deum*.[1] With Cyprian this 'righteousness of works' became systematically explicit. 'God must be appeased by our satisfaction.'[2] Forgiveness is certainly given freely in baptism; but thereafter 'the remedy for propitiating God, provided by the word of God himself, is that we must satisfy him with righteous deeds'.[3] Quoting Eccl. iii. 30 ('alms make an atonement for sins') he continues, 'thus the flame of punishment is quenched by alms and righteous works'.[4] 'Whatever defilement we may contract we may wash away with almsgiving.'[5] 'After baptism the Christian man must establish his claim upon God the Judge, by sacrifices.'[6] This figurative reference to the sacrificial cultus of the Jewish Temple means that Cyprian sees the New Testament through the Old, rather

[1] Power of reconciling God in his anger.

[2] dominus nostra satisfactione placandus est (*de Lapsis*, XVIII).

[3] remedia propitiando deo ipsius dei verbis data sunt...operationibus justis deo satisfieri (*de Opere et Eleemosynis*, II).

[4] ita eleemosynis atque operationibus justis delictorum flamma sopitur (*ibid.*).

[5] ut sordes...quascunque contrahimus eleemosynis alluamus (*de Opere et Eleemosynis*, I).

[6] promereri deum judicem post baptismum sacrificiis (*ibid.* I).

than all Scripture through Christ. He brings back the old wineskins, and the result is a new Judaism. His whole theory as to the legal nature of the Christian man's new relationship to God, and his constant description of this relationship in terms derived from Roman Law, continued to prevail in the West until St Augustine's day; and, with modifications, from St Augustine's day until now.

What were those modifications? This is the crucial question in the historic issue between Catholicism and classic Protestantism.[1]

St Augustine, one of the greatest figures in the history of Christianity, is also one of the most complex. His genius embraces philosophical, mystical, ecclesiastical, sacramental, juridical and popular elements which defy neat and systematic synthesis. He is, however, unmistakably evangelical; and the dominant influence in the compromise which he represents and transmits to subsequent ages is that of St Paul. In his thought of man, sin and redemption he goes deeper than any of his predecessors because the Pauline gospel of grace is his by experience. But he modifies it, nevertheless, by making it two-fold. Primarily, grace is the forgiveness of sins, declared and given in baptism. But secondarily and at the same time, this infusion of grace into the sinner's heart now makes good works possible. It therefore makes merit possible. As we have noticed already, *gratia* was described as *infusa* because the forgiving love of God was poured into or 'shed

[1] 'Classic' Protestantism, because modern Protestantism—either ignorant of or embarrassed by the older evangelical terminology (original sin, grace, justification, sanctification)—has largely returned to the legalistic or moralistic way of thinking about the Christian Gospel. Too often 'the natural man is a born Catholic' (Rudolf Sohm) even though he may call himself a Protestant.

abroad' in the sinner's heart. But *gratia* was at the same time described as *efficiens*; this is, having an effect, and making something possible which was before impossible—namely works which are meritorious in the sight of God. In crowning our merits (*merita*) with rewards (*munera*) God is but crowning his own gift of grace. All is of God; not only his grace, but also our faith which responds to it and our merits which are its result. Indeed, this result is required; merit is demanded; the ultimate reward (*merces*), which is eternal life, may not be had without it. 'Unde et ipsam vitam aeternam, quae certe merces est operum bonorum, gratiam dei appellat apostolus.' (And so eternal life itself, which is indeed the payment due for good works, is called by the Apostle the grace of God: *Enchir.* cvii.)[1] Again, in one of his best-known treatises, St Augustine writes: 'For grace is given not because we have done good works, but in order that we may be able to do them: that is, not because we have fulfilled the law, but that we may be enabled to do so.'[2]

St Augustine and the Middle Ages which followed him were well aware that grace, strictly defined, excludes merit. All is of God. Thus merit is always due to the initiating act and gift of God; and as it is possible only on this basis of his grace, in the last resort it *is* grace; it is ultimately nothing but grace. *Da quod jubes et jube quod vis* (give what Thou commandest, and command what Thou wilt). In short, three statements may be regarded as axiomatic for medieval theology here. First, without grace there is no merit. Second, without merit there is no salvation. Third, grace makes it possible, therefore, for man to win salvation; but merit *must* win it.

[1] Cf. the exactly parallel words of St Bernard, quoted p. 46 n. 1.
[2] *de Spiritu et Littera*, XVII.

The vast and intricate theological system built up by medieval theologians and schoolmen, and known as scholasticism, was ultimately an elaborate attempt to find a rational resolution of this antinomy between grace and merit. A comprehensive synthesis of the material which had come down through the centuries from philosophy, Scripture and the growing body of ecclesiastical tradition and precedent, it was at the same time an analytical system of countless distinctions: in this problem of grace, for example, there were distinctions between general grace and saving grace; between grace as uncreated and grace as created; between grace as *gratis data* (the initial act of God's love, freely given) and grace as *gratum faciens* (the grace which makes its subject acceptable to God); between faith which is *informis* (unformed) and faith which is *caritate formata* (formed by love); between merit which is *condignus* and merit which is *congruus*; between grace which is *operans* and grace which is *co-operans*. Our concern with this impressive mass of consecrated subtlety lies in its tendency to diverge from St Augustine; to qualify his strict anti-Pelagian logic, and to find room even for an imperfect or relative 'merit' in the man who, aided by initial grace, does 'what in him lies' (*quod in eo est.*) For us, this tendency finds its most significant illustration, perhaps, in Alexander of Hales, who invented the famous distinction (denounced by Luther as a monstrosity) between *meritum condigni* (merit in the strict sense and, as such, alone acceptable to God) and *meritum congrui* (the relative 'merit' allowed by God's immutable generosity to the man who does what is in him by 'disposing' himself towards the good).

An even more pertinent illustration is found in the famous Thomist formula *fides caritate formata*. Indeed, it invites careful comparison with the Lutheran *sola fide* which challenged it. As we have seen, medieval Catholicism could speak of justification by faith; but by 'faith' it here meant 'faith perfected by love'; and, with St Thomas Aquinas, it began to substitute for this the more consciously Aristotelian expression, faith *formed* by love. Form (εἶδος) is for Aristotle that element of value which, by imprinting its stamp upon 'matter' (ὕλη), imparts distinctive value to matter. All existing finite things are examples of 'formed' matter, man himself being no exception. For example, in a piece of marble, that which constitutes its distinctive individual excellence is its 'form'; and it is its 'form' which makes it serviceable to the sculptor—as butter or sand or steel would not be.

Medieval Catholicism applied this Aristotelian category to the relationship between *fides* and *caritas*, faith and love. Faith is 'matter', and as such it is without distinctive substance or virtue. Love is 'form', the formative principle which lends to faith its true being and worth, leaving its impress on it. Without the 'form' of love, faith is formless (*informis*). The bearing of this careful definition of faith on our problem is plain: it means that ultimately man is justified—and so attains to fellowship with God—not by faith, but by love. Whence comes this preference for love? The answer is that love is the fulfilling of the Law, the whole claim of the Law being comprised in love to God and love to the neighbour; and when man has this love all righteousness will be fulfilled, and he will be justified. He will be justified by grace, but his justification will take place at the divine level of holiness rather than on the human level of sin. *Fides caritate formata* becomes the classic expression for fellowship with God, not on that common level of sin where the sons of Adam all live, but on the level of that holiness without which no man shall see the Lord. Indeed, as Nygren puts it, the true contrast between the medieval and the reformed conceptions of grace is that the former regards grace as essentially a means for man's meritorious ascent to God.

At first sight this seems proper and right, given the Augustinian presuppositions: here morality is religious, and religion is moral. But at once the crucial, age-long difficulty emerges. Free and full forgiveness is declared and given in baptism—that effective sign of God's redeeming love in Christ crucified and risen from the dead. But thereafter the baptized person must stand on his own feet, so to speak; he has to earn, and thus become entitled to, his justification.[1] And he is justified, therefore, only by stages as his life goes on. He is assisted by the grace of the sacraments, notably that of penance; he has his moral victories and defeats, of course, as he strives to love God and his neighbour with a pure heart. There is sometimes more, sometimes less, standing against him or to his credit in the eternal account-sheet which will be balanced and closed in the day of judgement—*dies irae, dies illa.* Justification, in short, is not an abiding attitude of the Father towards the contrite prodigal from the beginning: it is the last stage of a long series, by means of which the prodigal is to 'make good' and become righteously worthy of the robe, the feast and the ring. Justification is thus confused with sanctification (which is perhaps the most serious Roman heresy). Pardon is ultimately equated with purification. So far from being a finished act—

> 'Tis done, the great transaction's done;
> I am my Lord's, and He is mine—

---

[1] In Luther's words: 'Genug zu tun um einen gnädigen Gott zu kriegen.'

the sinner's justification is still a *process*, which ends only in death. Christian must carry his burden on his back all the way from the cross to the Celestial City. There is no evangelical doctrine of Assurance here, even for the great Augustine. God in his distributive justice must fix his acceptance or rejection of men in accordance with the measure of their meritorious attainment, at the last.

The doctrine of Justification is a twofold doctrine, therefore, from St Augustine onwards. Justification is both an event and a process. It is the remission of sins at baptism (event), and thereafter the infusion of grace through the sacramental-penitential system of the Church (process). This process is inevitably a precarious process, its ultimate outcome being necessarily uncertain. Forgiveness of sins committed after baptism is certainly provided for through sacraments other than baptism, whereby the redeeming grace of God precedes, accompanies and follows all good works (*quae virtus bona opera semper antecedit et concomitatur et subsequitur*).[1] But this only serves to deepen the anxiety and suspense of any man who takes his sin—and its correlative, guilt—in deadly earnest. Have I done enough? Have I earned sufficient merit? The penitential conditions under which forgiveness is still made available to the sinner burdened with his guilt, sustain this scrupulous temper of uncertainty.[2] It is the incontestable evidence of church history that they sometimes exploit it. Indeed, the medieval church regarded such uncertainty as a healthy dis-

[1] *Conc. Trid.* sess. VI, c. 16.
[2] See Heiler, *op. cit.* pp. 261–9 on *Die Skrupulosität* with its first-hand modern evidence from Catholic sources of the way in which this synthesis of grace and merit now consoles and now tortures the tender conscience. 'Anyone intimately acquainted with living Catholic piety knows the devastating harm caused by this vicious soul sickness.' 'Die Skrupulosität ist geradezu die Seelenkrankheit der römischen Frömmigkeit.'

cipline;[1] it tended to look suspiciously on 'joy and peace in believing' (Rom. xv. 13) as a form of presumption. As Pope Gregory the Great put it, with the bland arrogance of all paternalism: *Sancta ecclesia fidelibus suis...spem miscet et metum* (Holy Church mingles hope and fear for her faithful children).[2] Replying to one of the ladies-in-waiting at the Imperial Court, who had written to him for assurance, the great Pope replied: *secura de peccatis tuis fieri non debes* (thou shouldst not become easy in mind about thy sins).[3] In one sense, this is unexceptionable theology; such a warning bears witness to a true and inescapable element in that paradoxical doctrine of Assurance which the Reformers rediscovered in the New Testament, and which forms by natural sequence the next section in this book. But, to use an exact though crude metaphor, the medieval Church came to trade on this insecurity; the whole degrading trade in Indulgences which became a moral outrage in the early sixteenth century, shows that the scrupulous Catholic did not know and might not know on what terms he stood, so to speak, with God. Luther felt that he must know. In fact it was Luther—not Hus nor Wyclif nor any of the so-called Protestants before the Reformation—who first broke decisively and conclusively with the whole tradition of ecclesiastical legalism, and went back to St Paul. He sought to expel the idea of merit from contemporary religion. He knew that men may never establish any claim upon God. He would have felt it blasphemy to say with Tertullian: *Bonum factum deum habet debitorem* (the good deed puts God in your debt). He knew that when we have done all, we are still unprofitable servants. The sinner becomes justified, right with

---

[1] Cf. Tert. *de Pudic.* 1.   [2] *Moralium Libri*, xx, 5, 13.
[3] *Ep.* VII, 25.

God, not on the unattainable level of that divine holiness which is of purer eyes than to behold iniquity, but solely on the human level where holiness comes down in the immeasurable condescension of redeeming love. The sinner is justified solely in virtue of the divine compassion and his own humble trust in it, the grace of our Lord Jesus Christ who loves and seeks, who pardons and renews. *Sola gratia; sola fide.*

By faith alone. But here too we must ask the question: is it credible that Christian theology knew nothing of faith, in this sense of *fiducia* (personal trust), before Luther's day? The question is its own answer, of course. The hymns of the Church sufficiently refute the suggestion. St Bernard is no longer thought to be the author of the rhyming Jubilus on the Name of Jesus; but the anonymous medieval author (*c.* A.D. 1200) of its wonderful verses

> Nec lingua valet dicere
> Nec littera exprimere,
> Expertus potest credere
> Quid sit Jesum diligere.
>
> Jesu, spes poenitentibus,
> Quam pius es petentibus;
> Quam bonus te quaerentibus;
> Sed quid invenientibus—

has there given an exposition (and far more) of faith as *fiducia.*[1]

But, on the other hand, questions involving the history of doctrine may not be settled by hymnology, and it is a

---

[1] The serious defect in Edward Caswall's well-known version of this untranslatable hymn is his misrendering of 'quid sit Jesum diligere'.

> 'The love of Jesus, what it is,
> None but who love him know'

would be preferable to 'his loved ones'.

matter of history that, from the very beginnings of systematic theology in the second century, faith was defined as assent to Christian truth: more particularly, assent to formal Christian doctrine—the *regula fidei*—and therefore to the articles of the creed. Faith is thus *assensus*; it is the Faith, a body of divinely revealed truths which are to be believed (*credenda*). To anticipate the useful terminology of later centuries for a moment, it is *fides quae creditur*; that is, the Faith which is believed.

Faith, however, is obviously more than knowing truths *about* God; it is knowing God himself. And the great Alexandrians, Clement and Origen, enlarged and deepened the merely intellectual concept of faith by interpreting it as the true gnosis, or knowledge. Until assent to historical or philosophical statements of truth is transformed into the knowledge of that truth, it is rudimentary and imperfect.

St Augustine and the medieval theologians who followed him went further. Being concerned especially with man, sin and salvation, they thought of faith as saving faith. The Philippian jailor's question is Everyman's (Adam's) question: 'What must I do to be saved?' And, as we have already seen, the medieval Church taught that belief (*assensus*), in order to become saving faith (*fides*), needed to be 'formed' by love—the principle of merit. *Fides caritate formata* is the true meaning of faith. But for the great medieval schoolmen, faith is still assent rather than confidence, *assensus* rather than *fiducia*. According to Peter the Lombard, *fiducia* is possible only as hope, based on merit; hope apart from merit is presumption.

What of the greatest of the schoolmen, 'the angelic doctor', St Thomas Aquinas? He is, above all, rational, as befits the disciple and Christian interpreter of Aristotle, 'the master of them that know'. Religion is conceived of as a form of knowing (*intelligere*), and the rationalism of the Aristotelian idea of God pervades, if it does not dominate, the vast architectonic unity of the *Summa*. Hebrew prophecy and Christian revelation are defined in terms of intellectual knowing; and the beatific vision in heaven—the final meaning and goal of human existence—is itself the perfect knowing of God (*perfecta dei cognitio*). Indeed, the intellect is the highest of the faculties of the soul, higher and nobler even than the will. Faith, therefore, is still thought of in terms of intellectual assent. It is defined by St Thomas as 'thinking with assent', in humble obedience to the authoritative doctrines of the Church. Its reward will be eternal life.

But neither the 'gnosis' which the Alexandrians add to intellectual assent, nor the 'faith formed by love' which for St Thomas is its supreme expression—is what Luther meant by faith. For him *fides* is *fiducia*; that is, confident trust. It does not exclude *assensus*; it presupposes assent to and belief in the articles of the creed (*fides* QUAE *creditur*): but it is supremely *fides* QUA *creditur*—the faith by which a sinner puts his humble, confident trust in the redeeming mercy of God.

In short, faith means trusting Jesus: just that, in its heartbreaking simplicity. And justification means that we sinners are put right with God, here and now, by that faith alone. If this is true, it is the most amazing truth under heaven. The Gospel declares that it is true. It is paradoxical, irrational and non-moral, that God should love the sinner and justify the ungodly. It is beyond reason and it makes nonsense of the wisdom of this world.[1] The Elder Brother was entirely right, on his strictly moralistic pre-

[1] ἡ σοφία τοῦ αἰῶνος τούτου: I Cor. ii. 6 f.

mises, in regarding it as unfair: it transcends every legal way of thinking, every system of moral book-keeping, every calculus of rewards and penalties; it refuses to put divine grace on a tariff. It is the Lord's doing, and it is marvellous.

Further, his discovery of this paradoxical Gospel sufficiently explains Luther's attitude to Aristotle[1] and to rational theology. His passionate and extravagant attacks on Reason as Frau Hulda, the Devil's bride, the Whore or the Fool, are the understandable and even necessary reaction of evangelical irrationalism against scholastic intellectualism. Luther attacks Aristotle as 'that monster', 'that blind heathen', because the great Greek philosopher had been consecrated as the high priest of reason by the later Middle Ages, and his *ipse dixit* had come to have a wholly unwarrantable authority over the disciples of Christ. Luther's protest against this alien influence, like Kierkegaard's scorn for Hegel's 'system', was a defence of biblical religion against rationalizing distortions and false simplifications of its paradoxical content.[2] 'Almost the whole of Aristotle's exceedingly bad ethic is hostile to grace.'[3] The 'Holy Ghost is greater than Aristotle.'[4]

---

[1] See Seeberg, *DG*[4], IV, i, 70, 76.

[2] See Jaroslav Pelikan, *From Luther to Kierkegaard* (Concordia, St Louis, Mo. 1950), p. 114. 'Intellectualism claims to have domesticated the truth and to have fitted it perfectly into its preconceived patterns....By its supposedly dispassionate analysis of the "objective" truth, external to all experience, it has completely perverted the truth. For truth is not a something with which I may deal as I choose, as though it were outside me. Truth is always personal, subjective. It comes in involvement, and it is hard to live with. The Hegelian assumption that a neatly-balanced system of reality can be constructed rationally from the truth is a tragic delusion. Only that is true which is true for me.'

[3] *Disputation against the Scholastic Theology* (1517), Art. 41; cf. Art. 43: 'It is erroneous to say that a man cannot become a theologian without Aristotle.'   [4] *WA*, VI, 511.

Luther saw that the rational speculations of theism are not only different from the Biblical revelation of the living God; the God of philosophical and rational theology is, of necessity, a God whose righteousness is retributive and punitive, whereas the 'righteousness of God' proclaimed in the Scriptures (Ps. xxxi, 1; Rom. i. 17) justifies the sinner and redeems him. Luther realized that reason is the necessary presupposition of legal righteousness: to argue that God must reward the good and punish the bad is part of its inevitable logic. A God who yearns after sinners in love (ἀγάπη), giving himself for them to the uttermost, so that his love becomes what Luther called 'eine verlorene Liebe' (a lost love; Matt. xxvii. 46)—this is and must be unintelligible to reason. It is 'wider alle Vernunft' (against all reason); to Greeks, from Aristotle onwards, it is foolishness (I Cor. i. 18–23; iii. 19). There is nothing rational about God's justification of the ungodly; so far from being a rational inference from the moral law of God, it contradicts that law. Indeed, Luther candidly recognizes that belief in the divine forgiveness of sins is not logically compatible with belief that morality is divine; the Christian man can only express it, therefore, in antinomies: it is 'gegen sein eigenes Gewissen' (against his own conscience); here he overcomes God with God ('Gott mit Gott überwindet'); here God's Word is contradicted by itself ('Gottes Wort wider Gottes Wort laut').[1]

In this paradox of justification, Luther is not merely rediscovering St Augustine. Trembling before the retribu-

---

[1] References in Holl, *op. cit.* 1, 37, 77. Cf. Shakespeare, *Richard II*, act v, scene 5:

> ...the Word itself against the Word,
> As thus: 'Come little ones.' And then again:
> 'It is as hard for you to come as for a camel
> To thread the postern of a needle's eye.'

tive righteousness of God and recognizing that its judgement of him is just, he is nevertheless enabled to pierce to the heart of its ultimate redemptive meaning. God's grace does not by-pass his righteousness; it acts *through* his righteousness. Even when the Holy One and the Just is bringing the sinful man down to the dust, crushing and virtually annihilating him, he imparts his own righteousness to that man by grace.[1] For it is his nature, not only to have mercy and to forgive; he gives and shares himself; ultimately he is nothing else than self-giving Goodness. Reason is not able to compass the heights and depths of this paradox of justification; but

> Where reason fails with all her powers,
> There faith prevails and love adores.[2]

Luther's open letter on the art of translating is largely a defence of his introduction of the word 'alone' into his German version of Rom. iii. 28. Excerpts from it may fittingly conclude this survey of the paradox of justification.

It would have been pointless to tell me that the word 'alone' is not found in the Latin or Greek texts here, for I was well aware of it....But the word has to be added if the sense of the passage is to be expressed clearly and with proper force in German. For it was not my wish to speak in Latin or Greek here, but in my own tongue....You must not ask the Latin language how to express itself in German...you must ask the mother in the home, the children in the street, the man in the market-place; you must notice how *they* speak, and translate accordingly; only so will they understand you....I can certify with a good conscience that I have laboured at this translation with the greatest fidelity, and that it has never been my intention to falsify the true text....Moreover, so far from being

---

[1] Isa. xxviii. 18, 21.
[2] This concluding couplet of 'We give immortal praise' (Isaac Watts) could have been written by St Thomas Aquinas.

too free with the text, my colleagues and I have striven for literal accuracy as far as this was feasible....But this art of translating does not belong to everyone. It requires a heart that is truly religious, believing, devoted, reverent, Christian, experienced and disciplined....And so I was not concerned exclusively with the Greek text when I added the word 'alone' to Rom. iii. 28: the text and the thought of St Paul imperiously demand it....'But', says someone, 'it sounds bad, and people will understand it as meaning that they need not do good works.' My dear man, let me ask you whether St Paul scandalizes us less by adding 'without the works of the Law'? 'By faith alone' is a formula which you might ingeniously get round and explain away: but this other formula—'without the works of the Law'—is so brutally explicit that no explanation can get round it....If it is not offensive to preach 'without works' or 'not by works', why should it be offensive to preach 'by faith alone'? Friend, St Paul and we his translators *wish* to scandalize here. The only reason why we attack works so strongly and exalt faith to pre-eminence is that people need to be scandalized, so that they may learn that they will not become religious by their works, but by the death and resurrection of Christ....I am not the first to have said that faith alone saves. St Ambrose and St Augustine said it before me, and a good many others. And he who would read St Paul with understanding cannot say anything different.

ADDITIONAL NOTE

Luther's conception of the Work of Christ

(*a*) For all Christian theologians, Catholic and Protestant, the death and resurrection of the Incarnate Son of God is the central, constitutive fact of the Church and the Christian religion. The doctrine common to medieval Schoolmen and the Reformers was (i) that what Christ did (his active obedience) and what he suffered (his passive obedience) has infinite and objective value; (ii) that this

Work of Christ atoned for the sin of humanity; it was
nothing less than God's act of redemption: he who is holy
Love was here reconciling the world unto Himself, without making light of the enormity of the world's sin;
(iii) that legal terminology (law, justice, satisfaction, merit)
was appropriate to describe and explain the Atonement
and the Gospel of Redemption. Luther and the Reformers
were thus in general theological agreement with their
medieval predecessors here. What were the essential
differences?

(b) For the broad medieval view we may go to the great
and representative figure of St Anselm (c. 1033–1109).
Here satisfaction was a concept taken from private law. It
meant compensation for wrong done. But man cannot, in
the nature of the case, make satisfaction for sin, since sin
concerns none other than God in his infinite perfection, and
its guilt is necessarily infinite. Sinful man cannot pay
what, nevertheless, he must pay. Yet he was created by God
for blessedness, and God's purpose may not be defeated.
Therefore, since the compensation required is infinite,
God himself is alone able to provide it, and in Christ He
becomes man; the eternal Son is united with humanity in
one person—that of the God-Man. The God-Man lives that
human life of complete and perfect obedience which is man's
supreme obligation. Since Adam, death has been the penalty
for sin but, as Christ is sinless, his willing surrender of his
life on Calvary is a debt which he does not owe. And since
it is his free gift to the Father, its merit is infinite, and the
requisite compensation for sin. In justice, it merits infinite
reward. But there is nothing which the Father can give
the Son for himself. Therefore the infinite merit of the
Son is passed on, so to speak, to sinful humanity, and it
takes the form of forgiveness of sins. As a sufficient and

75

superabundant satisfaction for sin the infinite merits of
Christ are available to the faithful, and dispensed to them
through the prescribed means of grace, the sacraments.

The strength, weakness and classic importance of this
famous exposition need no comment here. Its essential idea,
modified of course by later Schoolmen in various ways,
provided a rationale of the salvation proclaimed and made
available to men through the Church.

One modification of St Anselm's theory may be noted,
however, since it provides a link with the Reformers;
namely, the idea of penalty. Hugh and Richard of St
Victor, Alexander of Hales, Bonaventura and Aquinas conceive of Christ's satisfaction not only as compensatory but
also as penal. Aquinas, for example, defines satisfaction as
the vicarious endurance of another's punishment. Anselm
had deliberately excluded this. Setting out the alternatives
'either satisfaction or punishment', he ruled out punishment as being inadmissible and impossible here. But some
of his medieval successors included the penal concept.
Following Alexander of Hales, Aquinas writes: *unus autem
pro peccato alterius satisfacit, dum poenam pro peccato alterius
debitam in se suscepit* (one makes satisfaction for the sin of
another when he takes upon himself the due punishment
for another's sin). This brings us to Luther and the
Reformation.

(*c*) Luther broke away from the general medieval conception of Christ's Work, and went beyond it, in two
directions.

(i) For him, satisfaction was a concept taken from public
law, where God is not, so to speak, one who demands satisfaction from another in court, but the Judge. Here satisfaction means (what it had meant in a subsidiary sense for
Aquinas and other Schoolmen) forensic justice demanding

punishment. Anselm had said 'satisfaction or punishment'. The Reformers said 'satisfaction through punishment'. Thus Luther and the Reformers took an unambiguously penal view of Christ's death: as substitute for humanity he endured humanity's due punishment. 'In my place condemned he stood; sealed my pardon with his blood.' This penal concept springs from the Reformers' new sense—biblical in its austerity—of God's absolute sovereignty; and from its correlative, their new and more serious view of sin and guilt. Sin is not something which may be 'made good' by compensatory satisfaction, an idea which found its analogue and working illustration in the elaborately differentiated tariff of ecclesiastical penances and indulgences rather than in the scriptural 'Thus saith the Lord'. The Judge of all the earth is not to be 'bought off'. The transgressions of his Law which justly provoke his wrath can be satisfied only by punishment. 'Was it out of sheer grace', asks Luther, 'that our sin is not reckoned as such to us by God? No, God willed it otherwise. Before everything else his law and his righteousness had to be satisfied, and more than satisfied. This grace had first to be purchased and won from his righteousness on our behalf. Inasmuch, therefore, as that was an impossible task for us, he foreordained One to undertake for us and to stand in our place; to take all our deserved punishments upon himself, and to fulfil the law for us, turning the divine judgement away from us, and expiating the divine wrath' (*WA*, x, i, 1, 470). Luther links this thought with the cry of dereliction from the Cross (Matt. xxvii. 46), and drives it to its dire, logical conclusion, that Christ on the Cross felt himself to be under the wrath of God, the whole curse of the Law (Gal. iii. 13) being there heaped upon him (*WA*, xl, i, 449). Christ comes to us because the loving compassion of the Father saw us oppressed by the curse of the Law and sent him to save us. Indeed, Luther's extreme, and sometimes highly rhetorical expression of the idea of penal substitution (Christ as 'maledictus dei'; Christ as 'the greatest of all sinners because he assumed our sins in his body, to make satisfaction for them') is not only an expression of the Reformers' austere sense of God's sovereign holiness; it is also and equally their way of realizing the wonder and glory of the forgiveness of sins. *Theologia crucis* is also and at the same time *theologia gloriae*. This brings us to the second direction in which Luther went beyond Catholic conceptions of Christ's saving work.

(ii) For Luther, the cross and the resurrection belong indissociably together. He recovers the Pauline experience, according to which death and resurrection constitute an indivisible whole. He thus corrects the one-sidedness into which Western theology since Anselm had fallen, and into which it was to fall again under the influence of Melanchthon and Protestant Scholasticism; namely, the limitation of Christ's redeeming work to his death and cross. Luther realized that Christ's death, the satisfaction of divine justice, is not God's last word. *Er hat noch ein Wort!* This is an idea of which he is exceedingly fond, and which is expressed with dramatic vividness in his Easter hymns (see p. 101) and frequently elsewhere: the Cross and the Resurrection are a marvellous battle, wherein the Lord of Life wins the victory over Death and swallows it up: 'the Curse rushes upon him and wishes to destroy him, but cannot because he is eternal Blessing. The Curse has to yield, because if the Blessing in Christ could be conquered, God would be conquered.' Thus the Resurrection means (1) that we look through and beyond God's wrathful judgement to grace and blessing; (2) that Christ is now present

78

and effectively at work in the believer: Luther thus makes his own St Paul's so-called 'Christ Mysticism': 'he who has faith in Christ has Christ present in him like a precious stone in its setting' (*in einer Zang einen edlen Stein*): the believing soul is married to Christ, faith being the 'nuptual ring' (*WA*, XL, i. 233 and VII, 54–6); (3) that Christ is thus present not as the object of mystic ecstasy but as the source of power in the fight against sin; the Christ who rose from the dead rises again in the believer and, as the Lord Sabaoth, daily conducts his warfare against evil in the believer; (4) that the strengthening thus experienced by the believer is his assurance, not only that his sin is forgiven, but also that in the power of Christ he may overcome it. Thus faith deals as much with the power as with the guilt of sin. Because *theologia crucis* is also *theologia gloriae* Satan, Sin and Death are really defeated. The *salutaris hostia* is *Christus Victor*. Or, as St Augustine put it: 'ideo Victor quia Victima' (*Conf.* X, 43).

Professor (now Bishop) Gustav Aulén put modern theology in his debt with his stimulating and valuable book *Christus Victor*, which argued—probably rightly— that Luther's soteriology is characteristic of the Greek rather than of the Latin tradition. But the book is so one-sided as to be seriously misleading. Its author chooses to ignore altogether abundant evidence in all Luther's works from the beginning, where the accent is unmistakably that of the Latin west and its *theologia crucis*. All the standard histories of doctrine give the evidence.[1] J. K. Mozley's sound and judicious *The Doctrine of the Atonement* (Duckworth, 1927) is a useful corrective of Aulén's brilliant but tendentious treatment of the history of doctrine.

[1] See especially Seeberg, *DG*[4], IV, i, 237 ff.; and Holl, *op. cit.* I, 69–72.

The last word may lie with Karl Barth:

We may take it that the Western Church has a decided inclination towards the *theologia crucis*; that is, towards bringing out and emphasizing the fact that He was surrendered for our transgressions. Whereas the Eastern Church brings more into the foreground the fact that He was raised for our justification, and so inclines towards the *theologia gloriae*. In this matter there is no sense in wanting to play one off against the other. You know that from the beginning Luther strongly worked out the Western tendency—not *theologia gloriae* but *theologia crucis*. What Luther meant by that is right. But we ought not to erect and fix any opposition; for there is no *theologia crucis* which does not have its complement in the *theologia gloriae*. Of course there is no Easter without Good Friday, but equally certainly there is no Good Friday without Easter.[1]

[1] *Dogmatics in Outline,* tr. G. T. Thompson (S.C.M. 1949).

CHAPTER V

THE PARADOX OF THE BELIEVING SINNER'S ASSURANCE

LUTHER's third evangelical conviction springs out of the foregoing and is a paradox in itself; namely, the believer's assurance of being right with God though he is still a sinner, and though the old Adam may hang about his neck to the end.[1] In spite of the rapturous evangelical experience of being justified by faith alone, Luther knows that we are always unprofitable servants, *semper injusti, semper peccatores* (always unrighteous, always sinners). But he knows too that the believer who receives by faith the mercy of God in Christ is *simul peccator et justus* (at one and the same time, sinful and right with God). This means that our justification is more than a promise of something true in principle but awaiting verification. It is not a possibility which should become an actuality as time goes on; it is more than a proleptic foreshortening of the time-process, the spirit's leap of anticipation to truth which will only be consummated hereafter; in short, it is neither a legal fiction nor a pious hope, but a present, continuous, dependable and permanent fact. We have joy and peace in believing: not because we are arrogant or smug or just plain stupid; not because we are living in a fool's paradise, blind to the sin that is ever before us; but because the Author of our salvation is trustworthy and unchanging.

Only present tenses may fittingly describe this assurance, and in the New Testament they abound. Again and again

[1] 'Der alte Adam uns immer am Halse hängen bleibt.'

the future tenses of the Old Testament become present tenses in the New. Something *has come to pass* and now *is*. We *have* peace with God through our Lord Jesus Christ (Rom. v. 1). I *am* crucified with Christ; nevertheless *I am alive*; and yet not I, but Christ *is alive in me* (Gal. ii. 20). I *am* persuaded (Rom. viii. 38). We *know* that we *have passed* from death unto life (I John iii. 14). That ye may know that ye *have* eternal life (I John v. 13). Hereby *know* we that we *dwell* in him and he in us, because he hath given us of his Spirit (I John iv. 13). In the New Testament, assurance is not one doctrine among many, but the atmosphere in which all are proclaimed; it is the mood of the whole (I Thess. i. 5; Heb. x. 22). Discussing St Paul's so-called Christ-Mysticism, Professor Dodd observes that though the glory yet to come remains a background of thought, the foreground is more and more occupied with the riches of divine grace enjoyed here and now by those who are in Christ Jesus. In its final form, admittedly, the consummation of the supernatural order of life is still future and therefore a matter of hope. But the earnest or guarantee (ἀρραβών) of the inheritance is a present possession (II Cor. i. 22, v. 5; Eph. i. 14). An ἀρραβών is a sample of goods guaranteed to be of the same kind and quality as the main consignment.[1] An old Gospel hymn consciously recalls this:

> Blessed assurance, Jesus is mine;
> Oh, what a foretaste of glory divine,

and an older verse of Zinzendorf states it and its alternative:

> Er, er ist meine Zuversicht alleine,
> Sonst hab' ich keine.[2]

---

[1] See C. H. Dodd, *The Apostolic Preaching* (Hodder, 1936), p. 155, from which these references are substantially taken.

[2]   He is my Confidence alone;
               Else have I none.

Luther's doctrine has no other basis. We have assurance because the promises of God are Yea and Amen in Christ. God is trustworthy and unchanging. His grace may be relied on, however unreliable its objects may prove to be. The grace of God is not capricious, and therefore intermittent and precarious; it abides, even though we still fail and fall. The believer in God's grace may be steadily sure of it (Mark ix. 24).

> O happy day that fixed my choice
>   On Thee, my Saviour and my God:
> Well may this glowing heart rejoice,
>   And tell its raptures all abroad.
>
> 'Tis done, the great transaction's done;
>   I am my Lord's and He is mine.
> He drew me and I followed on,
>   Charmed to confess that voice divine.
>
> Now rest, my long divided heart,
>   Fixed on this blissful centre, rest:
> With ashes who would grudge to part
>   When called on angels' bread to feast?
>
> High heaven, that heard the solemn vow,
>   That vow renewed shall daily hear:
> Till in life's latest hour I bow
>   And bless in death a bond so dear.[1]

That is what the 'assurance' of the converted man means. As the late Prof. H. R. Mackintosh once observed, it is 'the glory of Protestantism'.

We have already noticed that for Pope Gregory I it was presumptuous to be assured of salvation. For Luther it was presumptuous and the sin of pride to doubt it. For

---

[1] Philip Doddridge, 1702–51.

Gregory, anxious fear was a duty, since assurance begets negligence.[1] For Luther, assurance was a duty, since the promises of God are, in effect, commands, Indeed, assurance is not merely permissible; it is an obligation; the believer ought to hope (*sperare debet*). Luther does not say that the believer may hope (*sperare licet*), nor does his use of the word hope here imply a lower level of assurance than faith, as though the believer's justification were still a matter of expectation. For Luther, as for St Paul, the present is the 'earnest' of a consummation in eternity; faith and hope involve one another, and to believe in Christ (*confidere in dominum*) is what hope means.[2] It is a Christian privilege to be assured that God will not cast us out (John vi. 37). Our relation to the Father, through the work of Christ for us and in us, is new and permanent. Luther was here sounding a note which had long been silent in Christendom.

This is no easy doctrine, of course;[3] and it was certainly never easy for Luther. Indeed, the sensitive conscience can never make light of the obvious difficulty and danger here. It is vividly illustrated by the question which Cromwell is said to have asked, as he lay dying: 'Tell me, is it possible to fall from grace?' After a moment his chaplain answered, 'It is not possible.' Cromwell said, 'I thank God, for I know I was in grace once'. But we recall Mrs C. F. Alexander's hymn, 'The roseate hues of early dawn' which

---

[1] mater neglegentiae solet esse securitas; habere ergo in hac vita non debes securitatem (*Ep. lib.* VII, 25).

[2] Holl, *Ges. Aufs.* I, 143 f., for this and the citations from Luther's lectures on Romans which follow.

[3] videtur ista doctrina facilis, sed quam res magna sit auditus fidei, experior ego et pii alii (that doctrine seems easy; but just how big a thing it is to hear God's word by faith, I know somewhat, and many a pious man does, too). *WA*, XL, i, 345.

contrasts the ideal and the actual, the aspirations and the shortcomings, in every Christian life, and ends

> Grant that we fall not from Thy grace,
> Nor cast away our crown,

and we understand, only too well, the common-sense answer which Catholic theology has always given to this cry for assurance. It steadily denies that in this life there can ever be an assurance of eternal salvation, and constantly cites the words of the Apostle about fear and trembling (Phil. ii. 12). As we have seen, this was the answer of Pope Gregory I to the lady at the court of the Empress Gregoria who longed passionately for religious assurance; and St Bernard of Clairvaux is typical of the whole Catholic tradition from Gregory to the Council of Trent in representing *sollicitudo* (care, anxiety) as part of the will of God for his children:

> What man can say, I am of the elect; I am among those who are predestined to life; I am of the number of the faithful? Who, I ask, can say such things?...We have no certainty: but we have the consolation of a trustworthy hope, which prevents our being tortured by an agony of doubt....God denies us assurance, but only that he may prevent us from growing careless. And so we must bow humbly beneath God's mighty hand, ever anxious, and in fear and trembling.[1]

The Anglican Professor Burnaby would not, presumably, endorse St Bernard's conclusion just as it stands, but he too is in line with Catholic tradition when he writes: 'To the Augustine whom Luther esteemed next to Holy Writ, the Lutheran assurance would have spelt deadly peril.'[2]

---

[1] 'semper solliciti et in timore et tremore' (*in Sept.* s. 1, 1; quoted by Heiler, *op. cit.* 580).   [2] *Op. cit.* p. 126.

There seems to be misunderstanding here, not of St Augustine, of course, but of Luther; and of what he meant (and did not mean) by assurance.

First, as to what he did not mean. All the Reformers were in entire and emphatic agreement with the opening words of St Bernard quoted above. No one could have been more explicit than were Luther and Calvin in repudiating all attempts to probe the final mystery of the divine predestination. God alone knows his elect, and no man may usurp a prerogative which is his alone. Assurance in this sense would be blasphemous presumption. Indeed, the Reformers constantly use St Augustine's own language about the *judicia inscrutabilia* of God, and ask his own rhetorical question: 'What man of the whole multitude of the faithful, as long as he is in this mortal life, may presume that he is numbered among the elect?'[1] They, too, quote Rom. xi. 20 in this connexion, as he does.[2] Indeed, Luther goes further in his definition of such presumption. He enlarges its area. He denies that the new life (*nova vita*) of the man who is justified by faith is an object of experience, which may be measured and spiritually evaluated. It is always veiled. No man enjoys such spiritual insight as to be disinterested about himself, not even the regenerate man. His self-love remains, even when he is living a new life under grace. No man knows his own secret motives; only God can judge them. No man can know whether he possesses grace as effective moral power; even the very elect may be deceived. Luther attacks the later scholastic doctrine, therefore, that signs of present grace (*signa presentis gratiae*) may be discernible in the justified believer.

---

[1] quis enim ex multitudine fidelium, quamdiu in hac mortalitate vivitur, in numero praedestinatorum se esse presumat? (*de corr. et gr.* XII, 40).

[2] 'Be not high-minded, but fear.'

He sees dangerous and destructive error here; for the signs of grace which we detect in ourselves may be that temptation of the devil to which Little Jack Horner succumbed ('What a good boy am I'). Luther does not deny that the new life in Christ must and does involve steady growth in grace and true freedom; but he denies that man may lift the veil to see how he is getting on. That would be presumption: 'For since we cannot know whether we are living in accordance with every word of God and denying none...we can never know whether we are justified and whether we believe.'[1] 'For no one knows by experience that he is living as a justified man; but he believes and hopes.'[2] This seems to mean, in short, that we can only have faith that we have faith; and that assurance, in the plain sense of the word, is ruled out altogether. But, tiresomely paradoxical though this is on Luther's part, his meaning seems clear: he is opposed only to that assurance which would appeal to a demonstrably acquired righteousness: the believer is still a sinner, and he always will be: the righteousness on which alone he confidently relies is never to be found in himself, but only in Christ. Because actual righteousness is his alone, it is always outside or external to the believer.[3]

Indeed, Luther insists that we have constantly to win anew our certainty of salvation. A man who is justified by faith will be constantly humble, continuously penitent, such penitence and contrition being the act and gift of God.

[1] quia cum non possumus scire an in omni verbo dei vivamus aut nullum negemus...nunquam scire possumus an justificati simus, an credamus (*Lectures on Romans*, II, 88).

[2] nemo enim scit se vivere aut experitur se esse justificatum; sed credit et sperat (*Ibid.* I, 54).

[3] extrinsecum nobis est omne bonum nostrum, quod est Christus (*Ibid.* II, 114).

The redeemed man must ever plead earnestly with God for this gift. 'Let him learn here who can learn; and let everyone also become an eagle that can soar aloft into the heights in such need. The Psalmist saith "I cried unto the Lord". Thou must learn to cry. Come now thou lazy rascal, fall down upon thy knees, and set forth thy need with tears before God.'[1] Luther is here addressing the believer; he is addressing himself. So much, then, for what he did not mean by assurance.

In the second place, what he did mean is best seen against the background of contemporary Catholic practice and doctrine. The Catholic sacrament of penance meant that God condescends to a renewal of the relationship of grace from time to time. The Council of Trent, answering the Reformers and initiating the Counter-Reformation, actually used the phrase 'magis justificari' (i.e. 'to be justified more and more').[2] Discussing what he describes as this 'curious and really sub-Christian idea that we are forgiven by degrees', the Edinburgh theologian H. R. Mackintosh observed that Rome did not ignore the urgent human desire for assurance, of course: indeed Rome contended that assurance of a kind is given to man in the voice of the Church, speaking through the absolving priest. But Protestantism has always felt that there are three evils here, which may be stated in an ascending order of seriousness. The first, and perhaps the least serious, is that the priest becomes an indispensable intermediary between the soul and God, an idea which is destitute of New Testa-

---

[1] *Lecture on Ps.* 118.

[2] I am aware that Luther himself used this phrase at least once. See Adolf Köberle's *The Way of Holiness*; its valuable excursus on the relationship of Justification to Sanctification as understood in the sixteenth century by Melanchthon, Osiander, Luther and Conc. Trid. respectively. Also Otto Ritschl, *DG des Protestantismus*, II, i, c. 28 f.

ment authority, and which is indubitably alien to the apostolic gospel. The second is that priestly absolution is made dependent on the performance of various satisfactions: about which one may relevantly say that the Father forgave the contrite prodigal freely and immediately, and without such conditions and technical guarantees as the elder brother doubtless thought necessary. But the most serious evil here is the third. It is, to quote Mackintosh, 'the doctrine implicit in the system as a whole; that with every new mortal sin the Christian forfeits his standing with the Father; that with each fall into transgression he ceases to be God's accepted child and must work his way back into grace by way of penance'.[1] Such forgiveness is conditional; it is subject to continuous revision and therefore precarious. 'Provisional pardon is an idea scarcely fitted to evoke a joy unspeakable and full of glory, or to inspire the tempted to unwavering courage.'[2] Such an idea would never have inspired the ecstatic gratitude and joy of countless hymns such as this:

> I've found a friend, oh such a friend,
>   He loved me ere I knew him:
> He drew me with the cords of love
>   And thus he bound me to him.
> And round my heart still closely twine
>   Those ties which nought can sever;
> For I am his and he is mine,
>   For ever and for ever.[3]

These lines illustrate not only the divine initiative but also that divine changelessness which is the true basis of the doctrine of assurance. Luther realized that just as God's judgement always rests on the believer, so does his promise.

---

[1] *The Christian Experience of Forgiveness* (Nisbet), p. 153.
[2] *Ibid.* p. 242. [3] J. G. Small (1817–78).

What he once wills, he wills continuously and permanently. His trustworthiness may not be broken or invalidated by man's disloyalties. 'For the counsel of God is not altered by any merits or demerits...it does not change because you have changed' (*quia nullis meritis neque demeritis mutatur consilium dei...non mutatur vobis mutatis*).[1]

Luther insists, often and emphatically, that fear of the coming judgement may never be eliminated from the believer's consciousness: assurance is his, yet even he has to think together as an indissoluble unity both God's utter rejection of him and His gracious acceptance of him. If this sounds paradoxical to the verge of absurdity, so be it: some antinomy is inescapable here, as those who have agonized over the problem know. But this may not be dismissed as a muddled attempt to go half-way back to the Roman position; and for two reasons. First, the Schoolmen and Luther think differently about hope. 'For hope does not proceed from merits...it has no other object, substance or foundation than the sheer mercy of God itself; certainly not our works.'[2] Second, for Luther the relationship between religion and morality differs from that in Catholicism. For him, morality is never the means whereby man 'wins through' to fellowship with God, such morality being the subtlest and most dangerous form of pride: but fellowship with God is the means whereby true morality becomes possible. The one demands a human righteousness as the price of divine friendship: the other gives that friendship, to the uttermost, and so builds righteousness on a new basis. It was while we were yet sinners that Christ

[1] Luther's *Lectures on Romans*, II, 264.
[2] quia spes non provenit ex meritis...nec habet objectum vel materiam seu fundamentum aliud quam ipsam nudam dei misericordiam; nequaquam opera nostra (*WA*, I, 428).

died for us. It was while the prodigal was yet a great way off that the Father saw him, and had compassion, and ran and fell on his neck and kissed him. We love because he first loved us.

This brings us to the fourth paradox which, along with the second, expressed the fundamental meaning of the Reformation.

CHAPTER VI

THE PARADOX OF 'GABE'
AND 'AUFGABE'

OUBTLESS more than one learned monograph has been written on the theological importance of the word 'therefore' (οὖν) in the New Testament. For the original Christian Gospel had a twofold structure. First, it proclaimed the revelation of God in what he had done for man, pre-eminently in the Incarnation: this gift of God placed man under the divine judgement and under the divine grace of forgiveness. Second, it proclaimed the moral obligation involved in the Christian's acceptance of the Incarnation. In the New Testament, the first element in this twofold proclamation is almost always followed by 'therefore' or its verbal equivalent. The divine gift (*Gabe*) involves responsive human activity (*Aufgabe*).

Rom. xii. 1 is a classic example. The great theological argument of the epistle comes to its tremendous climax in Rom. ix–xi, where the problems of time are set against the background of eternity, and the redemption of the world is seen in terms of the glory and the sole causality of God, 'from whom all comes, by whom all lives and in whom all ends'. The word 'therefore' follows immediately. It is the bridge from the ineffable mysteries of the supernatural order to the ethical obligations of daily living:

The teacher must mind his teaching, the speaker his words of counsel; the contributor must be liberal, the superintendent must be in earnest, the sick-visitor must be cheerful. Let your love be a real thing, with a loathing for evil and a bent for what is good. Put affection into your love for the brotherhood; be forward to honour one another; never let your zeal flag; maintain the spiritual glow; serve the Lord; let your hope be a joy to you; be steadfast in trouble; attend to prayer, contribute to needy saints, make a practice of hospitality.[1]

The Apostle means that our ethical obligations as Christians are founded upon and derived from our relation to the supernatural order. Being justified by faith, we have peace with God through our Lord Jesus Christ: *therefore* the love of the brethren is its inevitable expression.

The last but not the least of Luther's paradoxical convictions illustrates the same sequence: namely, that justification—not by works but by faith alone—so far from implying quietism, is the only true basis and source of Christian morality. It is *the* impulse to Christian action and the fulfilment of the Law of Christ. Faith without ethical consequences would be no faith, but a blasphemous imposture. *Glauben* and *Lieben* (believing and loving) are necessarily correlative. Luther was no more antinomian than was St Paul, who had to meet precisely the same slanderous misinterpretation.

It is true that later Lutheran orthodoxy, like later Reformed Pietism, did tend to quietism. What of Luther himself? Against the reproach constantly repeated by Catholics that he 'forbids good works', Luther defends himself frequently, emphatically and effectively. Did his doctrine of Justification by Faith encourage men to say: 'We will take our ease and do no good works, but be content with faith'? 'I answer', said Luther, 'not so, ye wicked men, not so.... I have not forbidden good works. I have simply declared that just as a tree must be good before it can bring forth good fruit, so men must be made good by

[1] Rom. xii. 7–13 (Moffatt).

God's grace before he can do good.'[1] Again: 'The Word is given that thou mayest be cleansed; it quickens thee to do good works, not to live at ease.'[2] Again: 'for God gives no one his grace that he may lie down and do nothing worth while any more.'[3] One of his Latin Propositions of 1520 succinctly states the paradox: 'Neither faith nor justification comes from works; but works come from faith and justification.'[4] Or, in his lively German: 'gute fromme Werke machen niemals einen guten frommen Mann; sondern ein guter frommer Mann macht gute fromme Werke.'[5] Luther is all the time fighting for the true evangelical perspective, and he therefore refuses the extravagant one-sidedness which is the insidious temptation in all controversy. For example, his friend and comrade Agricola assumed that the rejection of legalism meant the rejection of law. Luther denounced this, rightly, as antinomian. He knew, as he expressed it in another of his Propositions of 1520: 'It is impossible for faith to exist without assiduous, many and great works.' One glance at his two famous Catechisms shows the place which he gave to the Commandments of the Law; they have to be fulfilled.

Indeed, in his Preface to the *Epistle to the Romans* (1522) he distinguishes fulfilling the law from legalism, as follows:

Understand that to do the works of the law and to fulfil the law are two absolutely different things. The works of the law comprise all that a man can do by his own will and with his own resources. As all these works are done against the grain and with reluctance they accomplish nothing. This is St Paul's meaning in Rom. iii. 20 where he says that by the works of the

---

[1] See *Freiheit eines Christenmenschen*, §§ 19–25 (*WA*, vii, 20–38); and E. G. Rupp, *Luther's progress to the Diet of Worms*, p. 88 (S.C.M. 1951).

[2] *WA*, xv, 437.   [3] *WA*, x, iii, 287.   [4] *WA*, vii, 231.

[5] 'Good and pious works never make a good and pious man; but a good, pious man does good and pious works' (*Freiheit eines Christenmenschen*, § 23).

law shall no man be justified before God. But to fulfil the law is to do its works with a joyous heart, living a godly and good life quite spontaneously, without any constraint, as though there were no law and no sanctions. This verve, this spontaneous love, is created by the Spirit in the heart, as the fifth chapter declares: it is given only in conjunction with faith in Christ: it is created in us by the Word of God and by the Gospel which preaches Christ, Son of God and man, dead and raised up for us, as chapters iii, iv and x tell us. This is why faith alone justifies, and why faith alone fulfils the law. The Spirit creates in the heart that abandon and spontaneity which law demands; good works then proceed from faith itself. This is Paul's meaning in iii. 31 ...we establish the law, he says, by faith: that is, we fulfil it through faith.

A famous passage in the same Preface further illustrates the spontaneous character of faith:

Faith is not human day-dreaming which some people confuse with it...they say, 'Faith does not suffice; we must also do good deeds if we are to be religious and truly blessed.'... But true faith is a work of God in us which transforms and regenerates us by the power of God, slays the old Adam and makes us men whose hearts and faculties are entirely renewed by the Holy Spirit. Oh, it is a living, energizing, active, powerful thing—this faith! That it should not be ceaselessly active for good is just impossible. It does not ask whether there are good works to be done; for, before one can ask, it has already done them.... It is always in action.... One can no more separate works from faith than one can separate light and heat from a flame.

Or, as Luther had put it earlier: 'Just as 3 and 7 are not obliged to be 10, but are 10, and no law or rule need be sought for their being 10...so the justified man is not obliged to live rightly, but he lives rightly; and he needs no law to teach him to do so.'[1]

[1] WA, II, 596. It is Pascal's 'La vraie morale se moque de la morale' (genuine morality laughs at Morality), Pensées, Article VII, 34 (Havet).

Because Luther is here writing a Preface to Romans and making a general, running commentary on the argument of its successive chapters, it is not surprising that when he comes to the eighth chapter this distinction between doing the works of the Law and fulfilling the Law is expressed in terms of the liberating action of the Holy Spirit.

What is Law? By its very nature it is an imperative. It says: 'Thou shalt' (*du sollst*). It comes to man as demand. Man's motives in obeying are therefore fear of punishment and desire for reward. But these motives necessarily prevent that spontaneous and free obedience which alone would fulfil the Law's inmost intention. Obedience is, at best, external. Law can never evoke a truly spontaneous, free and willing response. That is why we may not speak, strictly, of a 'law of love'; for love is not an obligation which is enforceable. Every effort to enforce it negates it. 'Thou shalt love' is essentially self-contradictory as law. The 'law of love' is a norm rather than a law, and it may be realized only through the Holy Spirit in the heart. The Gospel brings new life to man because 'the law of the spirit of life in Christ Jesus hath made me free from the law of sin and death' (Rom. viii. 2 ff.). The new man needs no law. He is a new nature through the Spirit (*durch den Geist genaturt*). This is the key to Luther's frequent statement that the Holy Spirit comes not through the Law but through the preaching of the Gospel. The Spirit is effective only through the Gospel. 'If Law be there, Holy Spirit is not there...Law will not and cannot make a man good' (*ist Gesetz da so ist der Heilig Geist nicht da...das Gesetz woll und kann nicht fromm machen*). In short, Luther constantly comes back to the idea that whereas Law locks the mainspring of Christian activity, the Gospel releases it. Religion and morality are not only indissociable; it is religion alone which makes morality real.[1] How then are we to describe the Christian obligation (*Aufgabe*) to love? Luther constantly describes it in two ways.

First, it is *quellende Liebe*, a springing and overflowing of love in the heart, which requires nothing at all from outside for its stimulus. For the children of this world, love is ἔρως; it is aroused by something desirable in its object. For the Christian man it is ἀγάπη; it springs out of its own source, which is God's gift (*Gabe*) of fellowship with himself. As a man of faith, Luther always felt in his soul something of the religious power of this *quellende Liebe* which he so constantly praised. It goes far to explain his magnanimity, his freedom from envy, petty jealousies and anxious fears about the future. As a best-seller he might easily have been wealthy; but, casual about money, he was splendidly generous; there was a Falstaffian largeness about him; he knew no servile preoccupation with formal rules, and rarely bothered about 'was kommt hernach': that is, he did not calculate, and ask for security or guarantees from the future.[2] He was not tidy (and here I recall the shrewd word of an old London cook: 'Don't like tidy people; they're selfish'); indeed, he illustrates Paul Tillich's profound interpretation of Justification by Faith as willingness to live in 'the boundary situation'.[3] Böhmer adds that Luther thus presents a contrast to 'the good European' whose type has become familiar in the

[1] Commenting on the objection made against the Reformers that it is not enough to live by forgiveness 'alone', Karl Barth says: 'What folly! As though just this, the forgiveness of sins, were not the only thing by which we live....It is precisely when we are aware that "God is for me" that we are in the true sense *responsible*. For from that standpoint, and from that alone, is there a real ethic....Living by forgiveness is never passivity but Christian living in full activity' (*Dogmatics in Outline* (S.C.M. 1949), p. 152).

[2] So, Heinrich Böhmer, *Luther im Lichte der neueren Forschung* (Teubner, 1918), pp. 201 f.   [3] *The Protestant Era*, pp. 192–205.

modern era. Luther is neither 'gentleman' nor 'bourgeois' nor 'good citizen', none of whom have ever quite understood him. Reading his very human pages (for example, his characteristic letter to Peter the barber, who had asked his distinguished client to tell him how to pray) one understands what John Wesley meant by 'the old, coarse Gospel'; and what Foster described as 'the aversion of men of taste from evangelical religion'. *Quellende Liebe:* it is Luther's own experience of religious renewal; that result of his meeting with the God of judgement and grace which always remained for him a secret; a frightening, unfathomable and blessed mystery.[1]

In the second place, Christian love is love of the neighbour. *Quellende Liebe* involves the impulse to spend oneself in the patient, loving service of one's fellows. Only thus does the Christian fulfil the command in Matt. v. 48. If this sounds like the Religion of Brotherhood, the tame and wheezy moralism of Leigh Hunt's *Abou ben Adhem* ('Write me as one who loves his fellow men'), it meant for Luther something which transcended the horizontal plane of moral idealism; the dimension of the supernatural and the eternal is in it, and it involves the theology which is eschatology.

The neighbour is, first, God's Representative in this present evil world. He is appointed by God to receive the sacrifices of love and service which God does not need: or, rather, the *Aufgabe*—the new man's moral response to God's *Gabe*—is offered to God through the Neighbour. All is of God and all is for God, but the divine ἀγάπη comes down from the eternities as a parabolic curve which re-

[1] 'Daß der Gott, der so unbedingt das Güte will, zugleich so menschen-freundlich ist, bleibt ihm immer ein unergründliches Geheimnis, das in seiner Seele ständig den Affekt der Furcht und Ehrfurcht...wach erhält' (Böhmer, *op. cit.* p. 229).

turns thither by way of human priesthood; the priesthood of all believers to one another. A Christian is a channel, open upwards to heaven by faith, and outwards to the neighbour through love. All that the Christian possesses has been received from God that he may pass it on. He has nothing of his own to give; he is an instrument through which redeeming love is further mediated. Thus the Christian is called to be a Christ to his neighbour. *Ich soll mich meinem Nächsten als Christus geben* (I am to give myself as Christ to the man next to me).[1] *Jeder Christ dem andern ein Christus* (every Christian a Christ to the other man).[2]

Thus our neighbour, secondly, represents the invisible Christ. What we do to our neighbour we do not only in this present world order, but in the eternal world. Inasmuch as we have done it unto one of the least of Christ's brethren, we shall have done it unto him. For we are made to live in this order of creation—the world as it is, between the fall of Adam and Christ's second coming. It is a fallen world. Earth is no paradise, nor will it ever be; and though its 'orders' have a relative validity in the sight of God, and its powers are ordained by him as the result of sin and as the permitted remedy against it, this world's impermanence is the final truth about it. Our citizenship is beyond this world, in heaven. But we live with the neighbour in this world, and our sanctification here is a continuous process, since it is ever imperfect, and must continue until the Last Judgement. This process is the work of the Holy Spirit, who not only sanctifies the Church through the Word and the Sacraments, but also governs it. The Spirit is *spiritus rector*, since the spiritual life without the discipline of its ethical implications would be meaningless. My neighbour, like me, has his calling (*Beruf*). Our several callings—as

---

[1] *Freiheit eines Christenmenschen*, § 27.   [2] *Ibid.*

4-2

parents, magistrates, peasants, housemaids, princes, pastors, children or merchants—are God-given. We are to respect and accept them in faith as such[1] (I Cor. vii). To repudiate and retire from these orders of the world's common life—marriage, home, council-chamber, field, kitchen, court, congregation, market-place—as in monasticism: or to give them an authority and final sanctity as though they were ends in themselves (the *Eigengesetzlichkeit* of the natural order which Nazi Germany claimed to be Luther's teaching) is to sin against the supernatural meaning of our secular calling within this world. It is to forget that we are meant to be both at home here and not at home; that though our calling is *innerweltlich* (within the world), we are strangers and pilgrims in the earth; and that we look, beyond death and the fashion of this world that passeth away, to that city that hath foundations, whose builder and maker is God.

Thus the neighbour represents the invisible Christ in yet another way. He is the risen, triumphant Christ, victorious over Satan and the powers of darkness in man's dread battle with death. But all things are not yet put under man. Satan is still permitted to go about this world like a roaring lion, seeking whom he may devour. Our faith must therefore express that final victory of Christ, here and now, in worship: our life together in the Spirit must have that joy which is the foretaste and 'earnest' (ἀρραβών) of the final victory of the redeemed in heaven. Hence the well-known place which music held in Luther's life, and in the congregational worship of the Lutheran and Calvinist churches. Our common joy as neighbours who form one body (*Klumpen*) in Christ has an eschatological

[1] Luther saw that this would exclude some 'callings' therefore; the usurer's and even the banker's. See below, p. 109.

meaning. Singing together, like humour and laughter, is the joyous assertion by the Christian Church that the final defeat of Satan, and the end of the world itself, have already happened. Let loving Christians rejoice together (*Nun freut euch lieben Christen gemein*).[1] Christ is risen. Let us laugh together. In his earliest lecture-commentary on Romans (1513–16) Luther writes: 'None has made himself master of terrors save Christ, who has conquered death and all temporal evils; even eternal death. Wherefore all who believe on him are no longer subject to fear, but laugh at all these evils with joyous assurance.'[2] This recalls the *risus paschalis* (paschal laughter) in the rite of the Eastern Orthodox Church on Easter Day: it means that the final laughter of him that sitteth in the heavens (Ps. ii. 4) is a reality for believers who, in him, already share his victory. The human heart laughs; it is jocund and free.[3]

It is within this context of the ascended glory of the risen Christ, and only within it, that Luther's doctrine of the neighbour is to be understood. Indeed, there is a striking, not to say daring, passage in his works (Calvin could hardly have so expressed himself) where Luther's language recalls that of Irenaeus: 'We become divine', he writes,

---

[1] This is the theme of famous and oft-quoted hymns by Luther, e.g. 'Ein' feste Burg...', which was finely translated by Carlyle as 'A safe stronghold'....Also the Easter hymn which describes the Cross and the Resurrection as a battle between God and the Devil; between Life and Death. Life swallows up Death; Christ is victor.

> 'Die Schrift hat verkundet das
> Wie ein Tod den andern fraß;
> Ein Spott der Tod ist worden.'

> 'Scripture hath proclaimed
> How one Death devoured the other;
> Death has become a mockery.'

[2] Ficker's edition, II, 194.

[3] 'quo accepto (*sc.* spiritu sancto) cor fit hilare, jucundum, spontaneum' (*WA*, VII, 536).

'through love, which causes us to do good to our neighbour: for divine nature is nought else than the sheer doing of good.'[1] We become divine! Karl Holl observes that 'to become divine' was a phrase common to the Christian centuries, but its meaning varied. For Catholics, and especially for the Greek Orthodox, it meant to become immortal, or to become filled with supernatural powers. For mystics it meant to become one with the Infinite. For the typical man of the Middle Ages, the monk, it meant to become master of the passions and, therefore, of nature itself. For Luther it meant to become one who does good to others.

This brings us to the concept of the Calling (*Beruf*) and to its bearing, for ill as well as for good, on the Lutheran concept of the Church.

[1] *WA*, x, i, 100; quoted from Holl, *Ges. Aufs.* I, 101.

CHAPTER VII

THE CALLING AND THE CHURCH

THE writer of this book lived as a small child in a five-storied house of seventy-two stairs, overlooking Plymouth Sound. Built for the middle-class gentility of a century ago, it was a monument to domestic life at two distinct levels. 'Below stairs' were servants' quarters: basement, kitchen regions and—deeper still—a dark cellar fearsome to a child's imagination. 'Above stairs' were a pleasant dining-room and a library; and, higher still, on the first floor, a spacious 'withdrawing room', lit by three fine windows.

The social relationships symbolized by such architecture have long since disappeared with it. A vast number of people now live in bungalows or ranch-houses. In these single-storied homes, efficiently designed to eliminate drudgery, all activities take place at one common level: the ground level. There is no 'upstairs'.

This contrast may give us a rough analogy of the contrast between the medieval and the reformed conceptions of the religious life.

First, the medieval conception. Its genius was dualistic, in the sense that it envisaged human life at two levels: a lower and a higher; the natural and the supernatural. God had created Adam (man) with senses, reason and conscience at the natural level; immediately thereafter he had endowed his creature with the additional gift[1] of

[1] donum superadditum.

'original righteousness' from beyond the bounds of nature.[1] Through this gift man was to enjoy fellowship with his Maker at the supernatural level. But man fell through disobedience, and so lost the additional gift. He fell to the natural level. Whereas he had been intended for the full life 'above stairs', so to speak, he was expelled from the drawing-room to the ground floor. But no lower. For his natural endowment of sense, reason and conscience remained with him: though shaken and weak, it was and is still intact.

God has not left man in this sad condition, however. Through his saving revelation in Christ he restores the lost gift of supernatural grace, whereby fallen humanity is enabled to rise again to the supernatural level. There is thus a dualism between the natural religion of reason and conscience and the supernatural religion which is added to it by revelation. There is a corresponding dualism between the forms and orders of secular society at the lower, natural level and the forms and orders of ecclesiastical society at the higher, supernatural level. Society at the lower level is incomplete and insufficient in itself: it needs the perpetual interventions and controls of that higher society; for to his Church, and to it alone, God has entrusted the distribution of supernatural grace to humanity, from cradle to grave.

The forms of secular life at the natural level are not sinful as such, however; they enjoy a relative validity in the sight of God. For though they are the result and expression of sin in this fallen world, they are also the divinely permitted remedy against it; they are therefore, in one sense, an aspect of the long-suffering of God. But even at their noblest and best they somewhat hinder the full and

[1] ultra terminos naturae.

perfect operation of grace. The joys and cares of marriage, the privileges and responsibilities of landed wealth, the political power of rulers, the coercive power of judges, the stern execution of such powers through soldiery or hangman—all this, though divinely sanctioned (I Cor. vii; Rom. xiii. 1–7), falls short of the ideal standards of the Garden of Eden: mutual love and devotion in the ideal marriage do not exclude something of the tyrannous force of sensuality in the *furor sexualis*; there is arbitrary as well as legitimate exercise of power by the rulers of this world; the very justice dispensed in the court of the feudal overlord is always to some extent a rationalization of his own privileges and passions; ideally considered, even the most disinterested and precious expressions of human justice may be vain in the sight of God (Isa. xl. 23). Thus the ideal for man is to withdraw from the world: to give himself entirely to the supernatural order and its three counsels of poverty, chastity and obedience. He climbs, as it were, from the library and dining-room on the ground floor to the 'withdrawing-room' on the first floor. For the truly supernatural or religious life is the monastic life. Therefore the typical man of the Middle Ages is the monk, and he alone is designated as 'a Religious': to enter a convent is to enter upon religion.

Thus, between the natural and the supernatural there is a graded distinction rather than an abrupt opposition; and the classic system of St Thomas expresses this in its ingenious stairway of grades or stages from nature up to grace. Indeed, one of his most famous sentences may be said to summarize the architectonic principle of medieval Catholicism in its greatest period: 'Grace presupposes nature and does not repudiate it; grace is nature's consummation' (*gratia praesupponit naturam: gratia naturam non tollit sed perficit*). Whereas for St Paul and, in a measure, for St Augustine the heart of Christian theology is the anti-thesis of sin and grace, for St Thomas it is the graded distinction between nature and super-nature. The forms and orders of secular life constitute an ascending stairway from the lower level to that higher level which is attainable only by the 'athletes of the Spirit'. Further, this dualism necessarily involves a dual standard of ethics: the precepts of the Law for those at the lower levels; the counsels of evangelical perfection for the 'religious' at the highest attainable level of poverty, celibacy and obedience.

Before the end of the fifteenth century this medieval dualism was being challenged; with the coming of the Reformation it was expressly denied.

What then is the reformed conception of the religious life? Broadly speaking, the Reformers broke with medieval dualism in two ways.

First, they went back to St Paul, as Karl Barth and others have been doing in our own day: they denied that human reason can be the basis for any *saving* knowledge of God (I Cor. i. 17–ii. 14; Rom. iii. 9–23). Christian theology is a theology of the Word alone. This means that the Reformers took the fall of man and the consequent corruption of all human life with extreme (some would say extravagant) seriousness. They insisted, as we have noticed in earlier pages, that man's sin is a corruption which extends throughout the whole range of his nature, per-meating human life and experience at all its levels; that there is no activity of man's nature—neither his virtue nor even his religion—which is unaffected by it. Whereas Scholasticism had taught that the Fall left man's *naturalia* weak but intact, and that his reason and conscience are at least a basis for the saving knowledge of God, Luther insisted that our natural reason, apart from the renewing power of the Holy Spirit, is a snare and a delusion. Without the Word and the Spirit man is religiously in complete darkness (*nihil habet quam tenebras*): so far from being degraded merely to the ground floor, man has fallen 'below stairs' into the fearsome darkness of the cellar. With characteristic rashness Luther even goes so far as to say that sin is man's very essence (*essentia hominis*), and that he is nothing but sin (*nihil quam peccatum*). And if his bitterest critics (Gilson and Maritain today, for example) seize on such polemical extravagance and so misunderstand him, Luther has only himself to blame. For Luther had plenty of horse sense, and in the every-day world of family life, friendships, table talk, scholarship and music, Luther gladly recognized 'the magnificent light of reason and intelligence in man'. He was not obscurantist, in spite of his notorious sentence about Copernicus (Roman theologians were equally mistaken about Galileo). To suppose that the Reformation condemned reason and science is inexcusable error.[1] The positive point which Luther's discovery of the paradoxical wonder of the Gospel caused him to make so tirelessly, day in and day out, was that reason is a snare and a delusion—a courtesan—where men's urgent and agonizing concern is to find forgiveness and reconciliation with God. Here neither philosophical theology nor the logic of Aristotle have anything to say: so far from being a basis for the Gospel, or from pointing the way to a God who actually loves and seeks sinners, and dies for them—the rationalism and morality of the philosopher do just the opposite. It is the Gospel, in its sheer irrational wonder, which can alone pierce the

[1] See Seeberg, *DG*[4], IV, i, 50.

fearsome gloom of the cellar and bring the sinner out of darkness into marvellous light. The Spirit alone sets the prisoners free, and brings them up into the pleasant living-room of the children of God on the ground floor.

In the second place, therefore, the Reformers declare that the Gospel is God's word of redeeming power at one common level: the ground level, so to speak. The way of salvation is the same for all, since God is no respecter of persons (Rom. ii. 11). The virgin in the nunnery has no spiritual advantage over the pious mother in the home; the men who have embraced poverty in the cloister enjoy no surer hope of immortality than do believing peasants or masons who serve God with sickle or trowel. Christian discipleship knows no differences of caste. All are sinners saved by grace and by nothing else. Salvation through humble faith in Christ is as wonderful and sure for way-faring men in market-place, mill or council-chamber as for spiritual athletes who have withdrawn from these responsi-bilities into a monastic order. To be religious is not to be withdrawn from secular callings, as though marriage were spiritually inferior to celibacy, and a workman's shirt less pleasing to God than a hair shirt. Indeed, it is folly and worse to suppose that a man must flee the world to be religious, and that to keep oneself unspotted from the world (James i. 27) one must dissolve all ties with its privileges and duties. It is the consistent witness of the New Testament that the Christian must overcome the world just there where God's providence has placed him; he is not called upon to renounce the world in the monastic or ascetic sense.

Faith in Christ always involves renunciation, of course; there is no concord between Christ and Belial. And renouncing the hidden things of dishonesty will necessarily test many a 'calling' (that of the usurer, for example) whether it be of God. Indeed, the law of Christ makes stringent moral demands which will involve ascetic self-denial; but this will express itself *within* the world (*innerweltliche Askese*) rather than in flight from the world. A man's calling (*Beruf*) is therefore the normal context for the exercise of his Christian faith; his calling is the God-given means whereby he may serve and edify his neighbour in love. Luther was not the first thus to equate so-called 'secular' callings with those of priest and monk: he had been anticipated here by Tauler, Sebastian Brant and many a late medieval broadsheet and apocalypse.[1] But Luther was doing something new in affirming the inherently religious character of everyday life as the Christian is called by God to live it: the concept of the Calling had not been so interpreted before.

This evaluation of the Christian man's secular calling as something intrinsically sacred had implications of immense historical importance. Negatively it meant the end of ecclesiastical control over large areas of human life: the Christian man was no longer to be subject to the tutelage of priests. What did it mean positively? What was Luther's own concept of the Christian Church?

His main presupposition, of course, is that of ancient Christendom: Christ through his Spirit is ever present in the world to bring men into his kingdom. Two main principles follow.

His positive principle is that the Church is invisible: its members are united in spiritual communion by the powerful, albeit invisible, link of personal faith: this communion suffices to maintain the unity of Christianity. On

[1] See H. Böhmer's account of the *Apocalypse of Michael, op. cit.* pp. 218–19.

this positive principle Luther never wavered. He thus brought back into prominence the Augustinian doctrine of the Church as invisible and he maintained that it is the true scriptural doctrine.

His negative principle is that ecclesiastical institutions have not the divine character claimed for them: all are human, fallible and alterable; he attaches relatively little importance to ecclesiastical forms as such. He therefore breaks with the specifically medieval conception that Christ's kingdom is concretely and visibly manifested on earth as an institution hierarchically ordered; and governed, by divine authority, in terms of law. To the Church of history and law he opposes the Church of the Spirit which, ideally considered, has no need of a visible, corporate constitution to make it a reality in the world.

This repudiation of what the Middle Ages understood by the Church was not individualism. Unlike the mystics, Luther made no claim to a religious experience which is intrinsically individual and private. Just as his Christian faith does not start at the transcendental level where God is hidden and unknowable (*deus absconditus*), but at the human level where God is accessible (*deus revelatus*) in a manger, on a cross, at the font and at the altar; so his Christian discipleship does not begin or continue in mystic aloneness, but at the level of his urgent need. Luther is virtually saying: 'I cannot stand alone. Satan tempts me. I need my brother's voice as the human instrument by which God assures me of his Grace. God appoints my neighbour to be his representative. Through the voice of the brother, the preaching man, the power of the keys is exercised on my behalf, and I am assured of absolution and forgiveness.' For Luther, the power of the keys is entrusted, not to bishops or priests as such, but to the Church, and therefore to every individual Christian: for the power of the keys is the proclamation of salvation. Luther sees the true apostolic succession where one disciple of Christ, apprehended by grace, declares to another the word of reconciliation.

Thus, what the individual receives in Christ is fully realized only in and through community: and though *jeder Gläubige hat Christus ganz* it is equally true that *niemand hat Christus ganz*.[1] And he resolves the familiar paradox by adding: 'this is the communion of saints whereby all have all things in common.'[2] Because the Christian life is thus indefeasibly social Luther fights a constant battle against the *singulares*, the *monii*, as he calls them.[3] Indeed he is emphatic in his defence of the old maxim of Cyprian that there is no salvation apart from the Church; though he regards this, of course, as an evangelical and historical fact rather than as a legal injunction. 'Outside the Christian Church', he says, 'is no truth, no Christ, no blessedness.' But he goes further. Not only is the Church necessary to the individual; the Church is necessary to God himself. Just as 'God's folk cannot be without God's Word', so 'God's Word cannot be without God's folk.' And in a striking passage in his early lectures on the Psalms he says: 'Hadst thou no Church thou wouldst not be truly God' (*nullam ecclesiam haberes tunc non vere esses deus*).[4]

So much for Luther's ecclesiology in 1520 when he wrote his treatise on the Papacy. His thought and practice developed with experience. During the next two decades Melanchthon, Bucer and Calvin insisted in their different

---

[1] 'Every believer has Christ wholly'; 'no one has Christ wholly'.
[2] haec est communio sanctorum qua fit ut omnia omnium sint communia (*WA*, xiv, 714). See Holl, *Ges. Aufs.* i, 96 f.
[3] I.e. the 'singular' people; the 'I-myself-alone' type. Cf. Hosea viii. 9.
[4] *WA*, iii, 578.

ways on the necessity, efficacy and value of the Church as a visible institution charged with the responsibility of sustaining the Christian life and transmitting the evangelical faith to future generations. And as Luther's somewhat naïve confidence in the administrative efficacy of the preached and heard Word became shaken by the hard fact that his followers had neither the depth and richness of his own religion, nor the strength and energy of his own religious life, he found himself forced, albeit reluctantly, to agree with his younger colleagues. In January 1527 he writes to Spalatin: 'Up to now I have been cherishing the vain hope that men can be directed by the Gospel. But the fact is that they destroy the Gospel and wish to be constrained by law and sword *(volunt legibus et gladio cogi)*.'[1] Indeed, it is not surprising that the Reformers of the second generation found themselves compelled to distinguish between heresy and truth, to maintain the pure preaching of the Word through the machinery of faculties, synods, consistories, visitations and similar ecclesiastical institutions, and so to build up 'churches'. Thus, by the time Luther came to write his *Treatise on Councils and Churches*, part III, in 1539, he is doing very much what Calvin is doing in the second edition of the *Institutio*, published that same year[2]—namely, coming down to 'brass

[1] *De Wette*, III, 151. In the Preface to his *Deudsche Messe und Ordnung Gottisdiensts* (1526) Luther devotes a paragraph to summarizing what Evangelical Church Order should be *(die rechte art der Evangelischen ordnunge haben solte)* for worshippers in earnest about the gospel. He concludes, however: 'in short, if one had the people—individuals who earnestly desired to be Christians—fitting forms and uses would soon be established. But I cannot and may not set up or organize such a community or congregation, for the requisite throng of people and individuals is still lacking; nor is it yet in sight.' See *WA*, XIX, 72 f., or Hans Lietzmann's *Kleine Texte*, number 37, pp. 4–5.

[2] See pp. 146 f., below, on Calvin's doctrine of the Church in successive editions of the *Institutio*.

tacks', so to speak; defining the primary and secondary signs of the Church visible, and enumerating the seven principal means whereby it is sanctified as such.

But he is still 'Lutheran' rather than 'Calvinist'. In spite of concessions extorted from him by the hard realities of the situation, the sole *essential* function of the Church is to preach Christ through Word and Sacrament. As in his earlier period, he is still reluctant to say that the Church has an institutional and administrative function within society. Any outward forms and concrete details of polity which experience may find to be necessary have no more than pragmatic justification. God's redeeming work in society must and will be done by the Word. The Word, as preached and as conveyed through the Sacraments, remains the ultimate, constitutive reality of the Church of God.

There is great strength here; and weakness too. For, on Luther's presuppositions, in place of the sacerdotal hierarchy of medieval Christendom the Pastor suffices. Even in his later period, and under the pressure of hard facts, Luther is preoccupied with the provision of good pastors rather than with the organization of the Church as a visible body. He conceived the Church as a *Pastorenkirche*. The pastors, sharing in the common priesthood of believers, were those whose specialized function it was to conduct the public worship of the parish, from the pulpit, at the altar and at the font. Ideally this should have sufficed, since ideally the Church is made up of dedicated spirits, those who are 'in Christ' and who share the evangelical experience of the believing soul. Ideally, this *Volkskirche*, the generality of parishioners, should have been a *Heiligkeitskirche*, as on the day of Pentecost itself. But from St Paul's day to this (as Rome's profound wisdom has always recognized) this has never in fact been so: the contrast between the ideal and the actual, between the peak of vision and the level plain of mediocre attainment, has been the mark of the Church in every generation.

Luther was no sentimentalist, nor was he lacking in realism; he had to take his Germany as he found it. He had asserted the liberty of the Christian man, the right and duty of every individual Christian to discharge the obligations of his calling within the natural forms of secular society: the Church of the Word had no more right to legislate for a man's secular calling as a husband, merchant, peasant or ruler, than had the Papal Church. All that the Church might do, under God, was to permeate society with the regenerative power of the Word. But in actual practice this meant that over any issue of principle between Church and State a single man, the Pastor, was left to confront a single man, the Prince. And not all princes were like Duke Frederick of Saxony, nor had all pastors the personality and courage of Martin Luther. As a result, the Crown Rights of the Redeemer in his Church were not always vindicated. It is possible to argue that Melanchthon and Brenz were the chief offenders here; for Luther himself protested at times with characteristic vigour and effectiveness against this growing menace of Erastianism. But when the administrative efficacy of the preached Word proved to be a dream rather than a working reality; or when a bishop proved to be no true pastor in the evangelical sense, Luther acted as he had done in 1520 when he appealed *To the Christian Nobility of the German Nation*; he turned perforce to the Christian prince or ruler, and invited him to act virtually as *summus episcopus*.[1] In this way questions touching the deepest things by which men live

---

[1] This issue is discussed further on pp. 289 f. below.

often came within the competence of the civil authority. Lutheran churches were organized and ruled through Consistories which Lutheran princes nominated and so controlled.

The notorious subjection of German Lutheranism to political authority is an aspect of the problem of Church and State, and discussion of it is therefore appropriately deferred to a later section of this book.[1] We may notice here, however, that Luther's alleged lack of organizing ability is hardly an adequate explanation. The Lutheran theologian, Professor Otto Piper, has acutely observed that there are 'two tendencies in the German soul which seem to be opposed. People seldom realize that in the German soul the desire for absolute independence exists side by side with willingness to subordinate itself absolutely. Both traits form the polar expression of the German attitude towards others.'[2]

It is the second tendency or trait, however, which has been tragically dominant. To quote Doumergue: 'The passivity of the Lutheran temper dominates not only theory but practice.'[3] But this is a Calvinist's judgement: and without John Calvin we should certainly be interpreting the Protestant tradition with one eye shut. At this point, therefore, we turn to Geneva.

[1] See pp. 263 f.
[2] *Recent Developments in German Protestantism*, pp. 11–12; see also pp. 52–3.
[3] *Jean Calvin*, v, 20–1 (my translation).

PART II

CALVIN

CHAPTER VIII

SYSTEM

A BRILLIANT book appeared not long ago entitled *The Hedgehog and the Fox*. Its thesis was that great thinkers and writers may be divided, broadly speaking, into two main groups; those who would bring existence under a single organizing principle; and those who cannot help seeing existence in all its manifold variety and waywardness. In short, the hedgehog type of mind and the fox type. The hedgehog, a compact ball of defensive spikes, typifies the unassailable unity of a tightly articulated system. Reynard the fox typifies the agile, adventurous, creative mind, sensitively aware of the world of experience in all its concrete singularities, its strange contrariness and diversity. Isaiah Berlin, the critic who wrote this book, was largely concerned with Tolstoi, the creator of *War and Peace*: a thinker and writer who, though a fox by nature and genius, was always wanting to be a hedgehog. I make use of his thesis here only to point a familiar contrast between Calvin and Luther, the great twin brethren of the Reformation.

The contrast is often made and often exaggerated: yet Luther and Calvin do illustrate this difference between the creative and the systematizing mind. Luther's lack of system is notorious; it is alleged to be the result and the expression of his inexhaustible creative power; his fullness, originality and boldness: he has the defects of his qualities. Calvin is different. A powerful intellect rather than a profound mind,[1]

[1] 'Ein denkmächtiger aber unschöpferischer Kopf' (Wilhelm Dilthey, *Die Glaubenslehre der Reformatoren* (Preuss. Jahrb. 1894), p. 74).

he is less creative. He is an indispensable complement to Luther nevertheless.

Born a quarter of a century later, he belongs to the second generation of Reformers; indeed, he vividly illustrates what Troeltsch has called 'the doctrinaire logic of men of the second generation'. Trained in the discipline of legal and classical studies, this Frenchman had what Luther lacked—organizing genius. Luther's rediscovery of the personal religion of the New Testament is a mountain torrent, plunging grandly down from the heights in springtime; loosening rubble and mud in its course; destroying, purifying and refreshing; seeking its irregular channel in the valley below where tributary streams make it a river; and then pursuing its slower, somewhat uncertain way through the broad plain, where it has to come to terms with human mediocrity and inertia.

Calvin defined and cut a channel for this river, controlling the flood-waters, giving them direction, and making them a power in the world. If Luther was a creative genius in religion, Calvin was fitted by birth, temperament and intellect to be a great theologian and a great churchman. Whereas Luther trusted, with magnificent *naïveté*, to the Word, saying 'The Word must do it';[1] and whereas a

[1] Memorably illustrated in the eight sermons which he preached at Wittenberg in March 1522; in his *Manifesto to the Nobility*, § 24 (1520); also in his treatise *On the Competence of the Civil Power* (1523). Here he sets out the reforming method to which he remained faithful—in principle, at least—throughout his career. It is the Word of God alone which wins the victory over human hearts. We have to trust the Word and to wait in faith and patience for its victories. We may not use violence even to abolish abuses. We may not use force: otherwise hangmen and executioners would be the most effective theologians. We may not tyrannize over the tender conscience or the weak brother. We may not try to force God's hand by hurrying the march of events.

It should be remembered that for three years after Luther's return to Wittenberg, the Mass was publicly celebrated there.

dangerous tendency to quietism developed within him, especially as a result of the iconoclastic excesses of others, Calvin was a man of precise notions and constructive action. He introduced order, system and authority into a new world which Luther had opened but had not organized.

In short, Calvin's greatest gift to reformed Christendom was a sense of form, expressed in what is unquestionably his greatest achievement—the *Institutes*. This work is not only an enduring monument to his genius as the greatest theologian of that age; it is Protestantism's greatest treatise in systematic theology. If Luther stands with the giants of religious intuition—Paul, Augustine, Bernard of Clairvaux, George Fox—Calvin is in line with the great doctors and princes of the church—Tertullian, Athanasius, Gregory the Great, Thomas Aquinas, Hooker, Bellarmine. Indeed, what Aquinas did for classic Catholicism in his *Summa*, Calvin did for classic Protestantism in his *Institutio*.[1] It was not a piece of clever perversity, therefore, that a distinguished Anglican scholar at Oxford should have described Calvin a few years ago as 'the last and greatest of the Schoolmen'.[2]

But it may be objected at this point—is system so important or even desirable in religion? Surely the Christian Church always pays heavily for it. And as for scholastic system, the beginnings of which we see in Melanchthon's *Loci*, the *Augsburg Confession* in Germany, the *Helvetic Confession* in Switzerland, the *Thirty-nine Articles* in England, the *Formula of Concord*—to name only these[3]—has not all

---

[1] The plural form, *Institutes*, has long been the accepted English translation of *Institutio christianae religionis*.

[2] Canon B. H. Streeter in his Bampton Lectures.

[3] For the texts see E. F. K. Müller's *Bekenntnisschriften der reformierten Kirche*; also a comprehensive historical survey by A. W. Curtis in Hastings' *Encyclopaedia of Religion and Ethics* (art. Confessions).

this proved, on balance to be an embarrassing hindrance? Has it not too often been a millstone about the neck of living religion; and is it not incontestable that by the time the seventeenth century is reached there is little to choose between the more biblical Protestant and the more philosophical Catholic Scholasticisms, for sterility and deadness? Is it seriously contended, then, by the neo-Thomists or the neo-Calvinists of our time that we are in debt to the systematizers—to Aquinas and Trent, or to Melanchthon and Geneva? If so, are we not merely exchanging one hedgehog for another? Or, to put it as Milton did, is not new presbyter but old priest, writ large? There must be few modern Christians, however precise and unsentimental their theology, who have no sympathy at all with Friedrich Heiler's impassioned religious criticism of the hard, formal *Dogmatik* of all Confessions.[1] And here I may fittingly refer to the oft-repeated judgement of John Oman, one of the most profound religious thinkers of our time. This Presbyterian scholar (he could hardly be called a Calvinist) spent his life with the problems of authority and freedom in religion, and the following pregnant paragraph appears more than once in his writings in slightly varied forms:

Under the sense of chaos around us, I can find no sense in life and no meaning in history on the view that God is as much concerned with correct doctrine, approved action and regulated institution, as man is. To have made us all infallible in every judgement and undeviating in every action, would surely have been child's play for his omnipotence. But if the most perfect order be the freedom of God's children; and if this involve knowing God's mind of our own insight, and doing his will of our own discernment and consecration; and having

[1] *Der Katholizismus*, pp. 114, 360, 365, 369–72.

a relation to others which is a fellowship mutual both with God and man; and that in the end, God will not be content with less—we can see, dimly at least, the necessity of the long, hard way man has had to travel.[1]

To this, presumably, most readers would say Amen; incidentally, it is good Lutheranism. But, on Oman's own showing, man is not ready for this high way of freedom. Further, he is afraid of it, and prefers the 'long, hard way' of legalism, with its restrictions and rules, its precise credenda and agenda. He is at home with this and would rather have this than the freedom of the filial spirit. Further, it is useless to rail despairingly at such legalism in religion, since legalism is God's necessary way with us if we prefer the obedience of slaves to the freedom of God's children. And most of us do. The burden of freedom, save as a Paul or a Luther understands it, is too much.

Calvin knew this, and he faced it realistically. This Schoolman was a practical man. He never evaded awkward issues. Like a prime minister whose executive responsibilities do not allow him the luxury of formulating ideal programmes, since he has to act somehow, and decisively, this very evening: so Calvin did not run away from the real issue. He wrestled with the old problem of freedom and authority which was as inescapable under its sixteenth-century forms as it is under the ideological forms of our twentieth century. And the point which the historian may not forget is that in the sixteenth century the alternative to order, system and authority was chaos.

This is not rhetorical exaggeration. No period was more critical for the Reformation than those years 1530–40 which saw Calvin's appearance on the stage of world history. It is arguable that he appeared just in time. For

[1] Cf. *Honest Religion* (Cambridge), 1941, p. 18.

confusion and uncertainty were becoming widespread. The religious revolt against the medieval order, now nearly two decades old, seemed unable to move out of its first revolutionary phase, and to overcome its tendency to further division and disintegration. The individualism which its first leaders had let loose against the papal tradition of a thousand years was now recoiling upon themselves. Zwingli was ranged against Luther at Marburg, and both of them against radicals of the ecclesiastical Left, such as Carlstadt. Further, there was an increasing proliferation of new doctrines, sects, brotherhoods, mysticisms, apocalyptic dreamings; most of them pathetically quiet and innocuous, though not all. For with much feverish innovation there went also an occasional orgy of fanatical iconoclasm. Along with sectarian anarchy there went a dangerous intellectual anarchy. Some spiritual libertines in Holland and Germany were proclaiming the indifference of all outward forms and institutions in religion. Nor was this all. As the crypto-paganism of the Renaissance spread like a subtle poison among certain 'advanced' humanist circles, open paganism made its appearance, denying religion and its sanctions altogether, in the name of an explicit materialism. It is not surprising, therefore, that intellectual and spiritual anarchy occasionally led to downright moral anarchy. In the heaving ferment of new ideas, the lowest and worst came to the surface. Impostors duly appeared—such as the infamous John of Leiden—to disgrace the cause of religious reformation. His notorious utopia at Münster, with its licentious communism in wives, and its bloody tyranny, was certainly not typical of anabaptist or other prevalent movements of the Spirit. But it happened. Though unlike the tragic Peasants' Revolt of 1525, it was nevertheless like it in seeming to bring the cause of reform into discredit, and so playing into the hands of brutal reactionaries. Serious and discerning minds in the Protestant world were therefore beginning to feel alarm, and to think again about Christian unity. They realized that the Reformation itself was lost if it could not overcome this threat of chaos.

Further, such chaos was not due to the conflict of current religious 'ideologies' only: the feudal and agrarian structure of medieval society had been disintegrating for over a hundred years, long before Luther was born; and it, too, was now visibly crumbling and falling; the ecclesiastical, economic and political revolutions were proceeding *pari passu*. What new structure was there, then, under the shelter of which men and nations might live in safety? Politics and economics had already given their answer, which became more explicit as the sixteenth century went on: the national state, which was rising everywhere on the ruins of medieval institutions, was to be the new power, expressed through the person of King, Prince or Elector; or through a Council of Syndics or Magistrates. It was natural and understandable, therefore, that under the threat of ecclesiastical and confessional anarchy, the reformed religion should give a like, albeit reluctant, answer: King or Prince or Elector or Magistrate must put his power, the power of the new nationalism, at the service of the Gospel. If need be, he must undertake for the Church of Christ by organizing it himself. He must even be, like Henry VIII in England, 'supreme head of the Church'. In short, the Gospel which has escaped the tutelage of priests is now subjected to the menacing tutelage of princes: the new Protestant churches are everywhere State churches.

Now it is just at this point that Calvin's immense historical significance emerges. He saw that if the new evangel was to replace the ancient Church it had to learn the secret of her power, and to discover the evangelical counterpart of her authority, unity and universality. In short, Calvin perceived that the great need of the sixteenth century was a positive ecclesiastical polity. It was idle to criticize the defects of the old Church in the negative manner of Wyclif. It was not enough to recall men to the religion of personal faith, even in the positive and evangelical manner of Luther. Protestantism had produced its prophets, preachers and theologians, but it had not yet produced an ecclesiastical statesman; an architect on earth of that city whose builder and maker is God.[1] In Calvin he appeared: a man of order, strong as iron in his certainty of the majesty, the sole causality and the glory of God, and destined to leave his mark not only on the doctrines but also on the institutions of the Reformed Church in Switzerland, France, Holland, Scotland, England, New England and North America generally. From Geneva there went to the ends of the earth a conception of religion august in its authority, secure and venerable in its foundation, complete in the range of its application, thorough if not terrible in its logic. Mark Pattison was right: 'Calvinism saved Europe.'

This must not be taken to imply that there was any fundamental difference, much less any cleavage, between Luther and Calvin. They were different in several obvious respects, of course, and it is true that Luther's noticeably strong influence on his younger contemporary did abate somewhat, as Calvin proceeded steadily to build a system strongly marked by elements which Luther always sus-

[1] Cf. B. L. Manning, *The Making of Modern English Religion* (S.C.M. 1929), p. 95, to whom I am indebted for the substance of this and the three preceding sentences.

pected and sometimes disavowed; namely, law, an elaboration of ecclesiastical institutions, and ecclesiastical discipline. Yet Calvin could never forget what he owed to the great pioneer in reform. Though their ways tended to diverge, he always regarded Luther as virtually exempt from his criticism. On one occasion he said as much: 'If he called me the Devil I would always pay him reverence as the Servant and Messenger of God.'

What, then, did Mark Pattison mean? He meant, presumably, that it was Calvin rather than any other man whose work successfully held in check the extreme Right and the extreme Left in modern Christendom, and prevented the triumph of either. On the one side there was the Jesuit order, that spear-head of the Counter-Reformation; and on the other side there were fanatical and violently subversive elements, prophets and apocalyptists, who sought to exploit the contemporary religious upheaval in the interests of social and economic upheaval, and who were neither Protestants nor Christians in any classic and exact sense, but forerunners of the French Revolution and of Marxism. All the Reformers fought on two fronts in this way; but it was Calvin whose generalship won the war. The military metaphor is singularly appropriate since Calvin himself not only makes constant use of such metaphors in treatises, letters and sermons: his historic achievement in doctrine and churchmanship is probably best appraised in terms of his generalship, his long-term strategy, and his instinct for soldierly discipline. The 'appalling Calvin' as he has been called, not without some justification, is best understood if we see him as Captain-General of the Evangelical Faith in the day of reaction and disintegration. The test to be applied to him is ultimately empirical and pragmatic. If history has anything to say by way of testimony here, it is that the very elements in Calvin's theological system which are 'appalling' to the refined conscience of the atomic age, did nevertheless put iron into the marrow of Huguenots in France, Beggars in Holland, Covenanters in Scotland and Puritans in England, enabling them to stand in the evil day. Calvin is open to devastating criticisms which are endorsed even by the school of crisis-theologians who have been rediscovering him during the past three decades. Nevertheless, Calvinism has been vindicated by history. But for the Chief of the Protestant General Staff in his headquarters at Geneva our modern Protestantism might not be here at all. It is to Calvin that his modern Protestant critics owe their very survival, and the luxury of abusing his memory. Calvinism is supremely memorable, then, for its marching orders: that is, for its doctrine and its churchmanship. We must look at each in turn.

CHAPTER IX

DOCTRINE

THE doctrine of the *Institutes* is a complete system of
theology which defies summary. A comprehensive
account of it in a few pages would be either unintelli-
gent or so compressed and technical as to be unintelligible.
We may profitably isolate for discussion, however, two
facts which may fairly be said to dominate and illustrate
the whole. First, this doctrine is pre-eminently biblical.
Second, it is massively theocentric: from beginning to end
it is a doctrine of God.

First, then, the stark and massive biblicism which
Calvin, above all the Reformers, bequeathed to Protestant
Christendom: what are we to make of it? Is the celebrated
dictum of William Chillingworth true that 'the Bible and
the Bible alone is the religion of Protestants'? Certainly
neither Luther nor Calvin would have endorsed this easy
generalization just as it stands. Too far from the truth to be
a good epigram, and too near it to be a clever caricature, it
is a misstatement as crude as it is dull. Four centuries
before Matthew Arnold, the Protestantism which had
rediscovered biblical Christianity was not unaware that
the man who knows nothing but his Bible does not know
even that properly. The Reformers were trained and
learned theologians; Calvin was certainly the most
learned and acute biblical theologian of his age; which
means that ecclesiastical tradition played as vital a part in
his thought and practice as it did for the Tractarians a

century ago and as it does for the non-Roman Catholic to-day.[1] In preparing the *Ordonnances Ecclésiastiques* his first thought is recovery rather than iconoclasm; he asks *quid ex antiquitate restituendum*,[2] and by 'antiquity' he means the first five centuries of ancient catholic usage, *ante papatum*.[3] Further, even though Luther was irreconcilably hostile to the Aristotelian philosophy which, in his view, had disastrously perverted this ancient and good tradition, Calvin was neither ignorant of medieval scholasticism nor aggressively hostile to it. The same is only too true of the theologians from Melanchthon onwards, who followed Luther but betrayed the fundamental biblicism of his witness by initiating a new scholasticism.

It is well known that the Reformers, like their modern successors, spoke much of the Word: *das Wort, verbum dei*. What did they mean? At the close of his Latin preface to his critical edition of Calvin's *Opera Selecta*, Peter Barth signs himself as *verbi divini minister*, minister of the Word of God. What did the great phrase mean?

By *verbum* or *das Wort* the Reformers meant the organ of which the Holy Spirit makes use to show and convey the redeeming work of Christ to the world. The Word is the threefold testimony whereby 'he takes of the things of Christ and shows them unto us'. It is, first, the spoken and heard word of Christian preaching. Second, it is the visible, acted, liturgical word of the two Gospel Sacraments. Third, it is the written word of the Bible considered as an organic whole; the Book of Life because it reveals in its totality,

---

[1] For the impressive evidence of Calvin's patristic learning and critical insight see *Calvini Opera Selecta* (edd. P. Barth and G. Niesel), and Holl's *Calvinrede* (*Ges. Aufs.* III, 282).

[2] 'What ought to be restored from antiquity.'

[3] Cf. *Inst.* I, 13, 3 f.; II, 16, 5; IV, 9, 8; also I, 11, 13; II, 2, 7. See my *Christian Doctrine*, pp. 147–9.

rather than in isolated statements treated as proof-texts, the true meaning of our life in God's world; the lively oracles of God and the fount of divine wisdom, because everything in it, rightly approached and understood, points to Christ the Redeemer.

We may not say, of course, that for the Middle Ages the organ of the Spirit was the Church, whereas for the Reformers it was the Word. That would be a false antithesis. The Middle Ages did not ignore preaching; and the Reformers (notably Calvin) certainly did not ignore the Church. There was, however, a difference of emphasis. For the Middle Ages grace was mediated through the objective and external instrumentality of an Institution, its Priests and its Sacraments; for the Reformation, grace was experienced as a personal relationship through the three-fold ministry of the Word. For the one, the basic authority was the Church; for the other it was Holy Scripture.

Luther does not find equal value in or give equal weight to every sentence of Scripture, of course; and, in actual fact, no man does or ever did, not even the most rabid defender of the verbal inspiration and literal inerrancy of the Bible. The statistics of the Book of Numbers, for example, are clearly not *das Wort* in the sense that St John's Gospel is; and what Scripture says about the waters that stood above the firmament (Gen. i. 7) is obviously less important evangelically than its testimony as a whole to a crucified and risen Saviour. For Luther, the Scriptures from Genesis to Revelation—in spite of elements in the Book of Esther, the Epistle of James and the Revelation, which he freely criticizes—are 'the cradle wherein Christ is laid'.[1]

---

[1] For the medieval Church the Word did the preparatory work of the Law, while the Sacraments infused grace into the soul. For the Reformers, however, the Word is the actual medium of grace. In Luther's theology

At first sight Calvin is less free in his treatment of Scripture. His profound reverence for this wonderful work of the Holy Spirit embraced its detailed statements as well as its general substance. His legal training confirmed his native caution, and he had a sober suspicion of exegetical novelties. He disliked subtle interpretations of the plain sense of Scripture and said that allegory was often the work of the Devil. Luther was inclined to take his stand on the impregnable rock of the literal evidence only when it suited him. At Marburg, for example, he said 'the Word is too mighty for me', his ultimate argument against Zwingli being to stand pat on the text and to repeat doggedly 'es steht geschrieben'.[1] But what tended to be intuitive and occasional with Luther was Calvin's considered and consistent principle.

He was not blind to the problems of textual and historical criticism, or course; nor did he hold that rigidly automatic theory of verbal inspiration to which later Protestantism became grievously addicted. For anyone knowing the Scriptures as thoroughly as Calvin did, that was and is virtually impossible. He doubts the authenticity of II Peter, James and Jude; and says of the notable *crux interpretum* in Matt. xxvii. 9: 'I confess that I do not know how the name of Jeremiah comes to be here, and I do not worry overmuch about it' (*nec anxie laboro*). It is true that he dismissed Castellio for teaching that Canticles is a Hebrew love-song and is therefore to be interpreted his-

---

verbum virtually takes the place occupied by *gratia infusa* in the medieval theology of the eucharist. The Word corresponds to the infusion of grace in that it enters the believer with all the power of God's promise. Cf. Isa. lv. 11. As irresistible grace it is the divine hammer. In short, for Catholicism the preached word was the preparation for grace; for Protestantism it was the very channel and means of grace.

[1] 'It stands written.'

torically rather than allegorically or mystically; but his action was not necessarily wrong in the circumstances even though Castellio was undoubtedly right, and Calvin wrong, as to the facts.

The fundamental fact is that for Calvin the chief end of man is to know God, and that the Bible is ultimately the sole source of authority for this knowledge. The principle dominating his whole theological system is that we have to listen to the sovereign Lord of the Universe as he makes himself known to each of us through the revelation of Scripture. Scripture is thus the Word of God. Calvin restores authority to the ministry because, and only because, it is nothing less than the ministry of the Word of God. The Scriptures which the minister expounds are sacred scriptures. They are more than documents illustrative of religious history. Their several authors were not authors in the normal human sense but *amanuenses* of the Holy Spirit, at whose 'dictation' they wrote. When Calvin says that St John thunders from heaven he means precisely what the metaphor conveys.

At first sight then, it may seem that the Reformation is here consciously substituting for the authority of pope and ecclesiastical tradition, the authority of a book. Indeed, it is notorious that such biblicism fell little short of bibliolatry in later generations, with their grotesquely rigid insistence on verbal inerrancy.

But Calvin says something else here. It is he who introduces into Protestant theology at this point the famous doctrine of the inward testimony of the Holy Spirit (*testimonium spiritus sancti internum*). What Protestantism means by the authority of the Bible here finds its religious ground and true explanation. The Bible is authoritative because of the witness of the Spirit to its truth, in the heart. It is a consentient witness, therefore: there is an accord between the Spirit and the Word. As the hymn expresses it,

> Come, Holy Ghost, for moved by Thee
> The prophets wrote and spoke;
> Unlock the truth, Thyself the key,
> Unseal the sacred Book.

Calvin means that God's Word carries its credibility within itself because it is authenticated by the witness of the Holy Spirit within the believer's heart. Holy Spirit and Holy Scripture are two inseparable aspects of one and the same testimony.[1]

Here, again, Calvin is fighting on two fronts. On the right is Rome, for whom the authority of Scripture resides in interpretations determined by the Church. To give but one example where fifty spring to mind: the Gospels refer explicitly to the brothers and sisters of Jesus; but tradition early decided that they were his cousins, and as the growing cult of Mary required the dogma of her perpetual virginity this dogma had to overcome history—history recorded in the Gospels themselves.[2] To Calvin, any such tampering with the Word is blasphemous tyranny. The Bible, he says, has not 'a nose made of wax'. The authority of Scripture is authenticated not by the pronouncements of an ecclesiastical hierarchy but by the Holy Ghost. But at this point Calvin turns to the other front on which he is also fighting. Here on the left are the 'spirituals', so called because they claim to be concerned with and guided by the Spirit alone, loftily rejecting all outward forms in religion—including even the biblical record itself—as rudimentary; a mere

---

[1] Inseparable, in the sense that the concave and convex aspects of the same curve are inseparable.

[2] See Seeberg, *DG*⁴, II, 211–14 for the literary development of the ideas underlying the word ἀειπάρθενος, from the second to the fifth century.

alphabet for children; 'un A, B, C des rudes', as Calvin puts it with mordant irony. To him this, too, is blasphemy; phantasy masquerading as the revelation of the Holy Spirit; as though revealed truth in all its givenness and objectivity could possibly be thus shut up in the dungeon of sinful man's proud and irresponsible subjectivity. One is reminded of Edward Gibbon's cynical and devastating comment on the whirling dervishes of Magnesia: 'They mistook the giddiness of the head for the illumination of the Spirit.'[1] Exactly. The Spirit *is* inward, of course; it is *in* us. But, adds Calvin, it is not *of* us; it is of God, and historically mediated.

Plainly enough, the old and ever present issue of authority in religion here presses upon us. Calvin's attempted fusion of objective and subjective here: does it solve the problem? It does not. In the nineteenth century Strauss declared that this 'inward testimony of the Holy Spirit' is the Achilles-heel of Protestantism. He meant that this definition of authority is vulnerable because it is still at the mercy of private judgement. If the strength of a chain lies in its weakest link, how can this particular chain have binding force? Is not the inward testimony of the Spirit one thing for this man and another for that? To this cogent objection we can only reply that such subjectivism and relativity are inevitable. Like moral obligation, real authority in religion is not something which can ever be demonstrated or proved. Man on this earth cannot have such absolute authority, even though he long earnestly for it and ascribe infallibility to pope or book as guarantee of his wishful thinking. Calvin recognized that the authority of Scripture cannot be externally demonstrated in this way. Proof, as the word is popularly understood, is not possible—

---

[1] *The Decline and Fall of the Roman Empire* (ed. Bury), VII, 140.

save for him who believes in Christ and who hears for himself, in Scripture as an organic whole, the sovereign word of that revelation in all its majesty and comfort. As one of the greatest biblical theologians the world has seen, Calvin himself pre-eminently illustrates the authority of the Word. Indeed, his attitude to the divine authority of Scripture is what it has now become fashionable to call 'existential' (see p. 17, above). He deprecates speculation about the ultimate mysteries of the transcendent Godhead as academic, vain and essentially frivolous. God speaks his Word that we may know, not what he is in himself (*quid sit apud se*), but what he is in relation to us (*qualis erga nos*). In short, all true knowledge of God springs from obedience (*omnis recta dei cognitio ab obedientia nascitur*). There is a sober restraint about Calvin's exposition of the classic trinitarian theology of the creeds, because he realizes that true belief in God is not theistic speculation which merely flits about the brain (*tantum in cerebro volitat*),[1] but that existential faith in God which is deeply rooted in the heart (*radicem agat in corde*.)

In the second place, Calvin's biblical doctrine is supremely a doctrine of God. No theology was ever more theocentric. All is of God. If two Latin words (*sola fide*) express the genius of classic Lutheranism, there are three which are supremely distinctive of Calvinism: *soli deo gloria* (to God alone be the glory). Calvinist theology is informed throughout with an adoring sense of the transcendence, the sole and absolute causality, of God, before whose infinite majesty, incomprehensible essence, boundless power and eternal duration, man is utterly insignificant, save to illustrate the operation of God's grace in redemption.

[1] Cf. the similar stricture of John Smith, the Cambridge Platonist: 'this hovering and fluttering up and down about divinity' (*A prefatory discourse.* See *Select Discourses*, 4th ed., Cambridge, 1859).

But here we may want to say at once, as most critics of Calvin have done: Is this biblical, not to say Christian; this insistence on God's absolute omnipotence and man's consequent nothingness? Granted that once (and once only) St Paul expressed God's absolute sovereignty over man his creature in terms of the potter and the pot (Rom. ix. 20–21): still, when pressed to its logical conclusion, as Calvin does press it, such complete and absolute divine causality is surely nearer to the Mohammedan concept of Allah, or to Oriental philosophies of Fate, than to the witness of the Bible. If Calvin insists unflinchingly that the will of God is the sole cause of all that has ever been, is or will be, how does this differ from determinism? Calvin may deny it, but human freedom and responsibility are illusory if everything happens of necessity.

Well, Calvin does insist that the will of God is the necessity behind all things; but he also insists that man is responsible for what he is and does. Calvin does not run away from the old paradox of necessity and freedom which has never ceased to vex human thought. As a man of religion and a man of action, he lives with this antinomy: he faces it, wrestles with it, and does not pretend to solve its mystery. He refers to it as the 'Labyrinth' because human reason here loses itself. He insists that the will of God is the necessity of all that is; in the same breath he insists that man is nevertheless responsible. His writings contain concrete illustrations of this dilemma: here is one such. A brigand attacks and murders a traveller whose money he covets. He wills this crime and is entirely responsible for it. But, as nothing happens in this universe which is not willed by God, this crime is also God's will. Calvin rejects as frivolous subterfuge the suggestion that God's will is merely permissive of such evil, and that the knifing of the unfortunate traveller takes place *permissu quiescentis dei* (because a quiescent Deity so allows). God is never quiescent, if the great doctrine of God's providence means anything that matters. He is the cause of all that is; intimately concerned with the movement of this raindrop, the nagging of those two women, the number of hairs on that head (Job xxxviii. 28; I Sam. i. 6; Matt. x. 30). Just as the sparrow falls to the ground by his will so does this traveller. What! Are God's will and the murderer's will in accord then? God forbid. It *is* the will of God that the traveller dies: we do not know why; but it is not the will of God that the brigand kills him. This murder, like all murder, is contrary to God's will, yet it does not happen— nothing happens—apart from God's will. To the finite human intelligence this is sheer contradiction. Calvin admits it. But he says that, in a manner which is astounding and incomprehensible, that which takes place in opposition to God's will (*contra voluntatem ejus*) does not take place apart from God's will (*praeter voluntatem ejus*). To the plain man this sounds like sophistry and worse, but all serious thought has to grapple with this and kindred problems if it is to take God's providence seriously. The novelist Thornton Wilder did so in his notable story *The Bridge of San Luis Rey*; and the rabbinical theology of Judaism, like parallel speculations in Islam, constantly recurs to the same mystery of the relation between God and man.[1]

[1] The following illustrations of the antinomy are taken from the remarkable anthology *A Year of Grace* by Victor Gollancz (pp. 9, 93, 105, 230).

'For God freedom is necessary' (Vladimir Soloviev).

'Whatever is, is in God; and nothing can exist or be conceived without God' (Spinoza).

'I have learnt that the place wherein Thou art found unveiled is girt round with the coincidence of contraries [*coincidentia oppositorum*], and this is the wall of Paradise wherein Thou dost abide' (Nicholas of Cusa).

'Rabbi Bunam was once walking outside the city with some of his

Leibniz in the seventeenth century stated the antinomy in terms of the classic doctrine of the divine *concursus*: God concurs but he is not an accomplice.

Calvin's doctrine of God is tense throughout with this antinomy. He hotly repudiates the charge that his ostensibly biblical doctrine of God is really Stoic determinism; but many theologians judge that he nevertheless shares in the error which he formally repudiates: that he is like

> ...the big man on the Syndicate
> Who desired his position to vindicate;
> So he rose to deny
> That he meant to imply
> Just as much as his words seemed to indicate.

One wonders. Paradox is inescapable here, as the great religious philosophies—Jewish, Mohammedan and Hindu, for example—sufficiently testify. Calvin faced this paradox steadily and without flinching. Let those who are never guilty of intellectual cowardice mock at him. The relevant criticism seems to be that there is an unresolved dualism between Calvin's awed religious sense of the majesty and glory of God, and his intellectual statement of its implications. As a result, his God is not always the God of the Bible, the God of Abraham, Isaac and Jacob, the God and Father of our Lord Jesus Christ. Calvin's God is too often an abstraction. Indeed, some theologians complain that Calvinism is really built up round the idea of sovereignty considered as a logical notion. This is probably unfair to Calvin who warmly and bitterly disavows it. But his

disciples. He bent, picked up a speck of sand, looked at it, and put it back exactly where he had found it. "He who does not believe," he said, "that God wants this bit of sand to lie in this particular place, does not believe at all"' (Hasidic story).

I add the celebrated saying of Rabbi 'Aquibah: 'Everything is foreseen and free will is given' (*Pirque 'Abōth*, III, 24).

critics are certainly right in arguing that with a metaphysical deity as pure omnipotence real religion has no concern. And this brings us inevitably to the place where Calvin's doctrine of the divine causality reaches its notorious and appalling climax: the divine decrees, or the doctrine of double predestination.

Here again 'all is of God'. As man is a fallen creature and a sinner he merits nothing but damnation. Therefore the grace of God in forgiveness is absolute grace. It is a sheer gift which does not depend in any sense on man; not even on man's co-operation with God. God's choice of us is completely unconditioned by any excellence or merit of ours. As Calvin once put it with grim humour: 'When God elects us it is not because we are handsome' (*ce n'est pas pour nos beaux yeux*). You do not owe your election to your good looks.

In this positive doctrine of election there is nothing peculiar to Calvin of course; nor, indeed, to Protestantism generally with which he shares it. This is common ground for St Augustine and Jonathan Edwards; for Lollards and Jansenists; for John Wyclif and John Wesley. It is good Pauline doctrine. Indeed, this emphasis on the grace of God as unmerited and unconditioned is not even distinctively and exclusively Christian. Hinduism had its doctrine of justification by faith in the great doctrine of *bhakti*,[1] as worked out in the school of Rāmānuja: and the two parties into which it split over the doctrine of redeeming grace reproduced in Indian religion the difference between the medieval Schoolmen and the Reformers within Christianity.[2] The two parties were known as the

---

[1] More precisely, *bhakti* is the equivalent of *fides caritate formata*.

[2] A useful account of this is given, with translations from the Hindu sources, in Rudolf Otto's *Indiens Gnadenreligion und das Christentum* (Klotz Verlag, Gotha, 1930), pp. 38–40.

monkey-school and the cat-school respectively. For, on the approach of danger the baby monkey climbs on to its mother's back, holds on and, as the mother leaps away to safety, is saved along with her: primarily through the mother monkey's act, of course, but also through the co-operation of her offspring. But when danger threatens a mother cat, she takes her kitten by the scruff of the neck and, willy-nilly, saves it. The kitten does nothing: it contributes nothing at all to the process of its salvation ('not by works, lest any kitten should boast').

The point is that you have here a difference of accent or emphasis which distinguishes believing men in every age and which occurs independently in more than one great historic faith. You may think that thoroughgoing Augustinians are less convincing than semi-Pelagians: that Calvin is extreme where Aquinas is reasonable: that the synergism of the monkey-school is preferable to the fideism of the cat-school. But the positive evangelical meaning of God's saving grace, and of justifying faith as itself God's gift, is not in doubt.

The positive evangelical meaning. Why did Calvin go beyond it? One word may fairly be given in answer: Logic.

Calvin begins with an indisputable fact, that the Gospel calls all men. He proceeds to the next fact, which is as mysterious as it is indisputable, that men differ in their hearing of the Gospel. Some receive it while others refuse it. Calvin faces this fact in the light of the sole causality of God's sovereign grace. The faith which says Yes to the Gospel is solely the gift of God; the seed of God's Word takes root and bears fruit only in those whom God's election from eternity has so predestined: they alone will be heirs of his everlasting kingdom. What of others, then?

Calvin rightly sees, on his presuppositions, that it is *sotte et puérile* (idiotic and childish) to confess eternal salvation but to deny eternal reprobation. The one cannot be without the other as its logical counterpart. And so he proceeds to the logical conclusion, in all its stupefying horror, that those who have no faith are those who, by the same eternal decree of God, have been abandoned to the eternal damnation which all deserve. And since John Calvin was neither a knave nor a fool, he himself described this as *decretum horribile*, the horrible decree. To us it is not only horrible but incredible. Why was it not incredible to Calvin? The answer seems to be that his pitiless logic had its basis, at any rate, in Scripture. Whatever may be thought of his conclusions, his premisses are certainly scriptural; and if their source makes them authoritative, their authority is more widely attested and much stronger than is realized by a generation largely unfamiliar with the Bible as a whole, and with its hard sayings. The idea of Reprobation is found in the Bible alongside that of Election; not only as logical implicate of the latter but as explicit statement. 'Ye have not chosen me but I have chosen you' (election). 'Many are called but few are chosen' (reprobation). 'All that the Father hath given me shall come unto me; and him that cometh unto me I will in no wise cast out' (election). 'No man can come to me except the Father draw him' (reprobation). 'So then God hath mercy on whom he will' (election); 'and whom he will he hardeneth' (reprobation). 'That which Israel seeketh for, that he obtained not: but the elect obtained it and the rest were hardened' (election and reprobation).

This list could be amplified; but one supremely explicit statement may not be omitted: 'Jacob have I loved but Esau have I hated' (election and reprobation). It is a hard and awful statement. And yet the modern mind which is revolted by this doctrine of Election, cheerfully accepts the modern doctrine of Selection, and is not appalled by the thought: 'The warm-blooded mammals have I loved, but the Ichthyosauri have I hated.'

This catena of scriptural evidence is cited here only to underline the fact that Calvin's use of scriptural evidence was not daintily selective. He faced it all. It should be remembered here, too, that he always warned men against wishing to know too much about this final mystery of human existence, and trying blasphemously to pry into the inscrutable depths of the divine judgements. But he also warned men against an equally improper reserve which would avoid the mystery in complete silence. We may not explore what God has hidden, but we may not neglect what God has revealed.

Calvin, then, was here confronted by the witness of Scripture. But an all-important qualification must be added immediately. Just because the principle dominating his whole system is that we have to listen to the sovereign God as he makes himself known to us in Scripture, we have to control Calvin's interpretation of Scripture by Scripture itself. And the unflinching logic of double predestination is not typical of Scripture taken as a whole. The Bible nowhere directly asserts the *decretum horribile*. Calvin is really basing himself not on the teaching of the Bible but on a logical syllogism: 'if there be election there must be rejection; there must be eternal predestination to eternal perdition.' The Bible nowhere says this. St Paul is much nearer to the biblical 'nevertheless' which defies and transcends logic. 'I was as a beast before thee. Nevertheless I am continually with thee: thou hast holden me by my right hand. Thou shalt guide me with thy counsel and afterward receive me to glory'[1] (Ps. lxxiii, 22-3). It is St Paul, therefore, who expresses the true biblical non-logical doctrine of double predestination, when he says: 'For God hath shut up all unto disobedience, that he might have mercy upon all' (Rom. xi. 32). Non-biblical and appalling though Calvin's logic is in its final, negative issue, its positive meaning is for ever true. Here is an incredible (because excessively logical) appendix[2] to what alone matters—the positive, evangelical assurance that our salvation is the act of God's sovereign grace, untouchable by human activity or weakness and unshakable in its finality. Fatal to all papal, hierarchical and sacerdotal pretensions this, too, is the glory of Protestantism.

[1] Cf. Jer. xviii. 1-12 on the divine 'repentance'. Calvin explains this away, as is his wont where an isolated text of scripture contradicts his position. Imbart de la Tour gives further examples of this 'souplesse et dextérité' which, though rare in Calvin, does more honour to his intellectual agility than to his intellectual integrity. See *Les Origines de la Réforme*, IV, 184-5.

[2] Ritschl regarded it as an *Anhängsel* (appendage) to the doctrine of redemption, and not as the central idea in Calvin's theology (*Geschichte des Pietismus*, I, 134).

CHAPTER X

CHURCHMANSHIP

ALONG with doctrine, churchmanship is the second constitutive principle of Calvin's system. But at once we meet an obvious difficulty. In the light of his predestinarian doctrine, how could Calvin be what he undoubtedly was; namely, a great Churchman? When taken seriously and interpreted rigorously, election seems to be logically incompatible with all ecclesiastical forms and institutions. If the divine secret of my salvation be decreed from eternity, how can the ministry of Word and Sacraments make any difference? Must not predestination imply and lead inevitably to thoroughgoing individualism; the visible, empirical Church being thereby dissolved into its component atoms? How, then, can Christianity and Churchmanship be synonymous terms for Calvin, and by what process of logic can he devote one-third of the great *Institutio*, that systematic masterpiece of Reformation theology, to the Church—its nature, order, powers, discipline and its fourfold ministry of presbyters, teachers, elders and deacons—as the divinely ordained means of salvation?

Plainly, here is that same tension or antinomy which we have been noticing all along. Just as all is of God, and yet the indefeasible responsibility of the individual man remains; so, though all is of God, and the Church of his elect is invisible save to his eyes alone, nevertheless the visible institutions of the Church—its scriptures, sacraments, ministry and discipline—remain as the *means* of grace. This is the channel or mode whereby the eternal decree of God's grace is expressed and conveyed in historic time. Indeed, the crucified and risen Redeemer himself, so far from being rendered superfluous (!) by predestinating grace, is the supreme means of that grace. As prophet, priest and king[1] the incarnate Son is the actualization in time of the eternal Father's will to save us. The Church is, as it were, his outward and visible Body; it is not only relevant but indispensable. Thus the Church is both invisible and visible; and in the successive editions of the *Institutio* from 1536 onwards, we watch Calvin's mind as he lives and struggles with this paradox, and defines it with increasing precision.

For Calvin's doctrine of the Church did not leap fully grown from his mind. The ecclesiastical polity which he bequeathed to the Churches of the Reformed tradition was the final expression of a doctrine which passed through four well-marked stages, and which was never without its strong inner tensions.

The first edition of the *Institutio* makes this clear. Published in 1536 when its author was still in his twenty-seventh year, it was a small book in comparison with the succeeding editions of 1539 and 1543 into which it was to be expanded, and the definitive edition of 1559. It took the form of a masterly statement of the fundamental truths of the Christian religion from the Reformed standpoint. It contains only six chapters, the second of these being an exposition of the Apostles' Creed entitled *De Fide*. But when Calvin comes to deal with the fourth article of the creed, *credo sanctam ecclesiam catholicam, sanctorum communionem*, it is clear that there are conflicting ideas in his mind.

He begins by defining the Church as the whole company of the elect, not only men but angels, not only the living

[1] Calvin was the author of this concept of the *tria munera*.

but also the dead; one society, one people of God; one
Body, as it were, whose head is Christ, made up of those
who in all ages and places since the beginning of the world
have been called, united and sanctified according to the
eternal providence of God. This invisible Church of the
elect is one, universal and holy.[1] The novelty in this comprehensive definition is the emphasis on election as the
constitutive essence of the Church, hardly if ever found in
previous expositions of the creed. For the Roman, the
Church was primarily a visible institution, hierarchically
constituted, and ruled by the Pope as Christ's Vicar. For
Luther, and for Zwingli in his earlier period, the Church
was primarily made up of believers, and therefore invisible
in the Augustinian sense. For Calvin, who also went back
to St Augustine, the Church is the *universus electorum
numerus*. Such a definition makes it plain that, in this sense,
the Church is beyond the sight and reach of all ecclesiastical
officials and institutions: God's elect may even be outside the
Church as formally organized, and many inside it may not
be, in fact, of the elect. As St Augustine himself had put it:
'There are many sheep without and many lambs within.'[2]

That Calvin's definition, however, is not meant to dissolve the Church into its component atoms—the individual elect—is proved by his immediate concern with the
question which is unavoidable: How are the elect to be

---

[1] The Church is 'populus electorum dei'. 'Electi dei sic omnes in Christo
uniuntur ac coadunantur ut quemadmodum ab uno capite pendent ita in
unum velut corpus coalescant.' Christ is Lord and King 'in quo pater ab
aeterno elegit quos voluit esse suos ac in ecclesiae suae gregem referri' (I, 73,
72, 74). These passages illustrate the dominant idea of all Reformed ecclesiology: the headship and the 'crown rights' of Christ. Further, the Church
is both visible (*corpus*) and invisible (*electi*): and the word *velut* further safe-
guards the idea of invisibility.

[2] itaque secundum occultam dei praedestinationem plurimae sunt foris
oves, plurimi sunt lupi intus (*Homil. in Johan.* xlv).

known? To meet practical needs, at any rate, one cannot help asking: Who belongs to the Church, and who does not? For Calvin, as for the great predestinarian thinkers, such a question does not present a mystery to be probed by the intellect; it evokes the fundamental loyalty of one's life. He replies, therefore, that we have sufficiently clear assurance that we are both among the elect of God and members of his Church if we have fellowship with Christ.[1] That is, personal assurance of our salvation is grounded, not in our knowledge of the hidden decrees of God (a blasphemous notion) but in the conscious experience of our inward calling (*vocatio interna*) through faith in his Son. If we possess Christ in faith we may confidently conclude that in him we are elect as God's children and sharers in the eternal kingdom. Only that faith in the Church is worth anything which includes faith in one's own personal membership therein.[2]

All the Reformers were inclined to be preoccupied with the problem of predestination, but, as is well known, Luther learned from Staupitz to avoid such unhealthy and fruitless pondering, and to rest his assurance of election on

[1] satis clarum testimonium habemus nos et inter dei electos et ex ecclesia esse si Christo communicamus (1, 74).

[2] For Calvin's full statement on the *vocatio interna*, and the assurance of election and salvation, see *Inst.* III, xxiv, 8 (final edition); also I, xvii, 8. That the unsoundable depth of predestination can in fact become the pledge of our peace, the stimulus of our moral life and the basis of our glad humility, is the testimony of history. *The Memoirs of the Life of Colonel Hutchinson* provide an exact illustration from the seventeenth century. 'Mr Hutchinson, taking delight in the study of divinity, presently left off all foolish nice points, that tended to nothing but vain brangling, and employed his whole study in laying a foundation of sound and necessary principles, among which he gave the first place to this of God's absolute decrees. This was so far from producing a carelessness of life in him, a thing generally objected against this faith, that, on the other side, it excited him to a more strict and holy walking in thankfulness to God, who had been pleased to choose him out of the corrupted mass of lost mankind, to fix his love upon him, and give him the knowledge of himself by his ever-blessed Son' (Everyman's Library, p. 53).

the Word, and on the believing fellowship with Christ which it guarantees. Luther's influence on Calvin is clear and strong here, therefore. But the practical question presses if the Church is an actuality in time at all: namely, how stands it with others? Can we decide who among them is of the Church, and elect? Luther's influence again makes Calvin return a decisive negative: 'To judge whether others be of the Church or no, and to distinguish the elect from the reprobate, is not for us. This is God's prerogative alone. The eyes of God alone see who are to endure unto the end.' But though this is true, it does not meet the practical needs of the case; and Calvin knows it. He therefore finds the definitive marks of the Church (*notae ecclesiae*) whereby the elect and the reprobate are distinguishable, in the Bible and in his evangelical experience of biblical religion. After anxiously emphasizing the necessity of the spirit of toleration (*judicium caritatis*) he says that all those should be deemed elect of God and members of his Church who by confession of faith, exemplary life and participation in the sacraments, confess with us the same God and Christ.[1] On the other hand, unbelievers or merely nominal Christians or men of openly evil life are held 'not to be members of the Church at present'.[2]

Calvin thus reaches the postulate of excommunication or its equivalent; and he justifies it on the three grounds that its absence would dishonour God, expose the faithful to evil example and provide for the evildoer no stimulus to repentance and betterment. But he is plainly embarrassed by this admission which hard facts force him to make, and

---

[1] scriptura certas quasdam notas nobis describit...quibus electos et filios dei a reprobis et extraneis distinguamus...debent quodam caritatis judicio pro electis ac ecclesiae membris haberi omnes, qui et fidei confessione et vitae exemplo et sacramentorum participatione eundem nobiscum Deum et Christum profitentur (1, 75).   [2] non esse ad praesens ecclesiae membra.

in a significantly long excursus he anxiously guards against the supposition that the ban of the Church in the interests of Christian perfection trenches upon the inscrutable divine prerogative, either of judgement or of mercy. The inference that an excommunicated man is *eo ipso* excluded from the possibility of election would be blasphemous. Calvin speaks emphatically of charity, caution, patience, mildness and love in thus judging men. The ban of the Church may never be equated with the removal of the hope of blessedness; the rule is only a rough one for the guidance of our human practice; and it is the sacred duty of the Church to leave no means of love untried in order to bring back the excommunicated into Christian fellowship. Indeed, in a remarkable passage which unfortunately never appeared again in later editions of the *Institutio*, Calvin asserted that not only ought we to deal thus in love with erring Christians, but also with Turks, Saracens and other avowed enemies of the Faith. 'Far be it from us', he says, 'to approve as right those inhuman methods whereby many up to now have sought to force such people to accept our faith, denying them food, warmth and life's commonest amenities, and persecuting them with fire and sword.'[1] It is significant that this noble witness to Christian humaneness disappears in succeeding editions of the *Institutio*; but it is not surprising that Castellio and other pioneers of toleration cited this very passage against Calvin in the famous tract of 1544, *De haereticis an sint persequendi*.[2]

It was his growing realization that the ideal aspect of the Church is eclipsed by the claims of the actual which led

---

[1] I, 77. Cf. St Augustine's 'coge intrare'. Zwingli had spoken of the iron rod of Christ (*eiserne Rut Christi*), and Bucer in 1538 was to insist on the necessity of a rigid discipline. Calvin was not yet faced in Geneva with the problem of a Servetus. See pp. 189 f. below on the voluntary principle.

[2] 'Should heretics be persecuted?'

Calvin to set forth in a famous sentence, based on the *Augustana*, the real basis for his doctrine of the Church in all later editions of the *Institutio*: 'Where the Word of God is sincerely preached and heard, and where the Sacraments are administered according to the institution of Christ, there we cannot have any doubt that the Church of God has some existence' (*illic aliquam esse dei ecclesiam nullo modo ambigendum est*). But he adds at once that clearer or more specific evidence is not available on earth in the nature of things, since the Church is above all invisible and therefore an object of faith.[1]

Thanks to this strong tension within him between the claims of the ideal and the actual, Calvin tends to vacillate between three different positions, no one of which is strictly compatible with the other two. He conceives of the Church primarily as the invisible company of the elect, and beyond the possibility of precise definition by man: this was his heritage from the later Augustine. Again, he conceives of the Church, albeit secondarily, as the visible Church of believers, recognizable by the preaching and hearing of the Word and participation in the Sacraments, no other touchstone being available, his common sense reminding him of the abiding imperfection of the Christian life under grace: this was his heritage from Luther. Yet again, as an idealist and a puritan, he cannot but think of the Church in terms of Christian perfection, though well aware of its dangers, and he insists on discipline and even excommunication in the interests of that holiness without which no man shall see the Lord: this was his heritage from practical experience, in collaboration with his contemporaries. In short, he is playing at one and the

[1] non rem esse carnalem quae sensibus nostris subjici aut certo spatio circumscribi...debeat (I, 77).

same time the three roles of Augustine, Cyprian and Wesley: the successive editions of the *Institutio* with their increasingly articulate churchmanship are a tense synthesis of the predestinarian logic of the first, the explicit churchmanship of the second and the perfectionism of the third. No theory of Church order is yet formulated. Calvin at no time had any enthusiasm for the formless or irregular, of course; the idea of the priesthood of all believers was not decisive for his thinking or practice in any way, though he acknowledged its scriptural basis and its truth. During the early inchoate phase of the Reformation the formula 'all Christians are priests' meant the repudiation of hierarchical claims, and the recognition of the spiritual competence of the 'layman'; but this phase is now over. All evangelical churches have their special office(s) of the ministry ; Calvin himself had never known anything else. But anything like his later elaborate theory of a fourfold office of the ministry is absent as yet. He has two offices only in view: that of the Minister (the Bishop, Presbyter or Elder of the New Testament) and that of the Deacon, called to care for the poor and needy.[1]

In the edition of 1539 a different note is struck. The invisible Church of the elect recedes into the background and gives place to the visible, ecclesiastical society. And here we meet an illuminating paradox. In this edition Calvin appears for the first time as the great dogmatic theologian: into the framework of the first *Institutio* he introduces a mass of new material, the central dogmas of Paulinism proper (the so-called 'five points'): the second edition is Augustinian to the core. But whereas in this and succeeding editions the Augustinian doctrine of the decrees

[1] The congregational form of Calvinist polity perpetuates this.

develops more and more into a sharply defined system, the Augustinian doctrine that the Church is made up of the elect and is to be defined only in terms thereof, recedes more and more into the background. Henceforward, predestination is a constitutive principle of Calvin's theology rather than of his ecclesiology. He tends more and more to define and recognize election in terms of churchmanship, rather than churchmanship in terms of election. It is significant, for example, that he does not make adhesion to the doctrine of Double Predestination a condition of union with German Protestantism.[1] The ideal Church of the Elect now retires into the background, and Calvin concerns himself more and more with the Church in its empirical actuality, where holiness is potential rather than achieved, and is only in process of becoming. During that process much imperfection must be tolerated in the Church by an earnest Christian: yet it is the Church of God, the Mother of Believers, and outside it there is no practical possibility of Christian salvation.

Calvin now writes—like St Cyprian to Jubaianus—that rebirth to life eternal depends on being conceived in the womb and nourished at the bosom of *nostra omnium mater* 'within whom the Lord willed the treasure of His grace to be deposited.... Scripture pronounces that outside the unity of the Church there is no salvation.'[2] This is a new note. Calvin is here facing the great practical question of his age which caused the Reformers, who had themselves separated from Rome, such acute embarrassment. Is separation justifiable, even on the high conscientious ground of 'reformation without tarrying for any'? When

[1] See Eugène Choisy, *Calvin et le Calvinisme*, p. 79.
[2] I, 539. He quotes Isa. xlvi. 13, Joel ii. 32 and Ezek. xiii. 9 in support.

is a break with the existing Church a duty, and when is it a sin? How far may admitted defects exist in a church without thereby excusing separation from it? Granted that the Church is the visible society outside which there is, in principle, no salvation, is it to be understood as a *Heiligkeitskirche*, as the sixteenth-century Separatists contended, or is it rather a *Volkskirche* which wisely declines to set up too absolute a standard for wayfaring men, but contents itself with a fair average, and trusts the power of the creative Word?

The old rigorist challenge of Montanists, Novatians, Donatists and Cathari is represented in the sixteenth century by the 'Anabaptists', and fanatical *Schwärmer* of the sect-type. It is met by the Protestant Cyprian of that century, John Calvin. But in this second edition of the *Institutio* we can detect something of the pang it cost him to repudiate their separatist claims so decisively, in the uneasy and almost wistful sense of kinship which he shows with men whose ideals, in many cases, he respects but whom he must nevertheless fear and denounce. Calvin was always fighting on two fronts: not only against Rome, separation from its abuses seeming plainly justified; but also against the extreme Left-wing of the evangelical movement. Though he will never abandon perfection as the ideal and the goal, he insists that where the Word is purely preached and heard, and where the Sacraments are rightly administered, there is the Church, from which individuals have no right to separate. If they do so, Christ regards them as traitors and deserters.

I am unwilling to condone even the most trifling errors here, and to seem to encourage them through indolence or connivance. But I do say that because of sundry little differences of opinion we may not rashly desert a Church in which at least sound and undiminished doctrine is held, in which true religion stands firm and the use of the Lord's Sacraments is preserved.[1]

Speaking of the Rigorists or Perfectionists of his day, *esprits phrénétiques* as he calls them, he says: 'let them remember that the Word of God and His holy Sacraments have more virtue in conserving the Church than the vices of some of its members have in dissipating it.'[2] 'We have no right', he says in another place, 'lightly to abandon a Church because it is not perfect.'[3] Defects do not justify defection. But plainly Calvin cannot stop here. All his arguments against the new Separatists are grist to the mill of the Romanists, in whose eyes he himself (like all non-Romans) is a Separatist. The argument used by Calvin against 'Anabaptists' is Archbishop Sadolet's argument against Geneva. Therefore he cannot long postpone some positive definition which shall differentiate between the false and the true Church. It is in the third edition, of 1543, that he therefore expounds in detail the character, organization and function of the *legitima ecclesia:* that is, the *ecclesia verbo dei formata ac constituta.*

In the edition of 1543 there is again a new note and a new temper. If in the 1539 edition we 'descend' from the invisible to the visible Church, in 1543 this visible Church is embodied in and rigidly organized about the fourfold

---

[1] hic autem patrocinari erroribus vel minutissimis nolim, ut blandiendo et conniviendo censeam fovendos; sed dico, non temere ob quaslibet dissensiunculas deserendam nobis ecclesiam in qua duntaxat ea salva et illibata doctrina retineatur, qua constat incolumitas pietatis, et sacramentorum usus a domino institutus custodiatur (1, 545).

[2] *Inst.* IV, i. 16.

[3] *Inst.* IV, i, 12; II, 5. Cf. my *Christian Doctrine*, p. 137 and note. The issue is discussed below in terms of the sect-type and, later, of the modern œcumenical movement, pp. 189 ff.; pp. 317 ff.

office of the Ministry, as Christ's organ for the governance
and leadership of his Church on earth. Calvin here shows
to the full the organizing genius of the ecclesiastical
statesman. The earlier material is now worked over and
supplemented, the result being a positive, ecclesiastical
polity; a great structure resting on Scripture and ancient
ecclesiastical usage, cemented throughout with the sense
of order and discipline. But the dominant fact is the place
assigned to the Ministry. In the rule of his Church Christ
uses the activity of men who stand in his stead (*vicariam
operam*), making them his vicars (*les faisant comme ses
lieutenants*). 'For neither are the light and heat of the sun,
nor meat and drink, so necessary to maintain and cherish
the present life, as is the apostolic and pastoral office to
preserve a Church in the earth.' God's Word is uttered
by men like ourselves, common men who may even be
much inferior to us in dignity and importance. But when
some insignificant man is raised from the dust (*homuncio
quispiam ex pulvere emersus*) and ordained to the ministry of the
Word, he is God's own minister, to be revered and obeyed
as such.

This high Calvinist doctrine of the Ministry was not
being newly enunciated in 1543; it was being related in
detail to the developing ecclesiastical and social system at
Geneva. Already in the Genevan Catechism of 1537
Calvin had set forth this aspect of his high Churchmanship
with terrifying thoroughness:[1]

Since it is the Saviour's will that his Word and his Sacraments should be dispensed by the ministry of men, there must
be pastors ordained to the churches; men who, both in public
and in private, teach pure doctrine to the people, administer
the Sacraments, and by their good example instruct all in

[1] *Calvini Opera Selecta* (ed. P. Barth), I, 414.

holiness and purity of life....And in order that their ministry may not be impugned, they are equipped with a notable commission to bind and loose....But let us remember that this power attributed to pastors in the Scriptures is entirely contained in and limited by the Ministry of the Word; for Christ has not given this power to men as such (*proprement*), but to his Word whose ministers men are. Let them brave everything, however, by the Word of God whereof they are made the dispensers (*dispensateurs*): let them constrain all the virtue, glory and pomp of the world to give place to and to obey the majesty of the Word:[1] by means of it let them give commands to all from the greatest to the smallest: let them build up Christ's household: let them demolish the Kingdom of Satan: let them feed the sheep, slay the wolves, instruct and exhort the humble: let them engage, confute and overcome rebels; but all this in the Word of God (*en la parolle de Dieu*). If they turn away from it to the dreams and fancies of their own heads,[2] they are no longer to be received as pastors, but chased away as pernicious wolves. For Christ has certainly not commanded us to obey any other than those who teach us what they have received of his Word.

What ministerial offices, then, did Christ bequeath to his Church? Previously Calvin had treated exclusively of the preaching office and the diaconate. Now he sets himself to find scriptural authority for the fourfold order of Pastors, Teachers, College of Elders and Deacons. No easy task. The weakness of his scriptural evidence is obvious. He claims to hold firmly to what Christ has ordained; yet, in reality, his theory of a fourfold ministry rests on no word of Christ. And of the Pauline evidence to which he appeals (in Eph. iv. 11, I Cor. xii. 28, Rom. xii.

---

[1] When ministers seek their own interest and comfort 'there is no majesty of God seen in their ministry' (*Inst.* IV. viii).

[2] 'Quand nous montons en chaire ce n'est pas pour y apporter nos songes et resveries' (*Opera*, xxv, 646). As they hear the preacher the people should feel 'que c'est comme devant Dieu qu'il parle' (*Opera*, xxxiv, 554).

6–8 and elsewhere), he must needs explain away more than half of it, as being provisional and temporary.

He goes on to say that only a duly ordained man may preach the Word and administer the Sacraments. What then is requisite for the Church's act of ordination? Who is to be ordained; how; and by whom? Naturally the minister must correspond in character and gifts to his divine calling: further, the participation of the congregation is as essential as it is scriptural. Calvin here cites St Cyprian in support of this common right and liberty of God's people. 'The priest is to be chosen in presence of the people.' Ministers, he concludes, are legitimately called according to the Word of God when they are elected *ex populi consensu et approbatione* (with the consent and approval of the people). Other ministers, however, ought to preside at the election, lest any error should be committed by the general body.[1] As to the form of ordination and the rites to be observed, the New Testament gives no definite command; yet since the laying-on of hands was uniformly observed by the Apostles, it ought to be regarded as a precept; for if the Spirit of God has not instituted anything in the Church in vain, this ceremony of his appointing will be found useful, provided it be not super-

---

[1] It is possible to argue (see p. 223 below on the 'Sect-type') that Calvin, if not the father, was perhaps one of the aristocratic grandparents of modern democracy. But he himself was no democrat, whatever the ultimate implication of his principles; nor was he a monarchist. His preference is for the aristocratic, rather than for the monarchical or the democratic principle— both in church and State. He always mistrusted and feared the multitude. This is already noticeable in his earliest work, the commentary on Seneca's *De Clementia* (1531), about which Imbart de la Tour observes: 'Il ne croit pas le vulgaire capable de se diriger lui-même' (*op. cit.* p. 19). It is the more significant, therefore, that like Erasmus before him and Beza after him, Calvin takes χειροτονήσαντες in Acts xiv. 23 to mean election by popular suffrage. This is most unlikely; and in any case, χειροτονεῖν may mean 'to appoint to an office' in classical as well as in Hellenistic Greek.

stitiously abused. Calvin approved of this rite because he supposed it to be a good Hebraic custom for the consecrating of priests, which the Apostles took over and so perpetuated.

Detailed criticism of all this is not difficult: with regard to election by the congregation Calvin's scriptural proofs are again weak: without St Cyprian he has no strong case: and even so, election and mere presence at an election are two very different things.[1] As to the laying-on of hands he is hardly consistent, for in the earlier *Institutio* he had mocked at the dependence of the Catholic rite of consecration on the Mosaic Law, and what was done to Aaron. Yet here he approvingly deduces the laying-on of hands from the same Hebraic source.

But one can elaborate such criticisms and miss their real import. Calvin's ecclesiastical polity was no paper-project worked out in a study, nor did it depend for its authority on a fanatical biblicism. His scriptural justification of the four offices is weak; but no weaker than that claimed for other ecclesiastical polities, such as the so-called historic episcopate and the threefold office of bishop, priest and deacon. The choice of proof-texts, the subtle exegesis, the appeal to the Fathers—is all somewhat arbitrary. But in truth the four offices spring less from the Bible than from practical needs. Too much can be made of Calvin's stark biblicism, as though he knew the Scriptures only as an authoritative codex or law-book: in reality, his biblicism here is the façade of a structure built to correspond to

---

[1] For the meaning of the popular election of Western bishops in the fourth century (A.D. 374) see Homes Dudden's *St Ambrose*, vol. I, p. 70. Pope Caelestine, writing to the Bishops of Provence in 428, lays it down that *nullus invitis detur episcopus*, i.e. 'no bishop may be given to unwilling people'. By the fifth century, therefore, a bishop is 'given', though popular approval is still requisite; and he is still 'given' by the comprovincials.

experienced necessities. And in appealing to the early Church he is really appealing to the same wisdom, the same freedom from a fanatical historicism. For the early Church created as many offices as it needed, and experimented with more; they varied locally and at different times during the apostolic age, since they corresponded to the actualities of a changing situation. If Calvin's details seem arbitrarily forced on the New Testament, he remains true to its spirit nevertheless, for the New Testament knows no one ecclesiastical polity, and the story of ecclesiastical polity in the ancient Church is the story of the progressive standardization of an original diversity. As a man of order Calvin looked to apostolic custom and ancient church order; as a legislator he looked also to the sixteenth century and its needs. His attitude to episcopacy is akin to this. Though he quotes St Jerome in support of his conviction that in the New Testament 'bishop' and 'presbyter' were synonymous terms, and sees in the gradual subordination of the latter to the former an evolution in ecclesiastical practice which rested on no commandment of Christ—he recognizes nevertheless the inherent necessities of that ancient development and respects them.[1] Nor does he raise any doctrinaire objection to bishop, archbishop or patriarch, so long as these men, like the presbyters, exercise their calling to preach the Word and administer the Sacraments, and do not play the monarch.

The final, definitive edition of the *Institutio* (1559) makes the ideas of 1543 more explicit, supplements and re-orders the existing materials in the light of experience (and

---

[1] *Inst.* IV, iv, 2, 4; cf. *Opera*, XV, 332 for Calvin's letter to the king of Poland explaining on what conditions the episcopate appears to him to be tolerable in that kingdom.

controversy), and thus becomes a much larger and more coherent corpus of theological and ecclesiological doctrine. One quotation suffices to illustrate the temper of its famous fourth book, which insists on the necessity of the Church for the assured salvation of every individual soul.

It is not enough to embrace with the mind and spirit the assembly of the elect. There is no entering into life unless the Church conceives us in her womb, brings us to birth, nourishes us at her bosom and preserves us by her guardianship and discipline.... *Extra ejus gremium nulla est speranda peccatorum remissio, nec ulla salus* (no forgiveness of sins is to be hoped for beyond her embrace, nor any salvation).[1]

This is perhaps a practical caveat rather than a divine dogma; it is saying that the hope of blessedness (note the word *speranda*) is never to be entertained apart from Christian nurture within the Church. For the old tension remains even here where the successive editions of the *Institutio* reach their final form. The Church is the outward, indispensable means: yet Calvin does not cease to proclaim that all is of God and his sovereign grace. The *Institutio* is a magnificent monument to the paradox which all systems of 'conveyance' or 'mediation' attempt to resolve. Calvin's radical predestinarian faith declares that God alone is the source of our ultimate blessedness; yet in practice this is historically conditioned by means of the fellowship and discipline of the Church. He has indeed become the Cyprian of the Reformation era; and yet his high churchmanship is a tree planted deep—as it was for St Augustine—in the soil of that personal experience of God's grace of which election is the symbol. He thinks both ideas through with almost defiant thoroughness,

[1] *Inst.* IV, i, 4. For his defence of the legitimacy of historical development see a letter to Farel (*Opera*, XI, 393).

proclaiming the *decretum horribile* at the close of the third book, and opening the fourth with the idea which rings through it like a trumpet: *de vera Ecclesia, cum qua nobis colenda est unitas: quia piorum omnium mater est.*[1] Only the strongest natures can hold such tensions within the soul. Calvin felt deep within him that the one emphasis with which he began in 1536 demands this other with which he ends in 1559, as its complement and its final explanation.[2]

[1] 'Concerning the true Church, and that unity with her which is ours to cherish: for she is the mother of all believers.'

[2] We should notice, in conclusion, that Calvin's dread of schism springs mainly from his mysticism. For him the Church *is* Christ, as his commentaries on Corinthians and Ephesians (1546–8) make clear. The difficulty of knowing whether he is speaking of the Church invisible or visible is due to his practice of speaking continually of both. He speaks of the one and the same Church which is at once visible and invisible.

CHAPTER XI

THE CHURCH IN THE WORLD

C ALVIN'S first creative achievement was a Book, the *Institutio*; his second was a city, Geneva. Book and city were complementary. In the one, doctrine was systematically formulated; in the other it was systematically applied. The differences between Lutheranism and Calvinism here become a contrast.

As we have already seen, for Luther the Church was primarily a fellowship of believing souls, united by love; an invisible society, having little need of outward forms to give it actuality and identity. When experience demonstrated the necessity of such forms, he virtually left their organization and control to the territorial prince. Not so Calvin. Though he recognizes and venerates the existence of that Church invisible which is the fellowship of the elect and the communion of saints, his creative concern is with the visible society founded by Christ; an organized, disciplined community; *une église dressée*. The headship of Christ over his Church abolishes the dignity claimed by the sovereign pontiff; but Calvin has no intention of letting prince, seigneurie or parliament take his place. New presbyter is like old priest in proclaiming the distinction in not the separation of the spiritual and temporal powers. The Church is not unrelated to the State, of course, any more than the soul is to the body or the moral life to the physical; this dualism in human nature implies a like dualism in human society, and there is neither primacy nor subordination of either element in relation to the other. The civil and ecclesiastical powers (Seigneurie and Vénérable Compagnie) are equal in dignity, their spheres being conterminous.

'The two swords go not into one sheath', wrote Freidank the Minnesinger in the early thirteenth century: but just as this parallelism of the two powers, as defined by Pope Gelasius, had been powerfully challenged by Gregory VII and had yielded to papal autocracy under Innocent III, so the Genevan theocracy became a clerical dictatorship; and in the end Messieurs de Genève ceased to dispute the absolute authority of their 'pope', John Calvin.

This contrast with Lutheranism is the expression of a deeper contrast. Calvin is a man of law. Whereas Luther distinguishes Law and Gospel and ever gives the preeminence to the latter, Calvin unites them; sometimes he comes near to transforming the Gospel into a new Law. He insists that Christ has not abrogated the Law; he has fulfilled it. The Christian liberty which he gave to his Church meant the abolition of particular Jewish rites and observances which had no place in the new dispensation; it also meant, by implication, the abolition of rules and traditions of human invention such as celibacy, vows, abstinences and outward disciplines which had begun by being voluntary but had come to be an intolerable tyranny over man's conscience. But the moral law, the law of Christ, is by no means abrogated. Indeed its rule is now extended from the sphere of outward performance to the thoughts and intents of the heart. The divine work of grace in us does not cease with our justification: it continues to the end in the long process of sanctification: and the sternly militant puritanism of Geneva (a beleaguered city of refuge for thousands of persecuted Protestants fleeing thither from all parts of Europe) conceives this process in terms of discipline, rule, obedience, sobriety, resolve and strenuous action.

But that Calvin's emphasis on the divine law as the rule of life could be truly Christian and evangelical will be clear to anyone who reads the profound and searching seventh chapter of the third book of the *Institutio*, entitled: *A Summary of the Christian Life: Of Self-denial*. It moves throughout on an exalted level and must surely rank with the best and wisest things ever written on the theme 'ye are not your own'. It is a moving Christian exposition of Rom. xii. 1:

The great point, then, is that we are consecrated and dedicated to God and, therefore, should not henceforth think, speak, design or act without a view to his glory....We are not our own; therefore, as far as possible, let us forget ourselves and the things that are ours....We belong to God: to him, then, as the only legitimate end, let every part of our life be directed.... For as the surest source of destruction to men is to obey themselves, so the only haven of safety is to have no other will, no other wisdom, than to follow the Lord wherever he leads. Let this, then, be the first step: to abandon ourselves, and to devote the whole energy of our minds to the service of God. By service I mean not only that which consists in verbal obedience but that by which the mind, divested of its own carnal feelings, implicitly obeys the call of the Spirit of God.

Calvin proceeds to expound Titus ii. 11–14, dwelling on the three adverbs 'soberly, righteously and godly', as a summary of that self-discipline, that justice and equity in our dealings with our fellows, and above all that godliness which together constitute Christian perfection.

All the endowments which we possess are divine deposits entrusted to us for the very purpose of being distributed for the good of our neighbour....Thus, whatever the pious man can do, he is bound to do for his brethren, not consulting his own interest in any other way than by striving earnestly for the common edification of the Church....We are God's stewards and are bound to give an account of our stewardship; moreover the only right mode of administration is that which is regulated by love.... The Lord enjoins us to do good to all without exception, though the greater part, if estimated by their own merit, are most unworthy of it. But Scripture subjoins a most excellent reason, when it tells us that we are not to look to what men in themselves deserve, but to attend to the image of God which exists in all, and to which we owe all honour and love.... Therefore, whoever be the man that is presented to you as needing your assistance, you have no ground for declining to give it to him. Say he is a stranger. The Lord has given him a mark which ought to be familiar to you: for which reason he forbids you to despise your own flesh (Gal. vi. 10). Say he is mean and of no consideration. The Lord points him out as one whom he has distinguished by the lustre of his own image (Isa. lviii. 7). Say that you are bound to him by no ties of duty. The Lord has substituted him as it were into his own place, that in him you may recognize the many great obligations under which the Lord has laid you to himself.... But if he not only merits no good but has provoked you by infamy and mischief, still there is no good reason why you should not embrace him in love and visit him with offices of love.... In this way only we attain to what is not only difficult but also against nature, to love those that hate us, to render good for evil, and blessing for cursing, remembering that we are not to reflect on the wickedness of men but to look on the image of God in them.... We shall thus succeed in mortifying ourselves if we fulfil all the duties of charity. Those duties, however, are not fulfilled by the mere discharge of them, though none be omitted, unless it is done from a pure feeling of love.[1]

There is probably nothing here which could not have been written by Luther. Indeed, the whole chapter illustrates his doctrine of the neighbour.[2] But whereas Luther —after 1527 at least—virtually leaves the Christian ethic

---

[1] *Inst.* iii, vii, 1–7 (Beveridge's translation). [2] See p. 99 above.

on these heights of personal piety, the strenuous compulsions and controls in Calvin's system are aimed at making this ethic effective on the level plain of the common life. Calvin never fails to think in terms of community. In this he differs from Luther on the one hand, and from the anabaptist sectaries on the other. He agrees with Luther, against the Anabaptists, that the Church is a *Volkskirche*; it is for the general public, the whole people of Geneva, and not merely for a gathered sect of the elect (*Heiligkeitskirche*). Calvin's activity embraces the whole of Geneva, and he defends infant baptism there as energetically as Luther does in Germany. But, on the other hand, he cannot be content with Luther's quietism, preaching the Word and leaving the multitude to make of it what it will. Whereas Luther insisted that 'the Word must do it', Calvin's livelier sense of the practical ends to be attained made him what Luther never was, 'le grand organisateur de la communauté ecclésiastique'.

In short, for Lutheranism the ecclesiastical community was not unlike the medieval parish, a geographical expression for people—what Calvinist Independents in England a century later were to call 'the parish muster', scornfully rejecting it (as Calvin himself did not) in favour of their own 'anabaptist' ideal of 'the gathered church'. Lutheranism is nearer to medieval Catholicism and its thought of the community as the *object* of ecclesiastical ministrations: for classic Calvinism, the community is not only the object of pastoral care, direction and discipline: it is also the conscious *subject* of ecclesiastical life. For the Lutheran pastor the parish came to mean pasture: for the Calvinist pastor it always meant the flock. In 1688 a Hamburg pastor complained of having thirty thousand people in his parish: no effective cure of souls was possible.

The Faculty of Theology of Leipzig gave its formal opinion that 'it certainly is a large number; but the prophet Jonah had a hundred and twenty thousand souls in his parish at Nineveh.... It is incredible that Jonah should have had a cure *in specie et individue* (in the particular, individual sense) for each of his hearers'.[1] The Faculty of theology at Geneva could not have thought or spoken in this way. The cure of souls being the prime necessity, parishes and *dizaines* were defined and organized accordingly; there was a close personal relationship (some Genevans found it *too* close!) between the official ministry and every member of the Church. The Reformed Church has always conceived of the Christian life in terms of a living community.

How is this community to be understood? The question is crucial because it is divisive. Three main types of churchmanship which have played a notable part in the history of Western Christendom represent three different answers to it: the 'Catholic' type, the 'Protestant' type, and the 'Sect' type. As we are now within sight of the latter we must briefly compare the first two, since the comparison gives the key to the understanding of the third.

The great difference between the 'Catholic' and the 'Protestant' conceptions of the Church lies in the role of the community. For Rome, the community is relatively unimportant. Here the priesthood is the constitutive and solely essential fact. The Roman Church could subsist without the community; Mass can be said privately and without the presence of a congregation. The community is a valuable manifestation of the Christian qualities of the Church, of course, but it is not strictly necessary to the existence of the Church. For Protestantism, on the other

[1] Doumergue, *Jean Calvin*, v, 60.

hand, the community is essential and fundamental; all that it understands by the Church, its worship and its life would be inconceivable without it: here the faithful people are the constitutive and essential fact; without them the *societas fidelium* would be meaningless.

Speaking very broadly, catholic ecclesiology is here making use of a philosophical notion as old as Plato: the reality of Universals. Protestantism is more inclined to assert the reality of Particulars. A rough illustration of these terms may help us here. Is there a Universal Redness—of which red rubies, red sealing-wax, red wine and red blood are only the particular, phenomenal expression? That is the old 'realist' position: the Universal is the real; it is prior to the particular (*universalia ante rem*). Or, are Universals no more than abstractions distilled, so to speak, from the prior concreteness of Particulars—Beauty being no more than a name (*nomen*) apart from beautiful sunset or face, beautiful fugue or sonnet? That is the old 'nominalist' position: the Particular is the real; it is prior to the Universal (*universalia post rem*). The debate between these two main positions recurs, albeit with changing categories and subtle variations, in each generation. It dominates, for example, the perennial question of political philosophy, the relation of the individual to society. In the Christian theology of the saving work of Christ it divides those who conceive of 'human nature' as a reality prior to and independent of Tom, Dick and Harry; and those who decline to subordinate each separate man's moral individuality to abstract 'solidary' or 'societary' images.

For Catholicism, then—both Eastern and Western—the Church is not so much an association of believing minds and dedicated spirits as an institution: an indivisible, impersonal Magnitude, endowed with immutable attributes and preserving its 'mystical' being through the ages, independently of the actual thought and conduct of the individuals who, in aggregate, are its visible representation. As such, the Church is personified as the Mother of her children. She is the 'milk-white hind' of Dryden's poem, 'immortal and unchanged':

> Without unspotted, innocent within,
> She feared no danger, for she knew no sin.

What of classic Protestantism here? It did not repudiate the exalted concepts of the Church as the mystical Body of Christ, as the Bride of Christ, and therefore as the supra-personal and supra-temporal reality prior in thought and fact to the aggregate of individuals composing it on earth at any one time. The objective 'givenness' of the Church was as real for Calvin as it was for Cardinal Bellarmine: no man can doubt it who will read the early paragraphs of the fourth book of the *Institutio* which contain the words *Incipiam autem ab Ecclesia*.[1] And though Luther was not an *institutional* High-Churchman as was Calvin, the stark realism of his eucharistic thought, his devotion to the mystic theme of *Christus Victor*, his doctrine of Christ's bodily ubiquity and his complete credal orthodoxy—all place him in close rapport with the Christianity of the patristic era; he has notable links with Irenaeus.

But the vital point here is that the Reformers added to this institutional concept the further concept of the Church as an association of believing souls; a community. The Church is not only an *église-institution*; it is at the same time an *église-association*. As we have already noticed, it was Calvin in particular who recognized this twofold aspect of the Church: as the Institution to which every inhabitant

---

[1] 'My starting-point, however, is the Church.'

of Geneva was required to belong, it was a people's or State Church (*Volkskirche*): but as an association, fellowship or community slowly but surely generated by this institutional discipline and training, it was also a confessional church (*Bekenntniskirche*) of believers.

What of future developments, however; especially in countries or territories where the Reformed Church was neither dominant nor established as the State Church? John Knox will do in Scotland what Theodore Beza will continue in Geneva; but in England, Germany and Eastern Europe, Calvinism will inevitably become, as it were, decentralized into local communities or gathered churches. The Church will tend to lose its twofold aspect, the Institution being absorbed into local associations of the sect-type. Calvin strove ceaselessly to avoid this. Indeed the Reformers of the sixteenth century were ruthlessly opposed to separatism and to the autonomy of the local community, however much they might strive to foster its inner freedom. Though they themselves had separated from a church for which anything like a dissident and free Church was meaningless and impossible, they nevertheless looked with active and persecuting disfavour on local, congregational independency of the sect-type, which would have meant the absorption of the Church into churches; and they took all possible precautions against it.

It is a matter of history that later Calvinism did develop in the direction of the sect-type, however. That type of churchmanship—in its strength and in its weakness—is a part of the Protestant tradition which has had great historical influence and importance. To it we must now turn.

PART III

THE SECT-TYPE

CHAPTER XII

DISSENT

I T is an impressive monument to the empire of the Caesars
that on the continent of Europe all roads lead to Rome.
It is a still more impressive monument to the empire of
the Popes that for pious Roman Catholics throughout the
world all roads lead to St Peter's. When he arrives at the
great basilica the pilgrim enters and advances along the
vast nave with its flanking chapels until he stands beneath
the dome. Looking up at its inner circumference he sees
famous words from the Latin Vulgate in giant letters of
gold against a background of lapis lazuli: 'Thou art Peter,
and upon this rock will I build my church, and the gates of
hell shall not prevail against it.'

Bramante began to build St Peter's in 1506 (when
Luther was twenty-three years old). A century and a half
later Bernini was adding the famed elliptical piazza, a level
expanse stretching for nearly a quarter of a mile from the
great front of the basilica and bounded by two curving
quadruple colonnades, which have sometimes looked to
the non-Roman eye like gigantic arms, outstretched to
embrace and gather in her obedient children—not to
mention her disobedient children.

It is more than a coincidence that while Bernini was
building this symbol of papal imperialism in the seventeenth century, another type of churchmanship was struggling to establish itself in England and New England.
Nine years before Bernini began his work a ship set out
from Europe to found Plymouth plantation in America.

And the time being come that they must depart, they were accompanied with most of their brethren out of the citie, unto a towne sundrie miles off called Delfes haven, wher the ship lay ready to receive them. So they lefte the goodly and pleasant citie which had been their resting place near twelve years: but they knew they were pilgrims, and looked not much on those things but lift up their eyes to the heavens, their dearest countrie, and quieted their spirits.[1]

The departure of the *Mayflower* did not symbolize a new departure in Reformation churchmanship, since the sect-type—as Troeltsch has taught us to call it—had emerged at least a century earlier to embarrass the Reformers and to be savagely repressed by them, but to survive and grow nevertheless. Sectarianism is a generic term covering manifestations of the liberty of conscience bewildering in their variety: but here we may fittingly refer to the seventeenth-century form of dissent symbolized by the *Mayflower* because, while Bernini's piazza was being constructed from 1629 to 1667, the Long Parliament of Pym and Hampden, and the Commonwealth of Cromwell and the Puritans, were laying foundations of civil and religious liberty in England, on which the English-speaking world has been building to some purpose ever since.

Few contrasts could be more complete, however, than that presented by Rome and the sect-type today. The Pope exercises absolute spiritual jurisdiction over three hundred and seventy archiepiscopal sees, nearly a thousand resident bishoprics, five hundred apostolic delegations, vicariates or prefectures and—if figures may be trusted— over four hundred million souls. The Papal system is an impressive pyramid of hierarchical rule. With its doctrinal and administrative authority now centralized to a degree

[1] William Bradford, *History of Plymouth Plantation*, c. 7.

unknown in previous Roman history, the modern papacy disposes of vast spiritual and much political power which the forces of national and international politics cannot and do not ignore.

Modern Protestantism is notoriously different. Thanks to its impenitent sectarian temper, its churchmanship is not a seamless robe but a coat of many colours. We have to look to biology for a term to describe its divisions and subdivisions. Its developing life has been intermittently 'fissiparous': so far from realizing Calvin's dream of a world-wide organic unity, much of it has been a loose agglomeration of cells dividing by fission or schism into further cells. It is now possible to enumerate two hundred and fifty-six separate divisions within Protestant Christendom; and even the Churches recognized by and represented in the World Council number one hundred and sixty. That fact alone would sufficiently explain why the oecumenical movement has an inescapable urgency for Protestants who would take seriously the modern issues raised by their tradition of freedom in religion.

But the sect-type has had and still has great and precious importance. Dissent, not only from the centralized absolutism of Rome, but also from the State establishments of Protestantism in the Old World—is an historic fact of enduring influence. To account for the tradition of liberty in the 'free world' of today without reference to it would be to read modern history with one eye shut. Dissent, like all other forms of Christian association, has at times been grievously mistaken and blind: its temper has often been hard and bitter: during its classic pioneering period it had little thought of conceding to others the toleration which it claimed for itself: to extol the Pilgrim Fathers, for example, as champions of the principle of religious liberty for all, would be a grotesque delusion: they were children of their age.

But we are children of our age; and we are less confident than we were fifty years ago that we may look indulgently on such uncivilized shortcomings, from the height of our conscious superiority. It is hardly for the totalitarian twentieth century to make patronizing allowance for the intolerance of earlier, less enlightened generations. In the heyday of liberalism, when we took our democracy and religious freedom for granted, it seemed natural to appraise the struggles of the heroic past with easy detachment. We could toy academically with the 'evolution' of modern toleration, raising our eyebrows over Harnack's dictum that St Augustine was the first modern man, and discussing the rival claims of Frederick II, Marsiglio of Padua and Descartes. Indeed, we allowed generously for the awkward fact of human inconsistency. Was it not Tertullian's noble contention that 'it is no part of religion to compel religion, which should be adopted freely, not by force'? Yet Tertullian could be deplorably bigoted. Again, George Podiebrad was a truly tolerant monarch, born out of due time in medieval Bohemia; yet his wise and humane respect for the rights of conscience stopped short of its own logic at times. We remembered, with just a hint of patronage, that in this he anticipated the breadth and magnanimity of Cromwell (an Independent of the sect-type) who, when English Presbyterians were denouncing toleration as 'the great Diana of the Independents' and as 'the Devil's masterpiece', stood high above them in his treatment of Fox and Biddle. Yet we admitted of course that even he was something of a dictator, though we were mildly shocked that to the Irish Catholic he is still the Beast of the Apocalypse. We felt like Gibbon, who read the sermons of

Gregory the Great and admired their 'rude though pathetic eloquence'.

Today when the omnicompetent State threatens to control the individual from cradle to grave, prescribing with brutal thoroughness the way he is to think and the Leviathan he is to worship, the Spanish Inquisition or Alva's devilries in the Netherlands are not as far away as we thought; we are no longer in the comfortable front seats of the balcony, but in the arena. To use current jargon, our attitude is now existential rather than aesthetic, and the story of the vindication of our religious freedom in the teeth of three centuries of civil and ecclesiastical repression has a new and impressive relevance. Indeed, it is against the background of our own time that *we* have to evaluate the thoroughgoing Protestantism of the sects.

Thoroughgoing. 'But another sort there was, that disliked the whole constitution of the Church lately reformed, charging upon it many gross remainders of popery...insomuch that these latter separated themselves into private assemblies, meeting together not in churches but in private houses, where they had ministers of their own.'[1] In these words Strype notes the emergence, from the moderate or presbyterian puritanism of the Elizabethan age in England, of the extreme form of Puritanism which became separatist and sectarian. Instead of yielding reluctantly to the State-religion of the Elizabethan settlement, the separatists felt driven by loyalty to Christ to further reformation, 'without tarrying for anie'. They withdrew from the Establishment in the name of conscience instructed and controlled by the Word of God. To the moderates standing in the Genevan tradition, the Church meant congregations of baptized persons regularly attendant upon a duly authorized

[1] *Life of Archbishop Grindal*, I, c. xii (Oxford, 1821).

minister and subject to a duly elected eldership. To the separatist the Church meant a company of regenerate persons who confess direct responsibility to Christ for their own corporate self-government. The offices of the ministry might be the same in each case: those of pastor, teacher, elder, deacon and widow. But for the former, the power of the keys—power over admission to and expulsion from the Church—belonged to this official ministry as constituted in its presbytery or ruling eldership: for the latter it was regarded as the inalienable right of the whole congregation.

Rightly or wrongly these 'extremists' (that perennially useful word) were men and women who were beginning to be disillusioned by the Reformation, as a thing of compromise over first principles. Their protest against the national church established by the Tudors was a serious anticipation of Pitt's epigram two centuries later: 'We have a Calvinistic creed, a Popish liturgy and an Arminian clergy.'[1] When, in his controversy with Thomas Cartwright (the father of English Presbyterianism), John Whitgift (Master of Trinity College, Cambridge, and later Archbishop of Canterbury) classed Puritans with Papists as dissenters from the Church of England as by law established, Cartwright replied that Puritans attacked the Church of England just because it still had too much in common with Rome. Your Puritan, he said, wanted not only to unhorse the Pope but also to take away the stirrups, so that he might never climb into the saddle again.

These separatist companies of Protestant Christians may have had some lineal connexion with the medieval Lollards, with 'gospellers' in the reign of Henry VIII, and with 'the secret church' in the reign of 'Bloody Mary'. We catch glimpses of them during that reign (1553-8)

[1] Speech in the House of Lords, 19 May 1772.

assembling in private houses: of one Brooke, a salter of Queenhithe; at a fishmonger's wife's house, Mistress Barber's, in Fish Street; at the King's Head, Ratcliffe; at a dyer's house, Battle Bridge; at Sir John Carden's in Blackfriars; at an inn in Aldgate; in a cloth-worker's loft; in a cooper's house in Pudding Lane. They met several times on board the ship *Jesus* lying between Ratcliffe and Rotherhithe, where they had prayers, sermon and the Communion of the Lord's Supper. Picturesque details but a situation of great peril. In a riverside house in Thames Street they were once surrounded, at night. A mariner of the Company 'plucked off his slops and swam to the next boat and rowed the company over, using his shoes for oars'. Their numbers seem to have ranged from forty to two hundred. When John Rough and his fellow-members were arrested, they had assembled at the Saracen's Head, Islington, 'under the colour of coming to see a play' whereas—so their accusers said to Bonner, Bishop of London—they had made preparation to celebrate and to receive the Communion. Early in the reign of Elizabeth a separatist church, with Richard Fitz as minister and Thomas Bowland as deacon, seems to have met even in one of the London prisons. In 1567 they had assembled at Plumbers' Hall, between Thames Street and Cannon Street, ostensibly for a wedding, in order to shield the woman in charge of the building; but they were betrayed and imprisoned. A short statement, printed in black-letter, entitled 'Trewe markes of Christ's Church' and signed with the name of Richard Fitz as minister, is extant in the Record Office. It seems to have been addressed to the queen in 1571, petitioning that 'the glorious Evangel' be preached, 'freely and purely'; that the Sacraments be administered 'purely and only and altogether according to the institution and good word of Jesus Christ, without any tradition or invention of man'; further, 'not to have the filthy Canon Law, but discipline only and altogether agreeable to the heavenly and almighty word of our great Lord Jesus Christ'.

These familiar details illustrate more than the religious ferment of Elizabethan and Stuart England; *mutatis mutandis*, they are a picture of the sect-type as it emerged and spread, often to be brutally persecuted, from the Low Countries and the Rhineland to Switzerland, from Northern Italy to Hungary and the Vistula. With the varied details of this welter of sectarian witness—'anabaptist', mystical, antitrinitarian, apocalyptic, revolutionary, quietist or millenarian—we are not here concerned. In spite of their negations and their occasional crudity, they gave something positive to the modern world. As elements in the Protestant tradition their particular beliefs are less important than certain enduring principles of Christian faith and discipleship which they represent. These principles may be fairly summarized and evaluated under the three heads which follow.

CHAPTER XIII

THE PERSONAL PRINCIPLE

THE first of three principles which may be said to give unity to this sectarian multiplicity is that true religion is always an intensely personal matter. Christ's Church is made up only of his believing disciples who consciously take him as Master and Lord. A nominal Christianity is a contradiction in terms. 'The Lorde's people is of the willing sorte.' None, therefore, but local associations of professing Christians, who have experienced the grace of God in Christ for themselves, may be properly called churches. Here is the old ideal of the *Heiligkeitskirche* as opposed to and withdrawn from the *Volkskirche*.

But to insist that religion is indefeasibly personal, *and to become deliberately schismatic on so trite a basis*—is not this like defying all comers on behalf of the wetness of water? Does anyone deny what is obvious in the nature of things? Human thought and belief, like human life itself, are inherently and inescapably personal. No man goes to the dentist by proxy. So, too, 'no man may deliver his brother, nor make agreement unto God for him' (Ps. xlix. 7). Human life is pervaded with the vicarious principle, admittedly; but it operates within fixed limits; beyond them it is disallowed by the very structure of our life in the body as God has made it. To justify and practice schism on this basis, however, would—in the last resort—reduce Christianity to an atomistic individualism, and destroy the Church altogether: in strict logic, it should destroy the local, gathered church of believers too.

And is there not a further difficulty? The role of the 'professional' in most departments of human thought and activity, and the immemorial distinction between priest and layman in the sphere of religion, would seem to be part of the very 'stuff' of history. Whitehead's celebrated definition of religion as 'what a man does with his solitariness', though too near the truth to be ignored, is nevertheless too close to falsehood to be accepted. It is invalidated by history, which testifies that religion is not only personal but also indefeasibly social and corporate in its living expression: indeed it is surely qualified even by 'the priesthood of all believers', since this classic Protestant formula does not eliminate priesthood: it enlarges its meaning by making its range as wide as discipleship itself.

All this is true, and it may be fittingly stated at the out-set. But the free man's revolt against the claims of an exclusively mediatorial priesthood is also integral to the story of religion. This too belongs to the stuff of history. There is no salvation apart from the Church. True. The path to the mercy-seat is so narrow that two cannot walk abreast there. True also. As long as an arrogant sacer-dotalism claims that 'the hands of the priest are the indis-pensable link between the blessed Trinity and the ordinary believer', even the most wrong-headed sectarian fanaticism may be vindicating an evangelical truth which goes too easily by default. Again, the plain fact is that nominal religion is the enemy of real religion in all ages. It may be obvious, as theory, that religion is either one's own personal affair or it is nothing. But the theory is more easily enunciated in argument than vindicated in life; and sectarian repudiation of a worldly erastianism 'without tarrying for anie' was at least understandable if not justifiable, even though the Devil's work was too often accomplished in its name.

And there is a further answer, to match the 'further difficulty' set out above. The churches of the sect-type were not only challenging the erastian state-craft of the Reformation era, which virtually regarded the Church as a department of State: they were also defending the New Testament conception of the Church against the Roman conception, which finds the very *esse* of the Church in its priestly hierarchy rather than in the personal faith of its members. Consider, for example, the celebrated and oft-quoted definition given by Cardinal Bellarmine (1542–1621) in his *De ecclesia militante*, c. 2:

> Our doctrine of the Church is distinguished from the others in this, that while all others require inward qualities (*internas virtutes*) in everyone who is to be admitted to the Church, we believe that all the virtues, faith, hope, charity and the others, are to be found in the Church. We do not think that any inward disposition (*ullam internam virtutem*) is requisite from anyone in order that he may be said to be part of the true Church whereof the Scriptures speak: all that is necessary is an outward confession of faith and participation in the sacraments (*sed tantum externam professionem fidei et sacramentorum communionem*). The Church, in fact, is a company of men (*coetus hominum*) as visible and palpable as the assembly of the Roman people, or the Kingdom of France, or the Republic of Venice.

This clear and unambiguous definition explicitly excludes from the constitutive essence of the Church all subjective, personal elements. A Protestant admires its candour but he is astounded by its assumption that the Church of which the New Testament speaks could be so described. Not only for Anabaptists, Mennonites and Quakers, but also for Independents, Lutherans and Presbyterians, personal faith and discipleship is a fundamental presupposition of apostolic Christianity. Acts viii. 37 and xvi. 31 are not exceptional, but typical of what the Epistles and the Gospels are saying on every page. 'Only an outward profession of faith.' It is hardly surprising that serious men with the New Testament in their hands were outraged by so pitiful a caricature of New Testament Christianity. There is abundant evidence that they were neither unaware of the evil of schism, nor blind to the danger of spiritual pride; but from the Church as so defined they felt that they had no option but to separate themselves. Again, it is the old ideal of the *Heiligkeitskirche*; a 'gathered' church of those who could not trifle over that personal 'holiness without which no man shall see the Lord'. They believed that the Church of Christ cannot be restricted, on the one hand to a priestly caste, and on the other hand to a mixed multitude.

As Henry Barrow (1550–90), separatist and martyr, expressed it in his *Discovery of the False Church*, a true Church is a faithful people gathered by the Word unto Christ and submitting themselves to him in all things. 'The true planted and rightly established Church of Christ is a company of faithful people, separated from the unbelievers and heathen of the land, gathered in the name of Christ, whom they truly worship and readily obey as their only King, Priest and Prophet, and joined together as members of one body, ordered and governed by such offices and laws as Christ, in his last will and testament, hath thereunto ordained.' The public ministry of the Word and Sacraments is exercised by the pastor and the teacher; ruling Elders are responsible for discipline. These permanent officers are appointed and controlled by the whole congregation; they may not be imposed from without, nor are they lawfully called save by the congregation. Barrow magnified the office of the pastor but admitted no qualitative difference between pastor and people. All are spiritually, though not officially, equal. 'We hold all believers (to be) ecclesiastical and spiritual.... We know not what you mean by your old popish term of "laymen".' The clearest note of a true church, indeed, is its right and power to discipline itself; its elders, appointed for the exercise of this power, direct but do not dominate.[1]

The personal principle, as we have called it, and its implications for Christian churchmanship, were stated with formal precision and comprehensiveness by R. W. Dale in 1884. In a manual which has long since become a classic of ecclesiology, he enumerated and expounded five principles.

The first principle is that it is the will of Christ that all those who believe in him should be organized into churches. As in the apostolic age, so now, churches are the natural and necessary creation of the Christian faith, each particular church being a microcosm or representation of the Church universal.

The second principle is that in every Christian Church the will of Christ is the supreme authority.

The third principle is that it is the will of Christ that all the members of a Christian Church shall be Christians; and being a Christian means having personal faith in Christ. Apart from such personal faith can any man really be a Christian?

The fourth principle is that by the will of Christ all the members of a Christian Church are directly responsible to him for maintaining his authority in the Church. There is no reason for withdrawing from the commonalty of the Church the place and authority given to it in apostolic times and with apostolic sanction.

[1] See F. J. Powicke, *Henry Barrow* (Clarke, 1900), pp. 91 ff.

The fifth principle is that by the will of Christ every society of Christians organized for Christian worship, instruction and fellowship is a Christian Church and is independent of external control. The ground of this principle is the ground of the whole; namely, the presence of Christ with those who are gathered in his Name. 'Where two or three are gathered together in my name, there am I in the midst of them' (Matt. xviii. 20). These words are the charter and guarantee not only of the personal principle, but also of the voluntary principle. This is the second broad principle which gives unity to the multiplicity of the sect-type. We must consider it in the chapter which follows.

CHAPTER XIV

THE VOLUNTARY PRINCIPLE

A great number of people in divers parts of this realm...do wilfully and damnably before almighty God abstain and refuse to come to their parish churches.   *Second Act of Uniformity* (1552)

Your distinction betwixt the Church and the Commonwealth, if it were in Nero's or Diocletian's time, might be admitted without exception; but in my opinion it is not so fit at this time, and especially in this kingdom.... It cannot yet sink into my head that he should be a member of a Christian Commonwealth that is not also a member of the Church of Christ, concerning the outward society.

JOHN WHITGIFT, in answer to THOS. CARTWRIGHT (1574)[1]

When Christian churches are described as voluntary societies it is not meant that Christian people are at liberty to please themselves whether they will form churches or not, but that churches are to be formed in free obedience to the authority of Christ—not by the power of the State.   ROBERT WILLIAM DALE (1884)[2]

THREE HUNDRED YEARS of controversy over civil and religious liberty separate the first two of these statements from the third. The difference between Whitgift and Dale must be measured, in part, by the difference between their respective situations.

When Dale wrote, the civil and religious disabilities of dissenters from the State establishment of religion in England and Wales were largely at an end. Catholic emancipation had put an end to penal laws against papist recusants in 1829; and after the University Tests Act of 1871 all lay posts in the colleges as well as the Universities of Oxford and Cambridge were opened for the first time

---

[1] *Works*, I, 388 (Parker Society).
[2] *Manual*, p. 26 (Congregational Union of England and Wales), 8th ed. 1898.

to men of all creeds upon equal terms, without religious tests: dissenters who had long since vindicated their right to freedom of worship were no longer to be banned and disinherited in the academic sense. In short, the voluntary principle had been vindicated in England and Wales very largely by the sect-type of churchmanship represented by Independents, Baptists and Methodists, for whom the 'personal' and 'voluntary' principles were correlative; the first implying the second, and the second presupposing the first. Dale's situation, therefore, was very different from that of his separatist forerunners whom Elizabethan archbishops and bishops sent to prison and to death.

Archbishop Whitgift belonged to an age when the 'ideologies' dividing the European world into two camps were expressed not, as now, in terms of politics and economics, but in terms of theology, since religion was still one of the master passions of men. The presuppositions of all sovereign states being what modern democracy calls 'totalitarian', absolute conformity of faith and public worship within any state, Catholic or Protestant, was held to be a condition of public safety. Dissident religious opinions were dangerous opinions, and it was the universal belief (apart from exceptions to be noticed presently) that the force of the State, as the necessary and effective prophylactic against them, was a righteous exercise of a God-given power. The Tudor power which executed Sir Thomas More burned thirteen Dutch Anabaptists at the stake in the same year, but Sir Thomas More would have seen in their martyrdom an act of divine justice against the 'lewd leprosy of libertines'. Archbishop Cranmer who was martyred at the stake in Mary's reign had himself sent Anabaptists to the stake, the Flemish surgeon George van Paris among them.

It was a world, in short, in which dissidents from authoritative ecclesiastical order were burned or beheaded not only in Catholic Paris but also in Calvinist Geneva; not only in Anglican London but in Zwinglian Zürich. The horrors of the Spanish Inquisition are notorious and appalling; they have been excelled only by the tortures and mass-murders of our own time; but the ruthless liquidation of anabaptist and other innocent sectaries by German Lutheranism was part of the same totalitarian logic. Churchmanship itself was everywhere an aspect of patriotism; the religious recusancy of the Jesuit Campion and the Puritan Penry was regarded as political disaffection. Such extremists were 'liquidated', since such dissent involved not merely schism but treason. 'The vexed question whether the Romanists died for treason or for their faith implies an antithesis which had little meaning in that age of mingled politics and religion.'[1] Protestant England for example was menaced by the Armada of Catholic Spain; Englishmen were profoundly aware of the need for national unity; and if an Elizabethan bishop had not recognized the supremacy of the State in all causes, including ecclesiastical causes, he would not have remained a bishop very long. The monarch was the supreme head of the Church: the royal supremacy was one of the ways in which England, and all other States rising on the ruins of the medieval system, expressed the new principle of the indivisibility of sovereignty.[2] 'If you will have the Queen of England rule as monarch over all her dominions, then must you also give her leave to use one kind and form of government in all and every part of the

---

[1] Mandell Creighton.
[2] The problem of Church and State in the Reformation era is further discussed on pp. 288 ff. below.

same, and so to govern the Church in ecclesiastical affairs as she doth the Commonwealth in civil.' For the effect of dissent is

to divide one realm into two, and to spoil the Prince of one half of her jurisdiction and authority.... There is no reformed church that I can hear tell of but it hath a certain prescript and determinate order, as well touching ceremonies and discipline as doctrine, to the which all are constrained to give their consent; and why then may not this Church of England have so in like manner? Is it meet that every man should have his own fancy, or live as him list?[1]

To most men of the sixteenth century the answer to this rhetorical question was obvious. The concept of the Church-State being universal, uniformity was axiomatic, and conformity its self-evident corollary.

But a relatively small group of people gave a different answer. They asserted not only that the Church of Christ must be 'pure' (the personal principle), but also that it must be 'free' (the voluntary principle). They had no love of separatism for its own sake; indeed, they reflected the outlook of their age in that they became separatists only in the last resort and with great reluctance; further, they were certainly no less loyal to the reigning monarch, and no less zealous to uphold the just authority of the State, than were their conforming fellows. 'It is a woeful thing', said Barrow before the Privy Council at Whitehall, 'that our prince's sword should be drawn out against her faithful subjects.'[2] Nevertheless their positive principle of religious freedom involved them in denials which meant

---

[1] Whitgift, *op. cit.* II, 264; III, 321.

[2] 18 March 1588. Cf. Pastor Robinson: 'Do you imagine we account the kingdom of England Babylon or the city of Amsterdam Sion? It is the Church of England, or State Ecclesiastical which we account Babylon....'

either death or voluntary exile. In the autumn of 1581 Robert Browne and his little company 'all agreed and were fully persuaded that the Lord did call them out of England'; they stole away secretly to Middleburg in Zeeland which had been subject to the frightful cruelties of Spanish rule but had at last been set free by the Stadtholder of the Netherlands, William of Orange. The exiles from Scrooby were to leave the Lincolnshire coast in the same way and for the same reason, twenty years later. Robert Browne's classic treatise was published at Middleburg entitled, *A Treatise of Reformation without tarrying for Anie, and of the wickedness of those which will not reforme till the Magistrate command or compell them.* It contains the now familiar words: 'The Lord's people is of the willing sorte. It is conscience, not the power of man, that will drive us to seek the Lord's Kingdom. Therefore it belongeth not to the magistrate to compel religion, to plant churches by power, and to force a submission to ecclesiastical government by laws and penalties.' Yet even Browne betrays the temper of the age by adding—with an inconsistency which he defended to the last—that a church being once properly founded, the magistrate may take it under his charge and exercise 'outward justice' over it.

It was John Robinson therefore, rather than Browne, who first gave full and consistent expression to the voluntary principle of Independency. The main thought in his *Justification of Separation from the Church of England* (1610), which quotes II Cor. vi. 14 on its title-page, is the autonomy of each individual congregation; or, as Robinson expressed it in the Petition presented to James I in 1616, 'the right of spiritual administration and government in itself and over itself by the common and free consent of the people, independently and immediately under Christ'.

Writing of 'the proper subject of the power of Christ', he says, 'the Papists plant it in the Pope; the Protestants in the Bishops; the Puritans, as you (i.e. his episcopal opponents) term the reformed churches and those of their mind, in the Presbytery. We, whom you name Brownists, put it in the body of the Congregation, the multitude, called the church.' With an *a priori* disregard for all historical development Robinson is content to define the congregation in terms of Matt. xviii, 20. 'I do tell you that in what place soever, by what means soever—whether by preaching the Gospel by a true Minister, by a false Minister or by no Minister—two or three faithful people do arise, separating themselves from the world into the fellowship of the Gospel and covenant of Abraham, they are a Church, truly gathered, though never so weak.' Further, this autonomy of the local, gathered church excludes all subordination of one church to another, but it does not exclude fellowship ('consociation'). Robinson protests vigorously, therefore, against any such consociation becoming a national church or an *ecclesia catholica*. In his *Apology* he argues that the 'catholic church' is an ideal, not to be realized 'before the glorious second coming of Christ'. We should notice, too, that it was these ecclesiastical principles, and not theological considerations, which determined the attitude of these early Independents in England to other reformed churches. Robinson often said that in respect of faith he was in complete accord with the reformed faith of England, Germany and Holland. In this he anticipated the Independency of the later seventeenth century which was particularly careful to disavow anything like an independent theology. As John Owen put it in his *Letter concerning excommunication*: 'There is nothing determined by the ancient councils to belong unto Christian faith which Dissenters disbelieve...they own the doctrine of the Church of England as established by law, in nothing receding from it: nor have they any novel or uncatholic opinions of their own.'

But the autonomy of the local congregation being Robinson's main thought, its correlative was the principle of religious democracy (crude and misleading though the phrase obviously is). Clerical privilege was as alien and objectionable to these gathered congregations as was the intrusion of the secular power. Early Independency in England shows an untiring opposition to anything like priestly prerogative or office. Any essential difference between clergy and laity is repudiated. Nothing is commoner among these men and women than their polemic against the 'pharisaism of the time', by which they mean the tendency of priest or presbyter to presume on his school or university learning. 'It is a fond error', wrote no less a scholar than Milton, 'to think that the University makes a minister of the Gospel'. And, to anticipate our next section for a moment, the same protest comes, more understandably, from George Fox: 'At another time on a First Day morning, the Lord opened unto me that being bred at Oxford and Cambridge was not enough to fit and qualify men to be ministers of Christ.' In these autonomous assemblies where the voluntary principle was also the 'pentecostal' principle, all had the right to prophesy and to edify. The elders of the church were not lords but servants of the congregation. In his *Apology* Robinson by no means belittles the office of the minister or elder: the people are 'to give their assent to their elders' holy and lawful administration, that the ecclesiastical elections and censures may be ratified, and put into solemn execution by the elders'. But in his *Justification* he has already asserted what this may not mean. 'We may not acknowledge them for lords over God's heritage (I Pet. v. 3) as you would make them, controlling all, but to be controlled by none; much less essential unto the church, as though it could not be without them; least of all the church itself, as you would expound Matt. xviii.'

These words express, albeit negatively, the positive meaning of the voluntary principle. It is best appraised, indeed, not in terms of the particular concepts of three centuries ago, which time and experience have out-dated, but in terms of the spiritual maturity and competence of the ordinary humble believer. Such believers have not always been humble of course; the 'Saints' of the seventeenth century were not always saintly; they could be narrow, self-righteous and spiritually proud, though they had no monopoly of these common Christian failings. But they were being true to the first principles of the Reformation in believing that those who are in Christ should not be kept in tutelage as babes, but that, growing in grace, they should grow up, and so vindicate the freedom and the responsibility of God's adult children. A papal encyclical of the twentieth century shows, by contrast, what this means. In February 1906 Pope Pius X issued this definition of the Church:

The Church is the mystical Body of Christ, a Body ruled by Pastors and Teachers, a society of men headed by rulers having full and perfect powers of governing, instructing and judging. It follows that this Church is essentially an unequal society; that is to say, a society comprising two categories of persons; pastors and the flock; those who hold rank in the different degrees of the hierarchy, and the multitude of the faithful. And these categories are so distinct in themselves that in the pastoral body alone reside the necessary right and authority to guide and direct all the members towards the goal of the society. As for the multitude, it has no other right than of allowing itself to be led and, as a docile flock, to follow its shepherds.[1]

To multitudes of God's freemen this is so astonishing an interpretation of the mind of Christ as revealed in the New Testament, that they never cease to thank God for pastors of his flock such as John Robinson.

[1] *Vehementer*, 11 February 1906.

CHAPTER XV

THE SPIRITUAL PRINCIPLE

As certain Anabaptists do falsely boast
The Thirty-nine Articles: Art xxxviii,
'Of Christian men's goods'

WHO were these Anabaptists, and why have they been the victims of three centuries of persistent vilification? It is a large and complex question.

Anabaptism, which means re-baptism, was a general term of abuse covering several variants of an essential idea. It combined what we have called the personal and voluntary principles, by placing its main emphasis on the indwelling Spirit, Word or Light. Thus the sect-type here witnesses to a spiritual principle which is often consciously 'pentecostal'. One ironical result was that 'spiritual' became a term of abuse. The Anabaptists rejected infant baptism as an unscriptural corruption which makes the personal, voluntary and spiritual principles meaningless; they contended that believers' baptism is alone Christian in the apostolic, scriptural sense. Adults joining themselves to such Baptist communities of the Spirit were therefore re-baptized, even though they had already been baptized in infancy. 'Donatists new dipt' was Thomas Fuller's succinct caricature.[1] We may fittingly return to Luther, for a moment, to understand why Anabaptism, the *nomen horribile* of the sixteenth century, was not only treated with awful savagery by the Catholic Hapsburgs Charles V and his son Philip II in the Netherlands, but was also feared

[1] *Church History,* IV, 229.

and persecuted by Protestant rulers, with the approval of the Reformers.

From the moment when Luther climbs out of the valley of the shadow to his mountain height of evangelical vision, his natural conservatism makes him hesitate. He is like a mountaineer proceeding cautiously along a narrow ridge or 'striding edge', from which the ground falls steeply away on either side.

Below him, on the one side, is a sacerdotal and papal system from which the New Testament has delivered him. Knowing by agonizing experience that guilty man cannot put the Holy One in his debt, meriting acquittal or earning salvation, Luther discovers from the Epistle to the Romans that the redeeming love of God in Christ transcends such legal and commercial transactions altogether, and that men are justified by grace alone on God's part, and by faith alone on man's. There are three dark features of the Roman landscape, indeed, which he has left far below him: three related concepts which he repudiates as alien to the Gospel of the New Testament. The first is that priests are the exclusive purveyors of God's grace in forgiveness. The second is that they can repeat on the altar what the Crucified did once for all on Calvary. The third is that they may thus make the sacrifice of the Mass a meritorious 'work' on the sinner's part, which will be accounted to him for righteousness. To Luther, Calvin and Zwingli these three aspects of the Mass are the supreme abomination (*horrendae abominationis caput*).[1] The old order is at an end.

But on the other side of this mountain ridge there yawns for these reformers the dangerous abyss of radical individualism, sectarian 'spiritualism' and—as they had some justification for believing—the consequent anarchy of

[1] *Calvini Opera Selecta*, I, 152.

social revolution. The forces which Luther's example has released refuse to be controlled. The 'spirituals',[1] as they were contemptuously called, appeal too confidently to justification by faith alone: they thus become superior and hostile to almost all outward forms in religion, and so threaten to empty Christianity of its distinctive historical content. Indeed, whereas Luther had opposed the papacy with the Gospel, the Spirituals are now opposing the Gospel itself with 'the Spirit'. 'The Spirit of God', said Carlstadt, 'to which all things ought to be subjected, cannot be subject even to Scripture'—a bold formula which anticipates George Fox and Robert Barclay (to name only these), and which would make the individual conscience (lit, no doubt, by the Inner Light and animated by the spirit of Pentecost) the sole criterion of Christian truth. Luther is therefore gravely embarrassed. He feels about the Spirituals the same sense of indignation and outrage which the Papists feel about him. The principle which Luther has invoked against Leo X is invoked by Carlstadt and others of the emerging sect-type against Luther. Calvin faced the same problem with the *esprits phrénétiques*; that is, people given over to frenzied spiritual emotion, and gathering themselves into little dissident groups (*dissentiunculae*); though, as we have already noticed, the sect-type came to owe more to Calvinism than to Lutheranism as time went on.

One result of Luther's mingled irritation and fear was his onslaught in 1525, not only 'Against the heavenly prophets' (the anabaptist issue), but also against a depres-

---

[1] The German term of abuse for this 'pentecostal' mysticism was *Schwärmerei*, an expressive word describing what would happen if we brushed our teeth with shaving soap. It means 'swarming', 'foaming at the mouth'. It suggests, as it is meant to do, the frenzy of the epileptic or madman.

sed peasantry revolting by an inalienable human right against the tyrannous privilege of its feudal lords (the abiding issue of social justice). 'Therefore strike, throttle, stab, secretly or openly, he who can', writes the Reformer in a pamphlet of unforgettable savagery, 'and remember that there is nothing more poisonous, more hurtful or more devilish than a rebellious man.' This, from the great Rebel himself. This social and political quietism from one who had confronted the majesty and power of half the world at Worms, and publicly defied a papal bull. In spite of all that may be said in justification of Luther here, and of the massacre at Frankenhausen (1525), this is nevertheless the blackest blot on Luther's memory. To the disillusioned and despairing peasants, who were ultimately more right than wrong, Doctor Martin now becomes 'the flatterer of princes'; the triumph of social reaction is secure until the French Revolution. Indeed, just because Luther the magnificent religious rebel is at the same time the obstinate social conservative, he finds his freedom of movement on his reforming height much restricted, and it is difficult to avoid the conclusion that, in the last analysis, the vantage height from which he speaks is the State.[1]

But what, then, may be said in explanation and justification of the feeling of horror with which Anabaptism was universally repudiated and reviled in the sixteenth century? There is no smoke without fire; and though mass hysteria, fostered by the slanderous reports of enemies, will explain much, why was it that the charge or even the hint of sympathizing with Anabaptism at any point was the vilest mud which one could fling at an opponent, and which evoked on his part a feverish anxiety to clear himself? Was there any truth in the old calumny which has been so long

[1] On this issue, see pp. 289 ff. below.

in dying that Anabaptism was 'one of the wildest and fiercest sects ever bred within the pale of the Christian Church...a blood-red spectre which swept across Europe inspiring riot and rebellion',[1] and therefore fully explaining the savage measures taken against it—notoriously in the Catholic Netherlands, but also in Germany, Switzerland, Moravia and the Tyrol? Thousands were sent to deaths of every imaginable cruelty: there were innumerable torturings, burnings at the stake and drownings; women were regularly buried alive; the notorious Inquisitor Titelmann burned whole families at the stake, their only offence being the reading of the Bible in private.[2]

The truth seems to be that an innocent multitude suffered because of the guilt of a few. Thousands of quiet and pitiful people perished because a small minority of ruthless and violent visionaries did come to advocate insurrection and radical revolution—the greatest enormity of which the common man could be guilty in an age obsessed with maintaining the existing social order rather than with reforming it. Indeed, the leaders were often not Ana-

[1] Herzog, quoted by Powicke, *op. cit.* p. 201.

[2] The Regent for Charles V in the Netherlands was his sister the dowager Queen Mary, the 'Christian widow' admired by Erasmus. In 1533 she wrote to the Emperor urging that all heretics, whether repentant or not, should be put to death with the utmost severity, care being only taken that the Provinces should not be entirely depopulated. The imperial edict of 1535 authorized a system of wholesale murder, which the Christian widow put into execution: all heretics were condemned to death: repentant males to be executed with the sword, repentant females to be buried alive, the obstinate of both sexes to be burned. The edict was the law of the land for twenty years and it was rigidly enforced. On the accession of Philip II of Spain, the infamous edict of 1550 confirmed and intensified these measures. As he himself put it in a letter to Margaret of Parma, 'Why introduce the Spanish Inquisition? The Inquisition of the Netherlands is more pitiless than that of Spain (d'ailleurs l'inquisition des Pays-Bas est plus impitoyable que celle d'Espagne).' *Correspondence de Philippe II*, vol. I, 207 (quoted from Motley, *Rise of the Dutch Republic*, Part II, c. 3).

baptists in the strict sense at all. The notorious Thomas Münzer (1490–1525) was not; but claiming to be under the direct influence of the Spirit he had some early correspondence with them, until they discovered that his tenets were incongruous with their own—a fact which may have occasioned and perpetuated the calumny which identifies them with his bloodthirsty cause of communistic theocracy. Of the so-called Zwickau prophets, Nickel Storch was 'ein Kommunist und blutgieriger Apokalyptiker'.[1] Hänsel Hutt of Bibra, most wild and fanatical of all such apocalyptists, had a following in the Thuringian estates of the House of Saxony. It is not surprising therefore that in October 1531 the Wittenberg theologians decided, after discussion, that Anabaptists might legitimately be put to the sword. Luther added his vote on the characteristic ground that 'though it looks cruel to punish them with death, it would be more cruel that they should defile the function of the Word, repress true doctrine and advocate, to this end, the overthrow of the secular government'. He gave a like judgement, of course, on 20 October 1534, after the catastrophe of Münster which, more than any other fact, has done most to misrepresent the name of 'Anabaptist' and make it odious.[2]

Melchior Hoffman, preacher and popular leader, was attracted to Lutheranism, turned to Anabaptism in 1529, and succeeded for a time in introducing a new leaven of eschatological messianism into its pacificist and quietist tradition. He seems to have taught that the saints might justly wield the sword, and thus precipitate the coming of

[1] Böhmer, *op. cit.* p. 130 n.

[2] *Ibid.* pp. 248–50. But it should be noticed that as early as 1526 the anabaptist Felix Mants was put to death by drowning in Protestant Zürich in accordance with Zwingli's pithy formula: *qui iterum mergit mergatur* (let him who re-baptizes be drowned).

the Kingdom of Christ. He was opposed by many who disavowed this apocalyptic violence, holding steadily to Matt. v. 5. Others followed him, but allegorized his messianic gospel, and no more advocated political revolution than did the author of Eph. vi. 17: this was especially true of the Dutch 'Melchiorites'. But the Melchiorites— his confessed followers—were partially responsible for the excesses into which Anabaptism temporarily plunged. A similar fusion of mysticism with eschatology explains the violence of the Lutheran Rothmann, who taught that 'der unschuldige Abel muß die Waffen Kains ergreifen' (innocent Abel must seize Cain's weapons). The fall of Münster recalled Anabaptists, however, to their first principles, and after August 1536 all such violence was permanently repudiated. The leadership passed to Menno Simons who enunciated with convincing clarity and power the traditional Baptist distinction between the sphere of Christ and that of the State (the voluntary principle). Like Hans Denck, he revered the awakened and regenerate conscience of man as the dwelling place of the inward Word, Light or Spirit of God. The claim to spiritual freedom followed directly therefrom; the interference of the secular power with the inmost shrine of conscience is sacrilege. This has been the consistent witness of Baptist and Mennonite churches ever since. Thus the sect-type here enunciates the great concept of toleration. The Baptists were 'the first to see, the boldest to preach and the foremost to suffer for' the duty of a human soul to guide itself freely by the light of God's Spirit.[1]

---

[1] For a conspectus of the large modern literature on this subject, see *Handbuch der KG*, III (*Reformation und Gegenreformation*) by Hermelink and Maurer; the standard modern works on the history of the Baptists; the *Mennonite Quarterly*, which contains valuable modern research; and the many authoritative studies by Professor Roland Bainton of Yale on Left-

Perhaps David Joris (c. 1501–56) comes as near as anyone to being a fair representative of sixteenth-century
Anabaptism as a whole. Professor Roland Bainton has
enlarged our knowledge of the character and setting of the
movement, his important work on Joris being copiously
annotated from Dutch, German and Swiss sources, and
furnished with a hundred pages of original documents from
the Zürich and Basel archives. He uses two lines of research which decisively refute the tendentious inaccuracies
of earlier biographers.

In the first place he examines the different elements
which make up the spiritual environment within which
this mystic from the Netherlands moved and developed,
both by attraction and repulsion. His apocalyptic mysticism recalls the Franciscan spirituals; particularly Joachim
di Fiore,[1] who divided the history of humanity into three
ages; that of the Law or the Father; that of the Gospel or
the Son; and that of the Spirit, the *ultima aetas ecclesiae*,
when the whole world will become an order of *viri
spirituales*, the ecclesiastical hierarchy will efface itself, and
the end of the ages will come. Repelled by the violent
radicalism of Münzer, Rothmann and others, Joris shared
the allegorized messianic expectations of Melchiorites in
the Netherlands, but above all he was influenced by the

wing Protestantism of the sixteenth century. Particularly valuable is his
David Joris: Wiedertäufer und Kämpfer für Toleranz im 16. Jahrhundert (Ergän-
zungsband VI des *Archivs für Reformationsgeschichte*, Leipzig, 1937).

[1] Among the great mystics whom Dante placed in paradise—Anselm,
Hugh of St Victor and Bonaventura—he also placed this Calabrian
prophet: *Il calavrese abate Giovacchino*
           Di spirito profetico dotato.

Dante's lines may be an echo of the anthem sung on his feast day in the
Calabrian diocese: *Beatus Joachim, spiritu dotatus prophetico, decoratus intelli-
gentia, errore procul haeretico, dixit futura ut praesentia.* The words betray some
doubt as to his entire orthodoxy!

noble appeal of Hans Denck and Sebastian Franck to the cloister within the individual heart and to the 'inwardness' of the Word. Becoming more prominent when radical Anabaptism was compromised and discredited at Münster, and when many Anabaptists felt that Menno Simons had gone too far in repudiating radicalism altogether, Joris found himself mediating between the two groups and leading a sect as its inspired prophet.

In the second place Bainton's thorough knowledge of the prophet's extant writings and his critical comparison of the later edition of the *Twonder-boeck* with the first (1542), bring out for the first time certain significant developments and changes in Joris and his 'system' as he grew older and became steadily more quietist. Almost from the beginning his ecstatic messianism is moderated by his mysticism. Though his mother was executed at Delft because she confessed her son's prophecies to be as true as those of the prophets and the apostles, and though the less discerning undeniably regarded him as the promised 'third David' of the 'third age', Joris himself progressively spiritualized all such eschatological imagery. He urges every man to become David, killing his own Goliath. Joris is, with Franck, a man of the inward Word. Indeed, he becomes increasingly indifferent to theological controversy and to ecclesiastical forms. A letter to Schwenkfeld (1550) shows him appealing to the *ignorantia sacra* which declines to engage in current Christological disputes: 'I do not bother my head whether the Lord is above or here below (*droben ist oder hernieden*)...if I am of like disposition to him in heart, mind and spirit, that must suffice me.'

To meet the charge that his doctrine of the inner light was a claim to personal divinity (a claim alleged to have been made by James Nayler in England a century later)

Joris wrote two Apologies denying such transcendental implications. Here, too, as elsewhere he repudiates the stock charges of polygamy, murder and theft made against his sect,[1] and recognizes the authority of the law and of the temporal ruler. As for the motif of nudity appearing in some of his dreams and visions, Bainton concludes convincingly that its significance is ascetic rather than antinomian, having nothing to do with the erotic mysticism of the late Middle Ages and of Melchior Hoffmann, but with Isa. xx. 3. Indeed, Joris's general religious and 'theological' position, as discoverable in the numerous tractates, pamphlets, letters and books of his middle and later period, is neither exceptional nor extravagant, but typical of the spiritualism of the age.

After the grim story of his hunted existence in Holland, there follows the astonishing sequel of his arrival incognito in Basel, where he settles with his family to live the life of a propertied country gentleman, concealing his identity under the name of Johann van Brugge. For years the city fathers had no suspicion that this dignified and well-dressed refugee from Holland was a dangerous heretic. It is remarkable that the secret was kept so long. When the facts came out after Joris's death, one of his disgruntled disciples having acted as informer (and adding the charge of polygamy), the story reads like any modern thriller. After a judicial inquiry, tragi-comic in its pathetic sittings and interrogations, Joris's corpse was dug up and burnt, with his books. The Joris party, thirty in number, were imprisoned, admonished and solemnly pardoned, and the

---

[1] The horrible excesses of Münster were certainly not typical of Anabaptism, but public opinion throughout Europe refused to forget them; and authority used the memory unscrupulously. Cf. Whitgift, *op. cit.* I, 77, 125–39.

religious orthodoxy of the city thus vindicated. The whole story is an illuminating commentary on the abiding problem of freedom and authority.

The spiritual principle. Its vindication by the sect-type is not peculiar to the protestant era, of course; as the 'pentecostal' principle it has marked (and sometimes disfigured) the story of Christianity from the beginning. Indeed, the strength and weakness of the sect-type have to be appraised against a wider background than the sixteenth and seventeenth centuries afford. As a peg on which to hang the illustrative evidence of nineteen centuries we may legitimately look back for a moment to a famous heretic of the second century, Montanus, who—with the two women Prisca and Maximilla—provides the classic example of that spiritual or pentecostal enthusiasm which breaks out at intervals like a troublesome spring along the paved highway of ecclesiastical history. The ancient Catholic Church denounced Montanists as heretics, 'crawling', as Eusebius put it, 'over Asia and Phrygia like venomous reptiles'.[1] And the notorious heretic-hunter Epiphanius (c. 315–402) dismissed this father of the later

[1] *H.E.* v, 14–16. Mark Pattison said of satire that to be real it must exaggerate but that it is always an exaggeration of known and recognized facts. Satire never creates the sentiment to which it appeals. Many classic heresies in Christian history are patient of a like interpretation. Appealing to truth held in common by all the faithful they place disproportionate emphasis on a part and so distort the whole. Heresy is often exaggeration rather than innovation.

The menace of Marcion (*ipso Paulo paulinior*) lay in his exaggerated Paulinism. Arianism was the illegitimate distortion of the legitimate subordinationism of Origen and the East. The confident moralism of Pelagius threatened the very genius of Christianity as the religion of redeeming grace.

Indeed, such distortions repeatedly take their rise as reactions against dreaded error. Marcion feared the threatened eclipse of Paulinism. Arianism dreaded Sabellianism, and the pantheism which expresses its implicit

spirituals as 'that pitiful little creature, Montanus',[1] thereby anticipating the judgement of modern scholars that the
importance of his movement may easily be overestimated
and over-dramatized.[2] Why, then, did John Wesley
describe him as 'one of the holiest men of the second
century'? There are two main reasons.

First, Montanism is the classic example of a sect-type
destined to reappear constantly in the history of the Church
from that day to this. From I Corinthians onwards, emphasis on charismatic gifts, though a sign of life and power,
opens the door with notorious ease to an unbalanced
subjectivity; and Montanism is rightly regarded as the
prototype of those many religious revivals which have become separatist movements, thanks to their disapproval of
the Church as established, and to their restless sense of the
contrast between empirical and ideal Christianity.

Starting with the promises and apocalyptic visions of
scripture, nourished on the great word of Joel ii, and
dreaming of the lost pentecostal springtime of the Church,
visionary imaginations in all ages have gone the way of
Montanus and his followers, with their extravagant belief
in the presence and activity of the Spirit, to whose action
they have abandoned themselves in complete passivity
like the violin vibrating under the bow; and so emphasizing
the continuance of prophecy in the life of the Church, with
its spasmodic ecstasies, glossolalia and kindred manifestations. We may cite Gibbon's 'whirling dervishes' again,[3]

logic. Pelagius rightly feared the loss to the faith of a proper emphasis on
the will, and on moral effort.

Montanism provides an early and dramatic example of just such an exaggerated reaction.

[1] τὸ ἐλεεινὸν ἀνθρωπάριον Μοντανός (Panarion, XLVIII, 11).

[2] So Labriolle in *Les Sources de l'histoire du Montanisme* (1913), a collection
and translation of all the passages in early writers which refer to the movement; and in *La Crise Montaniste* (1913).   [3] P. 135 above.

and note that the phenomenon there caricatured recurs constantly, divergencies of race, environment and culture notwithstanding. The Montanist phenomenon has frequently reappeared throughout the course of history, and with each recurrence has followed an almost typical development; it has lived again, *mutatis mutandis*, in all religious movements whose promoters, believing in private revelation and a direct fellowship with God, have sought to quicken souls and to regenerate Christianity.

Thus, Montanism is the classic type of *Schwärmerei*, the first term in the long series made up of Novatians, Donatists, Cathari, Priscillianists, the followers of Joachim di Fiore, Fraticelli, Homines Intelligentiae, Flagellants, Anabaptists, Vaudois, Quakers, Herrnhuters, Swedenborgians, Mormons, Irvingites, Seventh Day Adventists and other modern revivalists. From Montanus to James Nayler, from Muggleton to Evan Roberts, the list could be extended indefinitely. That this sect-type has always criticized, irritated and menaced the official Church is understandable; chronologically, the head and front of the offence is Montanus.

In the second place, Montanism is of abiding interest because the issues which it dramatizes are not dead. They are still with a modern Christendom required to take account, say, of a group movement with its 'absolute' standards and its confident appeal to the direct guidance of the individual and the group by the Spirit. Again, the ministry of women, so far from being a dead issue, is likely to become a very live one before the present century is out. Again, while movements for reunion among the divided churches of Protestantism become more urgent, the history of the sect-type provides an eloquent comment on the fact that men do not necessarily become separatists out of obstinacy and caprice, but often because conscience and high principle compel them; and that until modern Protestantism has rediscovered for itself a high theology of the Church which, while true to its classic first principles, shall be demonstrably relevant to the need of the modern world, it will have no convincing answer to earnest, if fanatic, spirits who advocate 'reformation without tarrying for any'. Cromwell was not greatly distressed at the sects of his time: Ranters, Diggers, Quakers, Fifth Monarchy men and the like; he saw that the confusion of sects was a sign of life.[1] For a living Church men will pay the price even of sectarianism.

But the long story of the successive *ecclesiolae* of Christian history may well make men ask, too, whether separatism is not nearly always too big a price to pay. Writing of the Montanists Harnack observes: 'the effect on themselves was what usually follows in such circumstances. After their separation from the Church they became narrower and pettier in their conception of Christianity. Their asceticism degenerated into legalism, their claim to a monopoly of pure Christianity made them arrogant.' This easy generalization comes naturally from a German with little sympathy for the sects, and from a disciple of Ritschl to boot. His contemporary Troeltsch would hardly have endorsed it. But the evolution of Montanism has been repeated too often since the second century for modern revival movements and other consciously dissident groups to disregard it as easily. For more than two hundred years Muggletonians appear to have sung:

> I do believe in God alone,
> Likewise in Reeve and Muggleton.

[1] So G. N. Clark, *The Seventeenth Century* (2nd ed. Oxford, 1947) p. 312.

This is the Muggletonians' faith,
This is the God which we believe;
None salvation-knowledge hath
But those of Muggleton and Reeve;
Christ is the Muggletonians' King,
With Whom eternally they'll sing.

According to Mr Lytton Strachey—who found in this pathetic rubbish an opportunity for his ironic temper—one would be sorry if the time ever came when there were no more Muggletonians. But their tragedy, like that of the Montanists, is that they are such an unconscionable time a-dying after they have ceased really to live. Virtually dead in the fifth century, Montanism lingered on at Pepuza until John of Damascus' day,[1] and later; in Sir William Ramsay's view, it ceased to be only with the coming of the Turks. So tenacious of life can moribund religious enthusiasms be.

The truth seems to be that Montanism proper was at once conservative and radical, an old as well as a new thing. In its antiquarian idealism, its exaltation of the function and the authority of prophets, its charismatic ministry of women, its dissolution of existing marriages in the name of asceticism, it was reactionary: it was a protest against that ecclesiastical organization which was the answer of 'the great Church' to Gnosticism, and of which Irenaeus was the typical representative in the late second century. In opposing primitive spontaneity to regimentation in terms of creed, canon and episcopate (the Church's triple bulwark against Gnostic heresy) Montanism is essentially backward-looking. In its vindication of the liberty of prophesying, primitive Christian enthusiasm

[1] His *De Haeresibus*, c. 49, speaks of the Pepuziani who glorified Pepuza, which lay between Galatia and Cappadocia, and believed it to be 'Jerusalem'.

surges up again, both as a revival and as a survival. It is a protest against the naturalization of the Church in the world; and there is strength here, as well as weakness; truth as well as error. But the Church of Aviricius Marcellus had to deal with Montanus, just as Basil had to deal with Glycerius the Deacon, and Luther with the Zwickau prophets. Such reactions against the current externalizing of religion, with their naïve appeal to primitive simplicity, spontaneity and purity, naturally evoke both fanatic sympathy and fierce opposition. Phrygia in the second century, like Thuringia in the sixteenth, seems to have been temperamentally ready for a protest against the fact that 'apostles and prophets raised up by God were now giving place to Bishops and Elders appointed by men... that the laity were putting off the royal dignity of the universal priesthood on officials' (Gwatkin).

We are not here concerned with the astonishing initial success of the movement, its wide extension, and the alarums and excursions which it occasioned. Excommunicated[1] by the Asian bishops, the Montanists turned from Phrygia to the West, hoping to achieve in Rome the complete success denied them in the place of their origin. Just as the Irvingite Tongues spread from the West of Scotland into the heart of London in the nineteenth century, so the *nova prophetia* spread from Pepuza to Rome and Carthage, but with no more lasting success. The Tongues did not find in a Chalmers or a Carlyle that powerful advocacy which the new prophecy found in Tertullian; yet Montanism was as far from achieving its end as was the Catholic

---

[1] It is important to notice that Montanists were excommunicated for unorthodoxy not in belief, but in practice. Catholic opponents bear witness that Montanus did not deviate from received Church doctrine; he was content to affirm the *regula fidei*. 'About Father, Son and Holy Spirit they think as does the Holy Catholic Church' (Epiphanius).

Apostolic Church of the Irvingites. Violently repudiated everywhere, Montanists found themselves reduced to living on the fringe of the great Church: unable to capture it, they had perforce become a sect.

The late Professor H. M. Gwatkin's summary of three main results of the Montanist crisis is well known. He argued, first, that with distinct gain there went grievous loss. 'The failure of Montanism did much to fix on Western Christendom that deist conception of God as a King departed to a far country, which empties the world and common life of that which is divine and holy, and restores it but in part, through the mediation of the Church his representative, and by the ministry of sacraments.'

Second, that as a result of the Church's deep distrust of the prophetic and the charismatic in all its forms, the third century was an age of disillusion, like the eighteenth century in England. Enthusiasm was suspect, prophesyings despised and crushed, the Spirit quenched. 'This failure of Prophecy barred every plea of inspiration' (as Priscillian was to discover when he essayed to reopen the era of prophecy, in Spain), 'and helped to bar every plea of conscience not consistent with the actual order of the Church. Preaching was thrown into the background for a thousand years. The medieval conception of the priest's duty was helped forward.' We may add that just as the deism and rationalism of the eighteenth century was the price paid for the repudiation of Quakers, Seekers and other such sectaries of the seventeenth century, with their direct experience of God's activity as Spirit; so the institutional and sacramental emphasis of the medieval Church externalized the interpretation of Christian experience, and helped to obscure the enduring truth that the Spirit alone is primary and all else, however important, secondary. The Bible, the

Sacraments, the historical record of Christ's words and deeds—all are a channel of the Spirit: primary is the experienced fellowship of man's spirit with the Lord the Spirit. The doctrine of the Holy Spirit has too often been 'the stepchild of theology';[1] without this fire, religion is dead ashes. Historic Christianity does not escape this challenge by disavowing 'the squalid sluttery of fanatic conventicles'.

The third result, according to Gwatkin, was that a contrast began to be drawn between the apostolic age with its ministry of gifts (now ended!) and all subsequent Christian ages.

The official ministry seemed the one mediator with an absent king...the entire medieval system from the papacy downward is no more than a natural development of the unbelief which knows no working of the Spirit but one transmitted by outward ordinances from a distant past. To this development the failure of Montanism gave a greater impulse than the defeat of the Gnostics or the conversion of Constantine.

This over-strong language allows too much importance and influence to Montanism; but its positive point is one which the 'spirituals' have constantly made, often to the consternation of the official mind. When Henry Barrow in the Fleet prison was interrogated by Bishop Lancelot Andrewes, and claimed that the Word is interpreted by the Spirit, the following dialogue took place:

Andrewes: This savoureth of a private spirit.
Barrow: This is the Spirit of Christ and his Apostles, and most publicly they submitted their doctrines to the trial of all men. So do I.
Andrewes: What! Are you an Apostle?
Barrow: No, but I have the spirit of the Apostles.

[1] 'Der heilige Geist ist immer mehr oder weniger das Stiefkind der Theologie gewesen' (Brunner, *Das Mißverständnis der Kirche*, p. 51).

Andrewes: What! the spirit of the Apostles?

Barrow: Yes, the spirit of the Apostles.

Andrewes: What! in that measure?

Barrow: In that measure that God hath imparted unto me, though not in that measure that the Apostles had, by any comparison. Yet the same spirit. There is but one Spirit.[1]

This was shocking to the Whitgifts and even to the Burleighs of the age and, as we have seen, Barrow went to the block. He was anticipating Gwatkin's third contention. It is hardly fair, perhaps, to compare his modest speech with that of Tertullian fourteen centuries earlier. Tertullian became a Montanist, admittedly; and his passionate conviction of the unceasing activity of the Spirit was expressed with his unenviable command of sarcasm. Only *imbecillitas aut desperatio fidei*, he says, can pretend that the activity of the Spirit is confined to the apostolic age. He asks whether ecclesiastics (like Canute's courtiers at the sea's edge) will fix boundary stakes for the divine activity. 'Why not suppress God altogether? It is all that remains for you to do, such is your power.'

Montanism was, in some sense, the prototype of what we have called the spiritual or pentecostal principle. Its failure is now a matter of history, and not as important, perhaps, as Gwatkin suggested; the function of the prophet ceased partly because the logic of ecclesiastical development made it inevitable. But its essential principle could not be permanently forgotten or lost. In that age of reason, the eighteenth century, Novalis could witness to it, and so inspire the great word of Faust:

> Jetzt erst erkenn ich was der Weise spricht:
> 'Die Geisterwelt ist nicht verschlossen.'[2]

[1] Powicke, *op. cit.* p. 93.

[2] Only now do I understand the word of the Wise Man: 'The spirit world is not under lock and key.'

CHAPTER XVI

STRENGTH AND WEAKNESS

I N every truth which we receive there lurks some danger which has to be accepted with it. The sect-type is not peculiar in illustrating this familiar fact; and those who know it from within and believe in the principle which it embodies, love it too much to be unaware of its imperfections, or to pretend that there is no contrast between what it is ideally and what it is in fact.

It is easy to accuse the sixteenth-century Reformers of conservative reaction in their treatment of their colleagues of the Left-wing, but the sectarian course of much Protestant history at least explains and justifies their apprehensions, though it does not justify their repressive actions. For here we meet a recurrent historic issue; it is the old issue between order and ardour;[1] between authority imposed from without and vitality expressing itself from within; between the correct uniformity of law and the dynamic spontanceity of life; between the part regarded as having meaning only in the whole, and the whole regarded as no more than the sum of the parts. From the seventeenth century onwards, as we have already seen, it was to be the issue between the Church as a great Institution, established and ordered by the laws of state or hierarchy or both, and the Church as a free association of believers.

Discerning modern Protestants, especially those of the younger generation, are newly aware of and concerned with

[1] Dr John Mackay's phrase.

the related problems of authority and unity. They are thinking about the meaning of historical tradition. Mere individualism is seen to be anarchic; to think about men and things in isolation is to live in an unreal world. 'Like the rest of my generation', wrote the author of *The Testament of Youth*, 'I have had to learn again and again the terrible truth of George Eliot's words about the invasion of personal preoccupations by the larger destinies of mankind and at last to recognize that no life is really private or isolated or self-sufficient.'[1] The sects have never been unaware of this, of course, since the sense of community has been supremely distinctive of their genius. But the tendency of modern thought in many fields has required them to think again about community, not only in terms of the *ecclesiola* but also in terms of the *Ecclesia*.

Earlier in this century we spoke much of personality. We now see more clearly than we did that personality is mutual in its very being and that for all its sovereign individuality a self exists only in a community of selves. A philosophy of personality rightly insists on the sanctity and value of Tom, Dick and Harry as individual souls; but in its modern form it also insists that only as he presupposes Dick and Harry can Tom really *be* Tom. Strictly speaking, there is no such thing as Tom's private life. He has been a debtor from the beginning. Only by accepting the accumulated thought, tradition and criticism of the centuries could Tom ever begin, as he did when a very little child, to master and integrate his own experiences as a living person. Martin Buber has been teaching us a closely related truth by discussing what happens when person *meets* person: real human life is a matter of meeting, mutual confronting, personal 'togetherness'. To use his much-

[1] Vera Brittain.

quoted words: 'I find my being in thee; all real life is meeting' (*Ich werde am Du; alles wirkliche Leben ist Begegnung*). Indeed, it would be difficult to name any field of thought today where an earlier emphasis on the individual is not yielding to this new-old emphasis on organic relatedness. In the fields of economics and politics it is the dominant fact throughout at least three continents. The emphasis has changed too in the field of psychology. In the nineteenth century Matthew Arnold could still think (with the eighteenth century) of men as individual atoms, like lonely islands in the estranging sea;

> Dotting the shoreless, watery wild
> We mortal millions live alone.

But, as Rachel Carson's books about the sea remind us, insularity is half an illusion, since the islands are all part of one pelagic, submarine continent, deep down: and does not modern 'depth psychology', and our research on the unconscious, show that it is a *shared* unconscious, and that our seemingly individual separateness is also half an illusion?

In the field of theology we are not being allowed to distinguish as confidently as we did thirty years ago between Israel's strong sense of her corporate personality, and that new sense of the responsible, individual soul which is first clearly enunciated in Ezek. xviii. 20. For nearly all modern authorities on the Old Testament are agreed in denying that such a contrast between the corporate and the individual could become serious for the Hebrew mind, since the individual is rooted in his family, tribe and nation, and knows himself as such only in that larger context. It was as though each Hebrew, in spite of the emerging sense of exclusive individuality in the Book of Ezekiel, was always in some sense an adumbration of a corporate Israel animating the successive generations of an immemorial past. At the beginning of his *Ulysses*, therefore, James Joyce expresses this Semitic sense of solidarity, by making Daedalus ring up Adam and Eve through a telephone system of umbilical cords connecting the generations between. Is Joyce there suggesting that the race is eternal, and the individual is not? And if so, could even family, group, sect or nation itself have any ultimate significance?

But it is important to notice that while many modern Protestants of the sect-type are becoming critical and even afraid of a divisive sectarianism, the historic sect-type of churchmanship is arousing a new interest, sometimes in unlikely quarters. To-day when the omnicompetent police-state either standardizes or liquidates the non-conforming individual, the free world is recognizing something of the incalculable debt which it owes to the brave witness of despised and persecuted Christian sects. In spite of its criticizable limitations and weakness, the sect-type is being vindicated by a past which present experience is reinterpreting. Ever since Bismarck's *Kulturkampf* in the late nineteenth century began to suggest how far the centralized State can go in stifling independent centres of life within its borders, European thinkers of different persuasions—ranging from Catholic corporatism to syndicalism—have been looking to the local, self-governing group for the best protection against state absolutism on the one hand and anarchic individualism on the other. Further, students of Western politics realize that there is nothing inevitable about parliamentary democracy; it is not the only element in the Western political tradition; its permanence may never be taken for granted; it makes little appeal to the majority of human beings in the world at present, and it has an embarrassing trick of turning by corruption into its opposite (as Aristotle's *Politics* long ago made clear). We have come to see, indeed, that the spirit and meaning of our democracy is most truly defined not as the dominance of the majority but as the recognition by the majority that the rights of the minority are real, and that they are the best interpretation and guarantee of majority rule in the long run. If the shaping influence of the congregational principle of the gathered church on the British and American way of life can be preserved, the sect-type will be increasingly recognized as having meant far more than the mere 'dissidence of dissent' at which Matthew Arnold railed.

For to read the long story of Christianity with sympathy and imaginative insight is to understand Ranke's judgement that every historical epoch has its own direct significance in the sight of God. Ernst Troeltsch developed this relativist thought in his great work on the Christian Churches and Groups, warning us against the tendency of theologians to discover everywhere in the course of Christian history either corruptions of the Gospel or deviations from it. Troeltsch contended that the religious life, even that of Christianity, is something new and different in each of its great forms or types, and that each must first be understood as an independent phenomenon. The sect-type in all its variety is such a phenomenon. As we shall argue in our final chapter, the witness and power of modern Protestantism is dangerously weakened by its inherently schismatic tendencies, but that is not the main thing to be said about it, even in this day of oecumenical hopes. The worship, life and work of tens of thousands of gathered churches; the Christian social philosophy of Calvinist

Puritanism; the ultimacy of the spiritual in the Pietist movements—this and much else constitutes a genuine unity in spite of its superficial diversity.[1] Troeltsch argues impressively that for historical significance it may be fittingly compared with the medieval synthesis.

Further, churches of this type of Christian life—whatever their polities, formally considered—have spread far beyond the English-speaking world. The ideal of the gathered church has not only influenced the community life of the Presbyterian and Episcopalian churches of the United States; a very large proportion of Christians throughout the world now representatively associated in the World Council of Churches also confess substantially those personal and voluntary principles which we have been discussing and which were first clearly enunciated by the early Puritans and Anabaptists. In a paper presented to the first assembly of that World Council Karl Barth quoted the provocative and prophetic question of Friedrich Loofs: 'Who knows whether one day, when the national Churches of the Old World collapse, the congregational form of church order may not have a future among us?' Troeltsch had already been more emphatic: 'The days of the pure church-type within our present civilization are numbered' he wrote in 1911; 'more and more the central life of the church-type is being permeated with the vital energies of the sect and of mysticism.'

There is a refreshing vindication of the sect-type and its historical importance in Professor Roland Bainton's *Reformation of the Sixteenth Century*, but it caused one grateful reader some misgiving, nevertheless. Bainton discusses the Peace of Augsburg (1555) which established the fate-

---

[1] Cf. Heiler, *Katholizismus*, Vorwort, p. xxxiii.

ful territorial principle, *cuius regio ejus religio*; that is, 'the religion of a territory will be that of the prince who rules it'. This meant that Lutheranism had at last won legal recognition alongside of Catholicism in Germany. But it also meant that anabaptist sectaries, and even Calvinists, were excluded from this legal recognition. They were virtually outlawed; and, as we have seen, anabaptist groups were often stamped out by their fellow-Protestants with ferocious cruelty. Bainton adds:

> If only Lutheranism could have been subject to the stimulus of the criticism and competition of the sects, it could never have become so complacent and allied to the established order. The Anglican Church owes an incalculable debt to the Nonconformists. So completely were the Anabaptists exterminated that few Lutherans are aware that the principle of British dissent originated on German soil (p. 107).

Whether Bainton is right or not about British dissent, his estimate of its historic function recalls the characteristically fair judgement of Archbishop William Temple[1] that freedom in England had its origin 'chiefly in the claim of dissenters from the Established Church to worship God as their consciences might direct: it was rooted in faith... and the self-government of the local chapel has been a fruitful school of democratic procedure'. The ideals of those self-governing communities of the seventeenth century were partially expressed in a famous sentence of the Puritan, Colonel Rainborough: 'I think that the poorest he that is in England hath a life to live as the richest he.' In those tiny gathered congregations we had, albeit in miniature, something like democracy.

A member of the Society of Friends, Professor Bainton is an unabashed defender, not only of the sect-type but of

---

[1] *Christianity and the Social Order* (3rd ed. S.C.M., 1950), pp. 66–7.

sectarianism. He rightly argues that something precious had been gained at Augsburg; but he does not hesitate to rejoice in the fact that the principle of ecclesiastical solidarity had been formally as well as actually broken. Against the background of the savage passion for ecclesiastical uniformity in the sixteenth century, his defence of freedom is unanswerably right. But is he not out of line with the mind of the modern Church as it struggles to unlearn its sectarianism and to learn the way of oecumenical unity? He does not pretend to be ashamed of 'our unhappy divisions'. 'Those', he writes, 'who deplore any breach in unity as scandal and sin will bemoan the outcome at Augsburg. Those who prize liberty above universality will see here one step in the direction of freedom in religion.'[1] But must we be impaled on the horns of this dilemma? Can we not unanimously rejoice over this step towards religious liberty, and at the same time take active steps to heal a disunion which *has become* scandalous?

As an English Free Churchman the writer of this book cannot help feeling the weakness as well as the strength of the sect-type which he knows and loves. He feels that *reunion* 'without tarrying for any' is becoming as urgent as was the opposite principle for his spiritual ancestor Robert Browne. The weakness of sectarianism has been writ large across the Protestant era. Its sense of tradition has been gravely defective. At times it has been stubbornly and impenitently schismatic. The arrogance of its Catholic and Protestant detractors explains but hardly justifies its own too frequent lack of humility. Too often it has had little realization of the sacramental principle, and the mediation of the 'inward' through outward forms; the result has been not only liturgical barrenness, but a 'loss of

[1] *Op. cit.* pp. 155–6.

spiritual substance' which Tillich analyses with searching insight in his *Protestant Era*. It has been guilty of a radical and even anarchic individualism which its confident appeal to the New Testament cannot justify. It has been blind to the essential oneness of Christ's Body. But because this writer feels that its truth is still stronger than its weakness, the oecumenical issue is for him the surpreme issue for the Protestant tradition in the twentieth century.

PART IV

MODERN ISSUES

CHAPTER XVII

THE ROMAN CHURCH
AND TOLERATION

I. THE OUTLOOK FOR RELIGIOUS TOLERATION
IN THE MODERN WORLD

IF liberty is to be real, toleration must be its correlative. But the outlook for toleration is notoriously dim in the totalitarian climate of our time. That beacon light of truth for its own sake, lit by ancient Greeks, is often hardly discernible through the murk of twentieth-century propaganda. It must be admitted that, seated in the deck-chair of modern liberalism, we have sometimes talked sentimental nonsense about the Greeks: the culture of the citizens of Athens depended on the labour of slaves, and their religious intolerance made Socrates drink the hemlock. Yet we like to think that Socrates is remembered while his judges are forgotten; and that it is he who is an inalienable part of Europe's heritage. He taught us that, truth being what it is, the love of it must be disinterested; the questing human mind must be open and tolerant. We like to think that because John Stuart Mill was nurtured in the same tradition, his treatise *On Liberty* has become a classic apologia for toleration. It could be argued, too, that though Voltaire knew little and cared less about real religion and 'was in his way a bigot, an intolerant bigot';[1] and though his battle on behalf of the victims of a privileged and persecuting orthodoxy was prompted by dubious

---

[1] Gibbon, *Decline and Fall* (ed. Bury), VII, 139 n.

motives—he did care nevertheless for the free expression of opinion, and was sincere in writing to Helvétius, 'I disagree profoundly with what you say, but I will fight to the death for your right to say it'. And is it not Milton's main argument in the *Areopagitica* that the dangers consequent upon allowing full freedom of thought and expression are less than the dangers of suppressing that freedom, even though it should be done with the best of motives?

This light, the star by which Western man has steered. albeit fitfully, for over twenty centuries, now shines dimly. Indeed, our political philosophers and social analysts see it as a red light of warning. The Enlightenment, of which Voltaire and the Encyclopaedists boasted, has proved to be the prelude to an old darkness rather than a new dawn. After the judicial murder of Calas, Voltaire wrote: 'I am sowing a seed which will one day produce a harvest';[1] it now sounds ironical. The mordant and terrifying satire in Aldous Huxley's *Brave New World*, or in George Orwell's *1984* is prophetic warning that modern man is becoming depersonalized as the 'mass man'. Even among the peoples who assume, a little complacently, that they constitute the free world, this same mass-mental conformity can be so subtly pervasive that its victims do not notice it. Personal idiosyncracies of opinion, thought or belief are steadily ironed out, as mass suggestion—ceaselessly conveyed through radio, television, cinema, press headline, and the vast apparatus of high-pressure advertisement— does its menacing work of standardization. The human person loses his distinctive, individual significance. Community gives place to mere gregariousness. And this darkness which covereth the earth is, over a vast area, gross

[1] 'Je sème un grain qui pourra un jour produire une moisson' (*Traité sur la tolérance à l'occasion de la mort de Jean Calas* (1763), c. xxv).

darkness. Totalitarian systems leave no room at all for the dissident individual or minority. Thought itself is suspected and feared as dangerous. The outlook for toleration is grim.

Is the outlook any more reassuring in the sphere of religion; that is, at the deepest level of personal life where men stand in the liberty wherewith Christ has made them free? Few informed people would say so. Only a naïve liberalism would now assume that freedom of conscience is a permanently settled issue. Only wishful thinking would pronounce that Christendom cannot conceivably go back on that heroic vindication of Christian liberty which began, however uncertainly, with the Reformation. Such an assumption finds no support from the ecclesiastical situation in Spain, Quebec or parts of South America; and little from that in parts of Australia and Europe. Indeed, ecclesiastical intransigeance is growing rather than subsiding in our world, and there are many for whom religious toleration is only a polite name for woolly-mindedness and appeasement; it is a feather-bed for a dying Christian.

On the lowest level a man may be completely indifferent to all religion. He will feel, therefore, that its distinctions and differences mean nothing, and have neither relevance nor importance. His attitude is ultimately one of boredom or even contempt. He is not interested.

At the higher, existential level a man is not only interested: he cares so much that to disagree with him is to be excommunicated. To oppose him is heresy, and to claim liberty of conscience a particularly nauseating heresy. Theodore Beza, Calvin's successor at Geneva, stigmatized religious liberty as 'a most diabolical dogma, because it means that every man should be left to go to hell in his own way'.[1] The same logic was being used by his contemporary William Allen in England, a papal spokesman who contended strongly that it was against the laws of God and nature to persecute Romanists, but that heretics might lawfully be 'coerced'. Such bigotry is understandable, and not altogether indefensible: God help us if there is no passion in our religion.

But there is a higher level yet. A man may know that religion is a matter of the very greatest importance to any and every man that has it; so that everything relating to religion is sacred to that man, who cannot be expected to surrender the right of thinking and judging about it to any man or any body of men on this earth. In short, true religion means so much to that man that it lifts him even above the level of bigotry. Without compromising the truth which he himself knows, he shows genuine respect for the conviction of his neighbour. It is the toleration begotten not of indifference but of its opposite. In I Cor. xiii it is described as charity.

But even the most liberal-minded of men may ask whether—in spite of Socrates, Milton and Voltaire—there is not a necessary limit to this principle of toleration, especially in an era when politics have become a religion, and when Fascist, Nazi or Marxist ideologies are virtually systems of faith and worship. An academic issue fifty years ago, its relevance and urgency now are obvious. The political philosophy of the English-speaking world is, broadly speaking, liberal. We glory in the principle of toleration, that freedom of thought and speech to which we have been free-born out of the long travail of the centuries. But at what point do the intolerant ideologies of our day

[1] *Epistolae* (1575), xx. The quotation and reference are from Professor Roland Bainton's *The Travail of Religious Liberty*, pp. 114 and 263.

become intolerable? Is it right, in the name of the sacred principle of freedom, to tolerate the spread of ideas which, when powerful enough, will cynically repudiate the very principle of freedom which has made their rise possible? It is a first principle of democratic theory and of common sense that no man may claim from the State rights which he himself is unwilling to concede to his fellow-man. Obviously, therefore, democracies will have no scruples about taking action against those whose declared intention is to destroy democracy, and who would use a liberal philosophy of toleration as their instrument. Thus there *is* a limit to the tolerance which is natural and desirable in a free society; and it is reached when any organized enemies of freedom exploit that freedom to gain their absolutist ends.

And yet no believer in democracy's Four Freedoms[1] can subscribe to this without grave searchings of heart. History is eloquent of the way in which men become like their enemies in the very process of resisting them. The diseased mentality against which free men fight is dangerously contagious. How are we to check the enemies of liberty while at the same time preserving the precious tradition of liberty? How are we to balance the complementary demands of freedom and security?

This was the question which those protagonists of toleration, Milton and Locke, had to face even at the cost of inconsistency. As Professor Bainton has observed,[2] practical experience had taught John Locke that Roman Catholics could not be tolerated in seventeenth-century England because they were bound by their very presuppositions to

---

[1] See *The Universal Declaration of Human Rights*, approved by the United Nations Assembly, 10 December 1948.

[2] *Op. cit.* pp. 249–50.

persecute as soon as they had the power. The disabilities imposed on Romanists in the reigns of Charles II and James II (1660–88) were due largely to this legitimate fear of persecution. Englishmen could not believe that Romanism in power would long concede liberty. Locke saw that the Revocation of the Edict of Nantes by Louis XIV of France was true to the Roman logic. The same logic gave Milton pause. His tract entitled *True Religion, Heresy and Toleration*, written in the year before his death, actually exhorts Protestants to avoid contentions among themselves and to unite against popery. Here was a passionate protagonist of liberty, a Puritan and an Independent, who had spent his adult life in the service of Cromwell and the Commonwealth; the enemy of a state-church which rested on the twin pillars of monarchy and episcopacy. And yet he was writing here of that Church of England as 'our' Church, and adducing its authority for his argument, because he saw that the real danger was—if one may put it so—the papal International: a totalitarian system, inherently intolerant and repressive, as the dungeons of the Inquisition sufficiently testified.

The same issue appears in Lord Mansfield's summing-up at the trial of Lord George Gordon for high treason in 1781.[1] In 1700 an Act against popery had excluded Roman Catholics from the public services and from teaching. In 1778 Sir George Savile, M.P., a Protestant, introduced a bill removing the penalty of life-imprisonment from Roman Catholic priests carrying out their pastoral and educational work, on condition that they swore allegiance to King George, and fostered no Jacobitism; and that there should be no papal interference

---

[1] Howard, *State Trials*, xxi, 645. See pp. 499–502 for the facts of the case as presented for the Crown by the Attorney-General.

outside the spiritual sphere. Savile's Act was passed, but Lord George Gordon's Protestant Association was formed to petition Parliament against it. In the end there was rioting, and Gordon was indicted for high treason. The jury took but half an hour to bring in a verdict of 'Not Guilty'. He had, in fact accepted the presidency of the Protestant Association only after it was formed; and, in any case, the Association deplored the riots which it had not intended and for which it was hardly responsible. In his summing-up, Lord Mansfield the Chief Justice observed (almost as an aside):

> I cannot deny that, where the safety of the State is not concerned, my own opinion is that men should not be punished for mere matter of conscience and barely worshipping God in their own way: but where what is alleged as a matter of conscience is dangerous or prejudicial to the State, which is the case of popery, the safety of the State is the supreme law; and an erroneous religion, so far as upon principles of sound policy that safety requires, ought to be restrained and prohibited: no good man has ever defended the many penal laws against papists on another ground.

That this should be regarded as the only ground for religious intolerance, and yet good ground in 1781, is evidence that the fear, if not the threat, of papal political interference was a real one. Jacobitism was a dwindling cause, admittedly; but it was the contemporary illustration of the overriding of territorial by ideological loyalties.

2. ULTRAMONTANISM AND CONTEMPORARY IDEOLOGIES

The 'ideological' loyalty illustrated in these historical issues was, and still is, an international loyalty; for this is precisely what the word 'ultramontane' implies and means in church history. The Jesuit, for example, looked for his authority and his secret instructions *ultra montes* (beyond the mountains), those mountains being the Alps. Whatever his national loyalty, his ultimate loyalty lay beyond the national frontier.[1] His vow of absolute obedience meant that his life in its every detail was controlled by an iron 'party discipline'. Sometimes, to use a peculiarly exact modern parallel, he had to work underground. Indeed, Moscow and the Vatican today represent parallel ultramontane tactics. Karl Barth reminded us years ago that certain techniques of the Communist International have long been anticipated by the Roman. In this connexion it is instructive to notice that Marshal Tito's Jugoslavia is doing today precisely what Tudor England did under Henry VIII and Elizabeth in the Reformation era. Tito is taking severe action against the power of the Roman Church in his country because that Church (unlike the Reformed Church there) is an organization whose alleged hostility to Tito's regime is controlled from outside the country—from 'beyond the mountains'. Jugoslavia's objection to the Cominform and to Catholicism is that both are ultramontane.

The outlook for religious toleration in the mid-twentieth century is dim because liberty of conscience is ultimately

---

[1] As a witness to the truth that the Gospel transcends all national boundaries and limitations, such a protest against Erastianism was, as such, not unjustified. See p. 303 below for Heiler's comment.

incompatible with Fascist, Communist or Papist presuppositions.[1] No totalitarian ideology powerful enough to be effective can ultimately tolerate that freedom of thought and conscience which implicitly contradicts it. Pope Gregory XVI in his encyclical *Mirari vos* of August 1832 denounced this right of religious liberty as absurd and erroneous; or, rather, as a form of madness (*absurda illa ac erronea sententia, seu potius deliramentum*). The same pope's encyclical *Inter praecipuas* of May 1844 attacked the Bible Societies and the World Evangelical Alliance, describing religious liberty as poison, the poison of indifference (*religiosam libertatem, seu potius vesanum indifferentiae*). Nor may these papal dicta be courteously ignored and charitably dismissed as a pathetic echo of

> Old, unhappy, far-off things
> And battles long ago.

They are no mere archaeological survivals[2] from the fourth century of our era when Constantine accepted Christianity as the *religio licita* of his empire, and the Theodosian Code punished 'deviations' from it with increasing severity from A.D. 395 onwards.[3]

[1] That these presuppositions differ, especially in their attitude to Natural Law, is recognized below, p. 251.

[2] They do precisely recall, however, the language of the Imperial edict *Cunctos populos* of 27 February 380: 'It is our pleasure that all the nations which are governed by our Clemency and Moderation should steadfastly adhere to the religion which was taught by St Peter to the Romans....We authorize the followers of this doctrine to assume the title of Catholic Christians; and, as we judge that all others are poisonous madmen (*reliquos vero dementes vesanosque judicantes*), we brand them with the infamous name of heretics, and declare that their conventicles shall no longer usurp the name of churches. Besides the condemnation of divine justice, they must expect to suffer the penalties which our Authority, guided by Heavenly Wisdom, shall think proper to inflict on them' (*Cod. Theod.* lib. xvi, tit. i, c. 2).

[3] 'qui vel levi argumento a judicio catholicae religionis et tramite detecti fuerint *deviare*' (*Cod. Theod.* lib. xvi, tit. v, c. 28). Marxist in its connotation today, the italicized word has had an ecclesiastical connotation in the Roman Code for centuries.

Rome still makes her totalitarian temper unambiguously clear. The sympathetic message which French Cardinals and Archbishops addressed to the *Action Catholique Ouvrière* early in 1954 faithfully repeats the exclusive claim which— like the monotonous repetition of a gramophone record— is included in one form or another in every Roman pronouncement, year by year and century by century. 'There is only one Church charged with saving all men. This is the Catholic Church, missionary by its nature; there cannot be a missionary apostolate without it, outside it, or outside obedience to those whom the Holy Ghost has placed in authority over it.' The important Italian Jesuit review *La Civiltà Cattolica* consistently represents the same cool arrogance. In its issue of 3 April 1948, Fr F. Cavalli, S.J., wrote on 'The condition of the Protestants in Spain' as follows:

The Catholic Church, being convinced by reason of her divine prerogative that she is the one true Church, claims for herself alone the right to freedom; for this right may only be possessed by truth and never by error. Where the other religions are concerned, she will not take up the sword against them, but she will ask that, by lawful means worthy of the human creature, they shall not be allowed to propagate false doctrines. Consequently, in a State where the majority of the people are Catholic, the Church asks that error shall not be accorded a legal existence, and that if religious minorities exist they shall have a *de facto* existence only; not the opportunity of spreading their beliefs. Where material circumstances—whether the hostility of a Government or the numerical strength of the dissenting factions—do not allow this principle to be applied in its entirety, the Church requires that she shall have all possible concessions, confining herself to accepting as the least of all evils the *de jure* toleration of other forms of worship. In other countries, the Catholics are obliged themselves to ask for full liberty for all, resigning themselves to living together where they alone have the right to live. The Church does not in this way give up her theses, which remain the most imperative of all laws, but adapts herself....[1]

This has at least the merit of candour; it wraps nothing up. To Protestants, or those who hold other faiths with an equal seriousness and conviction, it would be pathetically comic, were it not the basic presupposition of active persecution. Protestants in Spain, for example, do not find it comic. The recent Concordat between the Spanish government and the Vatican illustrates the imperious pressure exercised by the Spanish hierarchy over the whole life of the State. Indeed, the Catholic priesthood in Spain holds a position of exclusive dominance, no other ministers of the Christian religion being recognized or allowed to exist as such. It is credibly reported by responsible journals that Protestant pastors have served long prison sentences in modern Spain merely because they are Protestant pastors. The Roman Catholic clergy are a caste apart, enjoying special privileges before the law. A prelate may not be brought to trial in the State courts, even on a criminal charge, save with the consent of the Holy See. Priests may not be tried, save with the consent of the bishop; and strict precautions against any publicity would be required for any such trials, which would have to be conducted in camera.[2] Ecclesiastical tribunals have exclusive control of all matrimonial causes. The Roman Church has exclusive control of all schools and of the appointment of all teachers. The teaching of Roman dogma is universal and compulsory on the ground that 'dogmatic

---

[1] Quoted from the translation given in *Christianity and Crisis* (1948), vol. VIII.

[2] Cf. *Codex juris canonici*, II (De personis), Can. 121: Clerici in omnibus causis sive contensiosis sive criminalibus apud judicem ecclesiasticum conveniri debent, nisi aliter pro locis particularibus legitime provisum fuerit.

intransigeance is essential to Catholicism'.[1] There is a toleration clause which grudgingly allows the withdrawal of the children of non-Catholic parents from this teaching, and the invidious position of those children can be imagined.[2] This clause seems to have been strongly resisted by Pedro, Cardinal Segura of Saenz, Archbishop of Seville. Public worship in any form is absolutely forbidden to Protestants. The only toleration which they enjoy in this regard is that they may not be molested as they pray privately at home. This, too, was actively resisted by the Cardinal. The Catholic Church receives an annual subsidy from the State, which means of course that the Protestant heretic is taxed for the support of the system which thus persecutes him. In short, the temper of this Concordat between 'two complete and perfect societies' recalls so glaringly the totalitarian temper of four centuries ago that it openly embarrasses Roman Catholics and Jesuits in the United States of America.[3] *The Indiana Catholic and Record*, official newspaper of the Indianapolis Archdiocese and the Evansville Diocese, was criticized by the Madrid Press in 1952 as having said that Spain, by refusing to permit 'complete religious freedom in our times, gives the impression of living four centuries behind in questions of religious peace and concord'.

And lest one should think that this totalitarian temper is a special anachronism peculiar to certain Mediterranean countries, we should notice that Monsignor Ronald Knox

[1] *Instructions*, issued by the Conference of Spanish Bishops on 28 May 1948.

[2] General Franco's message to the Cortes about the Concordat dwelt on this clause with a brief impatience which speaks for itself. It is not surprising that a great English newspaper of the liberal tradition, *The Manchester Guardian*, described the clause as 'preposterously inadequate'.

[3] See the article of 12 May 1952 by Camille M. Cianfarra in the *New York Times*.

in England seems to defend unambiguously the medieval argument for religious persecution.[1] His preface to Maycock's book on the Inquisition contains the sentence, 'the faith which is strong enough to make martyrs is strong enough to make persecutors'; and he seems to say this approvingly, for in his own book *The Belief of Catholics* (1927) he writes:

You cannot bind over the Catholic Church, as the price of your adhesion to her doctrines, to waive all right of invoking the secular arm in defence of her own principles. The circumstances in which such a possibility could be realized are sufficiently remote.... Given such circumstances, is it certain that the Catholic Government of the nation would have no right to insist on Catholic education being universal (which is a form of coercion) and even to deport or imprison those who unsettle the minds of its subjects with new doctrines? It is 'certain' that the Church would claim that right for the Catholic Government, even if considerations of prudence forbade its exercise in fact.... And for those reasons a body of Catholic patriots, entrusted with the government of a Catholic State, will not shrink from repressive measures in order to perpetuate the secure domination of Catholic principles among their fellow-countrymen.

That ominous phrase 'considerations of prudence' illustrates the changeless and impressive continuity of this Roman temper. In this the Roman Church is ever the same (*semper eadem*); as an undying Institution it can afford to take the long view, and to wait. Because it 'cannot err' it cannot repent. Rome's many saintly sons and daughters may do so individually, but Rome cannot officially, so to speak, confess to the sin and horror of the Inquisition.

[1] I quote here from Professor H. G. Wood's *Religious Liberty To-day*, pp. 97–8 (Cambridge University Press, 1949), which is an able, careful and fair analysis of the urgent current problem of religious intolerance.

Modern Protestants are appalled at the crime of Calvin's Geneva in burning Servetus at the stake, and they have erected an expiatory monument at Geneva, saying so.

Fils
respectueux et reconnaissants
de Calvin
notre grand réformateur
mais condamnant une erreur
qui fut celle de son siècle
et fermement attachés
à la liberté de conscience
selon les vrais principes
de la Réformation et de l'évangile
nous avons élevé
ce monument expiatoire.[1]

But is there—could there be—a similar 'monument expiatoire' on behalf of Thomas of Torquemada?[2] Not if the *Syllabus of Errors*, drawn up by Pius IX in 1864 is to be taken seriously. It was, to quote J. B. Bury, 'a drastic and authoritative reminder that the Papacy was as medieval as ever in its attitude to modern society and civilization, and uncompromisingly hostile to the ideas which commanded the assent of the most civilized sections of mankind'.[3] The

[1] 'Condemning an error which was that of his age, and firmly attached to liberty of conscience according to the true principles of the Reformation and the Gospel, we the respectful and grateful sons of Calvin our great Reformer have erected this expiatory monument.'

[2] On the contrary, in the *Analecta Ecclesiastica*, III, 29 ff. (1895) the Inquisition is ecstatically defended: 'O blessed flames of the stake by which, with the sacrifice of a few crafty wretches, hundreds and hundreds of regiments of souls were saved...! O glorious and venerable memory of Thomas Torquemada...!' (O benedictas rogorum flammas quibus e medio sublatis paucissimis et quidem vaferrimis homuncionibus, centenae centenaeque animarum phalanges a faucibus erroris et aeternae forsan damnationis ereptae fuere....O praeclaram venerandamque memoriam Thomae Torquemada, qui prudentissimo zelo..., etc.).

[3] Cf. *History of the Papacy in the Nineteenth Century* (Macmillan, 1930), pp. 2, 40.

Syllabus does not repudiate the medieval claim of the Papacy to depose secular princes and to abrogate secular laws. And in July 1871, the year following the announcement on papal infallibility, Pius IX expressly declared that 'the right to depose princes rests on temporal reasons and, as these do not now exist, the right is no longer used'. The right, we notice, is still a right, though it lies in abeyance. Indeed, Bury observes that one of the most important principles in ultramontane theory (a very embarrassing one to loyal Catholics in their respective countries) is that the Church has temporal power and the right to use force. We should be grateful, perhaps, that Monsignor Knox has stated with honourable candour that the relative toleration which modern Rome may find itself compelled to concede to other Christian Churches in the name of prudence cannot be more than a tactic of expediency. Rome is never abashed by the extreme implications of its logic. It was Leo XIII (1878–1903) who said, towards the end of the nineteenth century: 'Although in the extraordinary conditions of these times the Church usually acquiesces in certain modern liberties, not because she prefers them in themselves but because she judges it expedient to permit them, she would in happier times exercise her own liberty.' In happier times? That 'final euphemistic escape clause'[1] is, like Monsignor Knox's phrase quoted above, also ominous. It must be added, of course, that the official reissue of the *Corpus Juris Canonici* in May 1918 repeals every penalty for heresy save excommunication;[2] but in

---

[1] *The Christian Century*, 25 June 1952.

[2] 'Though it makes suitable changes, the Codex retains for the most part the discipline which has been in active operation until now. Any laws, general or particular, which are opposed to what is here prescribed, are annulled save for particular statements to the contrary. Penalties of which no mention is made in the Codex...may be considered as annulled. Anything

view of the clear, consistent and cumulative testimony of papal pronouncements through fifteen centuries, can modern men be blamed if they see that phrase 'in happier times' against the background of the thumbscrew and the stake?

And there is a further consideration. Sinful spiritual imperialism[1] takes many forms and Protestantism has not been guiltless of it. But no form of ecclesiastical arrogance is more astonishing or depressing than Rome's exclusive claim to the liberty which she denies on principle to others. Evidence for this abounds. Since she alone is the Church of Christ, all others being 'bogus',[2] her claim to religious

in other disciplinary laws which may have been operative up to now—if it is not explicitly or implicitly contained in the Codex—must be said to have lost all force.' (Codex vigentem huc usque disciplinam plerumque retinet, licet opportunas immutationes afferat. Itaque: 1°. Leges quaelibet, sive universales sive particulares, praescriptis hujus Codicis oppositae, abrogantur, nisi de particularibus legibus aliud expresse caveatur... 5°. Quod ad poenas attinet, quarum in Codice nulla fit mentio...eae tanquam abrogatae habeantur. 6°. Si qua ex ceteris disciplinaribus legibus, quae adhuc viguerunt, nec explicite nec implicite in Codice contineatur, ea vim omnem amississe dicenda est.) *Codex Juris Canonici*, 1 (Normae generales), Can. vi.

'No one may be compelled unwillingly to embrace the Catholic faith.' (Ad amplexandam fidem catholicam nemo invitus cogatur.) *Ibid.* Can. 1351.

[1] This is Reinhold Niebuhr's judgement on certain aspects of Anglo-Catholicism; *The Nature and Destiny of Man*, II, 225. See the whole section on 'the test of toleration', pp. 220–43.

[2] Cf. *A Catechism of Christian Doctrine*, revised ed. of the Baltimore Catechism (St Anthony Guild Press, Paterson, N.J.), Imprimatur 1948; § 160, pp. 123–4:

Q. How do we know that no other church but the Catholic Church is the true Church of Christ?

A. We know that no other church but the Catholic Church is the true Church of Christ because no other church has these four marks.

(*a*) All other churches lack essential unity. They recognize no authority in religious matters vested in an individual who is the vicar of Christ. In the worship of God many Christian sects are guided more by sentiment and personal conviction than by the objective truths given to the world by Our Lord.

(*b*) The founders of Christian sects were not saints and generally were freedom may not ultimately be shared; it must be a one-way traffic. Toleration may not be reciprocal. Roman Catholic leaders in South America, for example, seek to rob minority groups there of the very rights which Roman Catholicism freely enjoys as a minority group in North America. As the liberal Catholic Montalembert (1810–70) put it, with studied irony, during his losing battle with Ultramontanism: 'When I am the weaker, I ask you for liberty because it is your principle: but when I am the stronger I take it away from you because it is not my principle.' Montalembert's irony is not untrue to historic fact, however; indeed, it accurately interprets the historical situation which gave rise to the term 'Protestant'. We rightly insist that the term did not originally and does not now define a mere negation. The men of the evangelical and reformed tradition throughout Christendom are not merely objecting to grievous distortions and abuses; they are asserting the good news of God's grace; they are using the word 'protest' in the transitive, positive sense—as in Shakespeare's 'I do protest I love thee'. The first Reformers affirmed at Speyer that 'they must protest and

not holy or edifying men. The sects have not given saints to the world. Their truths are but fragments of the doctrines of the Catholic Church. The holiness of their members is due to the means that the sects have salvaged from Catholic worship. Moreover, these sects cannot point to miracles wrought in their favour.

(c) Not one of the Christian sects is universal or catholic; that is, not one has universality such as that of the Catholic Church.

(d) Not one of the Christian sects can trace its origin to the apostles.

(e) The Greek Orthodox or Schismatic Church began in the ninth century with its rejection of the authority of the Pope. From it have come various national churches, subject in some degree to civil authority. The Protestant churches began in the sixteenth century when their founders, rejecting certain doctrines of faith, broke away from Catholic unity. Many Protestant denominations are offshoots of the earliest sects. The Lutherans were founded by Martin Luther, the Presbyterians by John Knox, and the Methodists by John Wesley.

testify publicly before God that they could do nothing contrary to his Word'.[1] Yet the word Protestant bears the negative sense of objection, nevertheless, and for this further historic reason: when the followers of Luther thus met at the Imperial Diet of Speyer in 1529 they were weaker than they had been at the first diet (1526), and it was therefore decreed that whereas Catholic minorities were not to be disturbed in territories predominantly Lutheran, Lutheran minorities were not to be tolerated in Catholic territories. (Montalembert had hit the nail precisely on the head.) The Lutherans *protested* against an arrangement so cynically invidious, and they have been labelled Protestant ever since. But it is an honourable label even when it bears this limited, negative, sense; and it reminds us that protest against Roman intolerance has been part of the genius of Protestantism from the beginning.

3. DOGMA AS HISTORY

The issue of toleration is bound up with the deeper issue of historical truth. One of the most important acquisitions of the nineteenth century was the historical method. The father of our modern historiography was Ranke, who did his pioneering work a little over a century ago; and if the disinterested use of the historical method be the distinctive mark of the modern mind—as William Temple declared it to be—we like to feel that we are in Ranke's debt. For, to put it paradoxically, disinterestedness was Ranke's passionate interest. To write history without bias was his almost inhuman ideal. 'The naked truth without adornment (*nackte Wahrheit ohne Schmuck*)' was his heroic motto.

---

[1] Quoted by Bainton, *The Reformation of the Sixteenth Century* (Beacon Press, Boston, 1952), p. 149.

'I will merely record,' said Ranke 'how things actually happened' (*wie es eigentlich geschehen ist*). Insisting on the study of sources and original documents, he was one of the first men to study the Papacy and the Reformation with anything like scientific detachment. In short, Ranke conceived of historical study as the discipline which, among other things, prevents one from being partisan. So far from being 'existential', his work aimed at illustrating that aesthetic aloofness which is now fashionably decried as 'the gallery attitude'. Ranke was a splendid giant. But is not his ideal of disinterestedness dubious for more than one reason? Is a complete elimination of bias possible?[1] Is it even desirable when dullness is its almost inevitable result? We smile at the savage bigotry of Parson Thwackum in *Tom Jones*; it is satire, and not to be taken too seriously. But do we not ask of the historian of religion a 'right interest', as Runze called it,[2] if his work is to touch us where we live?

We are certainly less confident about the alleged *scientific* character of such historicism than we used to be, even though we have no intention of repudiating it as a method. We are more aware of the difficulties inherent in the use of the historical method than were the historians of the 'liberal' era who conceived of it as an exact science. Indeed, exact science itself no longer works with the presuppositions of a Clerk-Maxwell, as though its method were a matter of precise measurement and observation. According to the new physics, atoms or electrons are not 'things' directly observed; they are abstractions, or hypothetical constructions elaborated by the human mind to

[1] See above, p. 15 n.
[2] *Psychologie der Religion*, quoted and discussed by John Oman in *The Natural and the Supernatural*, p. 5.

account for the data of sense. The data recorded on delicate measuring instruments and photographic plates are 'pointer readings'; they are representations of phenomena which do not admit of being directly observed. In short, sense data and the inferences (sometimes the 'inspired guesses') which interpret them are inextricably blended. 'Matter has dissolved into mystery; electrons and quanta are not like those forces or materials with which we are familiar in the workshop.... They are an elaborate symbolism beneath which physics has no means of probing.'[1]

How does this bear on the understanding of history, and the writing of it, and the evaluation of it as written? The liberal historian conceived of his art as an exact science in the older sense of the term. For him, very properly, the past was *there*; it could not be altered. The great object of his research was the discovery of fact, tested by evidence. 'Comment is free, but facts are sacred.' To distort or omit fact would have been to falsify history and betray the truth.

Today, however, this common-sense attitude is being challenged over a wide field; not as untrue, but as inadequate and naïve. Modern thinkers who have wrestled with the difficult problem of the meaning of history (notably Croce), recognize that there is necessarily a subjective or relative element not only in the interpretation of historic facts but also in their actual selection: even the data recorded in an original document were no more than an arbitrary selection from the infinite number of recordable data which fill every moment of historic time. Is not historiography, then, an art rather than a science (unless science itself is in some sense Art)? If so, we can better understand the modern contention that history must at least be rewritten from epoch to epoch. A history of

[1] Whitehead, *Science and the Modern World*, p. 22.

Europe, for example, written towards the close of the nineteenth century would not do for the mid-twentieth century, because the point of view has changed. Our presuppositions are not what they were. Not only have we constantly to look at the past afresh, in the light of a new context of experience; the same principle of relativity requires us to recognize that an interpretation of European history written by a team made up of, say, Sir Richard Livingstone, Sir Winston Churchill, Dr A. N. Whitehead and the Archbishop of Canterbury, would be a seriously different thing from that written by an informed and competent team made up of a Japanese historian, a learned Confucian, a Hindu philosopher and a Kikuyu anthropologist. Trite though this is, its revolutionary import in a rapidly changing world can be a discovery both new and painful.

For this historical relativism is not only strange and baffling; in some of its modern expressions it is profoundly shocking and terrifying. To take an extreme instance: we have had to learn that organized lying is the common practice of statecraft in a totalitarian era. More than the propaganda technique which is practised (and defended as morally justifiable) in war-time, as a temporary expedient akin to military deception, this is something integral to the totalitarian philosophy itself. The lie is not merely a temporary device of propaganda but an enduring political method. Law itself is an instrument of politics; so far from being, in the words of Antigone, 'eternal in the heavens, not of today nor yesterday', law becomes whatever the omnicompetent State may find useful today. Tomorrow it may change with the changing will of the State. The philosophical basis of such relativism is a perverted pragmatism; that is, any 'falsehood' is 'truth' if it serves the purposes of policy. Thus, for this totalitarian mentality, history is something to be created rather than learned; it is not a constant pole by which to steer, but the powerful headlights proceeding from and directing its own energy of momentum. On such presuppositions the only valid theory of history is that which is based on what men are now making rather than on what is alleged to have occurred in the past. Who is alleging it? In his collected essays entitled *Shooting an Elephant* (pp. 110–11), George Orwell has argued that in societies where only one opinion is permissible (in biology, economics or history, for example) at any given date, the totalitarian mentality is really demanding the continuous alteration of the past, as circumstances or State policy may require: in the long run it is demanding a disbelief in the very existence of objective truth. It is a subjectivist epistemology applied to the politics of the herd. Monstrous sophistry though it is, it may not be dismissed out of hand since, as we have already seen, it contains a truth. When those giant historiographers Mommsen or Rostovstev wrote their histories of the Graeco-Roman world, how far were they unconsciously writing in terms of modern Prussia or Russia? An apologist for totalitarian pragmatism will argue, at any rate, that all historical records, like all historical writing, are necessarily selective and therefore biased. And a George Orwell will take him to mean that since absolute historic truth is not attainable, the appeal to history is a propagandist fallacy; and 'a big lie is no worse than a little one'.

No informed theologian would assert or suggest that the ultramontane view and use of history is totalitarian in this sense. As H. G. Wood observes, 'The Roman Church has consistently maintained certain principles which provide guarantees for civil and religious liberty'. One of these is 'the Catholic conception of Law which, as Troeltsch says, contrasts sharply with the modern doctrines of the creation of Law by the will of the state. It roots back in the conceptions of *lex naturae* and *jus gentium* to be found in Roman law. Catholic social doctrine conceives Natural Law as existing before the State.'[1] We may add a reference to the encyclical of Leo XIII which pronounces the study of Church History to comprise 'a body of dogmatic facts which are imposed upon faith and which no one may call in question' (*un ensemble de faits dogmatiques qui s'imposent à la foi et qu'il n'est permis à personne de révoquer en doute*). The human element in Church History must be studied, therefore, 'with great integrity' (*avec une grande probité*). As it is written in the book of Job (xiii. 7), 'God has no need of our lies' (*Dieu n'a pas besoin de nos mensonges*).[2]

What is incontestable, however, is that as ultramontanism begins and ends with dogmatic facts which faith may not question, its historic study of the evidence for those facts is of secondary rather than primary interest.

A notorious example is provided by the official Roman attitude to the received text of I John v. 7, which reads 'For there are three that bear record in heaven, the Father, the Word and the Holy Ghost: and these three are one.' The documentary spuriousness of this reading is undisputed. 'It is found in no Greek manuscript earlier than the fourteenth century, in no ancient Greek writer, in no ancient version other than Latin, and in no early manuscript of the Old Latin version or of Saint Jerome's Vulgate' (C. H. Dodd). First quoted as part of the text of I John by Priscillian, the Spanish heretic who was burned alive (the first to be so, under the Theodosian Code) at Treves in 385, it gradually made its way into the manuscripts of the Latin Vulgate until it was accepted as part of

---

[1] *Op. cit.* p. 90.   [2] *Depuis le jour*, 8 Sept. 1899.

the authorized Latin text. 'There is no doubt whatever', writes Professor Dodd, 'that the words are a spurious interpolation made first in the Latin version, and that the various forms in which they appear in Greek are all translations from the Latin.'[1] On 12 January 1897 the following question was submitted to the Congregation of the Inquisition (a committee of Cardinals): 'Whether it may be safely denied, or at least called in question, that the text of I John v. 7 is authentic?' The Cardinals replied in the negative and on 15 January 1897 Leo XIII approved and confirmed their decision.[2]

Whatever may be thought of the truth inherent in this spurious verse about the three heavenly witnesses, the Pope's own quotation from the book of Job is surely relevant: 'Dieu n'a pas besoin de nos mensonges.' But his self-contradiction illustrates the fact to which Bury constantly draws attention, that no conciliation is possible between the dogmatic point of view and the historical principle (*op. cit.* p. 45). We see the two traditions running parallel throughout the nineteenth century; the historical on the one hand, from Ranke down to Mommsen, Acton and Bury; the dogmatic on the other hand, from Gregory XVI down to Pius IX, the dogma of Infallibility and Leo XIII. In the early eighteenth century Fénelon (1650–1715) had argued that the Church is supreme over fact as well as over doctrine. He meant historic fact.[3] We remember the most

[1] C. H. Dodd, *Moffatt Commentary, The Johannine Epistles* (London, 1946), p. 127 n. 1. Cf. G. M. Young, *Gibbon* (Peter Davies, 1932), p. 123: 'In c. xxxvii he had remarked incidentally that the text...was spurious... Archdeacon Travis undertook to defend the text and was answered by Porson so conclusively that neither Travis nor the Three Witnesses could ever appear in scholarly company again.'

[2] See C. J. Cadoux, *Catholicism and Christianity*, p. 285.

[3] Cf. Bury, *Ancient Greek Historians*, p. 238. 'This was the first appearance of the principle which Cardinal Manning expressed.'

notorious sentence uttered during the whole debate on infallibility—Cardinal Manning's—namely that 'the dogma must overcome history'. It occurs in his Pastoral Letter on the Infallibility of the Roman Pontiff. Again, in his book *The Temporal Mission of the Holy Ghost* (p. 226), Manning throws down the ultramontane gauntlet before the modern mind with his truculent assertion that 'the appeal to antiquity is both a treason and a heresy: it is treason because it rejects the divine voice of the Church at this hour, and a heresy because it denies that voice to be divine'. After that, the words of Dupanloup, Archbishop of Orleans, come almost as light relief. 'Above all', he wrote, 'beware of sources (surtout méfiez-vous des sources).'

This obscurantist advice was hardly needed, for sources have been avoided in dramatic fashion, at least twice during the past hundred years. The dogmas of the Immaculate Conception of the Virgin Mary, and of her Bodily Assumption to heaven—proclaimed as dogmatic credenda —do not rest on a syllable of historical evidence. The dogmas have overcome history. As one Roman apologist put it with charming *naïveté*,[1] 'indeed, this most glorious Assumption of Mary is veiled in the mystery of silence: Scripture knows nothing of it'. Exactly. Roman theologians are required to teach that the bodily assumption of Mary is true; that it happened as an event in historic time: but they must teach at the same time that no one ever witnessed it. In short, it is dogma rather than history which is here victorious; dogmatic tradition is added to historic truth, and preferred to it.

---

[1] The Benedictine Fr. Bauer, in *Petitiones de Assumptione corporea B.V.M.* II, 422 (Rome, 1942) and quoted in F. Blanke's *Die leibliche Himmelfahrt des Jungfrau Maria* (Zürich, 1950). I owe the reference to Emil Brunner, *Das Mißverständnis der Kirche*, c. IV, n. 15.

But this should not surprise us, since the genius of the Roman system lies partly in its universalism. It is a huge synthesis. Vincent of Lerins prophesied more truly than he knew when he said of it *omnia fere universaliter comprehendit* (it holds almost everything in its universal embrace). The system is all-embracing in its syncretism. It does not exclude pre-Christian or extra-Christian ideas and practices, but assimilates and makes use of ancient paganism, Jewish legalism and its Temple cultus, Hellenistic liturgy, the folk-piety of the Mediterranean world (which is a euphemism for much primitive superstition), asceticism, mysticism, Neoplatonism, the classical philosophy of antiquity, the statecraft and legal genius of Rome. In historic Catholicism apostolic Christianity has come to terms with paganism; very largely by incorporating it.

In his Gifford Lectures, *Symbolism and Belief*, Professor Edwyn Bevan deals severely with one such pagan element in the long evolution of this multiplicity in unity—the historic origins of the Catholic mystical tradition which has had so rich a development. The main fountain-head of this tradition, says Professor Bevan, is to be found in the writings of the fifth-century impostor who pretended to be Dionysius the Areopagite, an immediate disciple of St Paul, and whose teachings were taken over wholesale from the pagan Neoplatonist Proclus.

It seems to be idle to defend the imposture by saying that it accorded with the ethical principles of the time. Professor Dodds, in his recent edition of Proclus's *Elements of Theology* calls the writings of the Pseudo-Dionysius outright a 'fraud', and adds in a footnote: 'It is for some reason customary to use a kinder term; but it is quite clear that the deception was deliberate' (p. xxvii). Considering the high place which the Roman Catholic Church has given to its Mystical Theology this taint of fraud in its origins is unfortunate....It is true, of course [adds Professor Bevan], that the immense majority of Roman Catholic scholars admit that the writings in question are not really by the first-century Christian by whom they pretend to have been written, but are products of the fifth century. Yet the fraudulent author is still regarded with respect as a Doctor of the Church, and some elements in the Catholic tradition which St Thomas took over from him, in the ingenuous belief that they were warranted by the authority of an immediate disciple of St Paul, remain there in the tradition of the Catholic schools undisturbed.[1]

In the course of this criticism Professor Bevan observes that 'it is strange to think what an immense influence has been exerted upon Catholic doctrine in two different fields by two bodies of writing which were definite impostures'.[2] But is it strange on the presuppositions of ultramontane historiography? If dogma is primary and not to be called in question (*révoqué en doute*) must it not overcome the troublesome historical evidence which stands in its way either by suppressing it or altering it or reinterpreting it from its special standpoint? Must not tradition be preferred to evidence, as the vehicle of the truth, whether God stands in need of our lies (*mensonges*) or not?

Tradition. One might suppose that the word (*traditio*) must necessarily translate that which has been handed down to us through the centuries; a living link between ourselves and apostolic testimony; for this was its meaning in the apostolic age, and in the undivided Catholic Church of the early centuries of the Christian era. But the Roman conception of tradition has developed into something very different from this: there are four main stages through which the development passes.

[1] *Symbolism and Belief* (Allen and Unwin, 1938), pp. 347–8.
[2] In addition to the Pseudo-Dionysius he is referring to the forged Decretals on which the temporal rights of the Papacy largely rested for many centuries, but which the Roman Church has now repudiated.

First, from the emergence of the Papacy proper in the sixth century to the mid-twelfth century, the canon law of the Roman curia was still mainly theological in its emphasis, for it was largely based on scripture, and on the interpretation of scripture by the Fathers and the great Councils.

The second stage began with the change from a theological to a juristic emphasis, towards the close of the twelfth century. Roman law, as distinct from the barbarized Roman law of the Visigoths in the sixth century, enjoyed a remarkable revival in the eleventh century, the four main centres of this legal renaissance being Provence, the cities of Lombardy, the old imperial city of Ravenna, and Bologna.[1] The long-term significance for the Church of this rebirth of classic Roman Law was hardly affected by the struggle between Guelphs and Ghibellines, the rivalry between the schools of Bologna and Montpellier or even between Roman law and English common law. For the tradition of Roman law steadily invaded the papal Curia, and the Catholic Church began to be thought of in terms of a corporation with ruling Pontiffs as its lawgivers, just as the Roman emperors had been the fountain head of Roman law. The Church is increasingly envisaged and constituted as a State. Christ now rules his earthly kingdom through an ecclesiastical corporation, juristically conceived and ordered. The *corpus juris civilis* of ancient Rome lives again as the *corpus juris canonici* of Catholic Christendom.

The third stage may be said to have opened with the Council of Trent and the Counter-Reformation. As though in answer to the Reformers and their reassertion of Biblical Christianity, Trent put non-scriptural tradition on

[1] See Vinogradoff, *Roman Law in Medieval Europe* (Harper, 1909) on 'Die Reception des römischen Rechts'.

the same level with Scripture itself.[1] This meant the formal recognition of the growing custom whereby the Christian faith as proclaimed by the Apostles could be supplemented, modified and even distorted from other sources described as 'traditions'. The context, text and meaning of Scripture were to be subject to the *auctoritas interpretativa* of the Church, in the name of tradition; which meant what at any period the Roman Church had come to hold, scriptural evidence and testimony notwithstanding. One implication of the concept of an unwritten tradition is clear, at least: the whole appeal to Scripture and to the Apostolic age of the Church can thus be rendered null and void.

The fourth and latest stage may be said to open with the decree of the Vatican Council on Papal Infallibility in 1870, and to reach its definitive climax with the new edition of the *Corpus juris canonici* in 1918. But is there any guarantee that this latest edition of the corpus of Canon Law is either definitive or a climax? The Pope has been described as 'the prisoner of the Vatican', but the enormously significant fact since 1870 is that everything in the doctrine and life of the Roman Church is now declared

[1] At its fourth session (8 April 1546) the Council claims to be fulfilling the command of Christ in Matt. xxviii. 18 f., 'perceiving that this truth and discipline are contained in scripture *and in traditions with no scriptural basis*' (perspiciensque hanc veritatem et disciplinam contineri in libris sanctis *et sine scripto traditionibus*). The Council '*accepts and venerates with an equal religious reverence* all the books of the Old Testament and the New, God being their Author; and *also those traditions pertaining to morals as well as to faith*, which are conserved by continuous succession within the Catholic Church...' (omnes libros tam veteris quam novi testamenti, cum utriusque Deus sit auctor, *nec non traditiones ipsas, tum ad fidem tum ad mores pertinentes... pari pietatis affectu ac reverentia suscipit et veneratur*) (sess. iv, Decretum de canonicis scripturis). Further, the Council anathematizes anyone who declines to accept these scriptures in whole and in part as sacred and canonical, in the old Latin Vulgate edition (*in veteri vulgata latina editione*) (*ibid.*). The decree is directed against the Reformers who have gone back from the Vulgate to the original Greek of the New Testament.

to be subject to the Pope: the whole body of Catholic dogma is subject to the papal *potestas jurisdictionis*. The Pope is not bound by what was formerly authoritative and valid for the Church. He can create new dogmas. He is no longer bound by the historic *consensus ecclesiae*. It is expressly decreed that he can create dogma 'of himself' (*ex sese*). He need not refer issues to General Council, Cardinalate or Episcopate. In short, tradition no longer means what it meant for St Irenaeus or St Augustine; namely, an unbroken chain of testimony linking each age of the Church to the controlling 'givenness' of apostolic experience and teaching. It has come to mean an absolute monarchy legislating *de jure*. Hence the notorious declaration of Pius IX at the time of the Vatican Council in 1870: *La Traditione son Io*.[1] The whole sacerdotal tradition here reaches its definitive climax because it has reached its apotheosis.

The final implicate of ultramontane logic is that the past means what it has come to mean. Tradition is now bound inextricably with the Papacy. No one with a sense of history will wish to deny that there is an impressive splendour about such a tradition. Too often Protestants have appeared content to leave to every individual man to define for himself what he means by professing faith in Jesus Christ as his Lord and Saviour: meanwhile Rome does them all the service of standing where she did, and of defining her terms with increasing precision. As the most thoroughly organized international 'pressure-group' which the world has yet seen she has often been and is still guilty of grievous political opportunism. She is nevertheless great in many senses of that word, the nursing mother of scholars and saints, and a Rock in the wilderness. But she

[1] 'I am Tradition.'

has little understanding of that evangelical liberty wherewith Christ has made believing men free. The ultimate differentia of her system, progressively defined and tightly articulated by her long tradition, is priesthood. The Protestant doctrine of the priesthood of all believers is easily misunderstood and caricatured; but it makes clear the line which separates justification by faith alone from all sacerdotal means of grace. Dogma as history is closely bound up with priesthood as power. Our discussion of the Roman Church and toleration may fittingly end with an impressive modern illustration of this, the ultimate, issue.

4. PRIESTHOOD AS POWER

On 2 February 1905 Johannes Katschtaler, Prince Bishop of Salzburg and Legatus Natus of the Holy See, issued a pastoral letter, its theme being the honour due to the priesthood. The letter is in two parts. The extracts given below are translated from the original German with strict accuracy, and nothing germane to the argument has been omitted.[1]

'Honour your priests.' Honour the priest because of the two inexpressibly high powers with which he is endowed through the goodness of God.

I. You know, most beloved, that the Catholic priest has power to forgive sins. 'Receive ye the Holy Ghost: Whose soever sins ye remit they are remitted unto them' (John xx. 22, 23). And these words, as you all know, concern not only the apostles, but also their legitimate successors; namely, the bishops and priests of the Catholic Church....

You see, most beloved, that the Catholic priest co-operates in this great act of God. What do I say? 'co-operates'? The word of the priest himself—the word 'I absolve you from your

[1] See Mirbt, *Quellen zur Geschichte des Papsttums*[4], pp. 497–9.

sins'—effects forgiveness. This word not only proclaims but effects (*bewirkt*) the forgiveness of sins and the justification of the sinner, as the holy Council of Trent teaches. God has, as it were, to this end surrendered his omnipotence for this moment to his representative on earth, the duly empowered priest. No, it is no empty, impotent word this, 'I absolve thee from thy sins', but a word of divine power; a word which has full validity even before the throne of God; a word at which the chains with which the devil has bound human souls are burst asunder, even though they be as hard as diamonds; a word at which the righteousness of God thrusts back the sword into its sheath; at which the evil spirits flee; at which the insatiable flames which were already prepared in hell for these sinners are quenched.

Of course the priest does not possess this altogether wonderful power of himself, but because of his ordination and because he is so empowered through the holy Church. . . .

Most beloved, where is there in the whole world a power to equal this? The power of rulers and kings? O the power of the Catholic priest is not inferior to theirs, but far exceeds it. The power of earthly emperors and kings extends only over the bodies but in no wise over the souls of men; it is limited to certain countries of this earth; but the power of the priest is active over the whole inhabited earth; indeed, what the priest looses and binds is valid not only on earth but also in heaven. Most beloved, where even in heaven is there such power? Look about you there and see the company of patriarchs, prophets, martyrs, confessors, holy virgins; the angels, archangels, thrones and principalities: can they loose thee from thy sins? No. The patriarchs with all their faith, the prophets with all their wisdom, the hermits with all their austerity, the virgins with all their purity—they cannot do it. The highly exalted spirits of heaven, the angels, archangels and principalities, the Cherubim and Seraphim, though they be the most exalted spirits in the Kingdom of Heaven, they can only beseech the Lord of Power that he will forgive our sins; but they themselves cannot forgive them. Nay more: even Mary, the Mother of God, Queen of Heaven—she cannot. Though she be the bride of the Holy Spirit, the Lady of the Universe, she can only pray for us that we may have forgiveness. Even she may not loose us from our sins.

Note well therefore, most beloved, how high, how sublime, how altogether wonderful is the power of the priest in forgiving sins. The Catholic priest, I say once more. Protestant pastors have not the priestly ordination through which this great power is transmitted according to the ordinance of Christ.

II. Honour the priests, because they have the power to consecrate.

Because of his ordination the Catholic priest and only he, and not the Protestant pastors (*und nicht die protestantische Pastoren*), has this wondrous power. The power to consecrate, to make present the Body of the Lord with the precious Blood, with his entire holy Manhood and his Godhead under the forms of bread and wine; to change bread and wine into the true Body and the precious Blood of our Lord—what a high, sublime, altogether wonderful power! Where in heaven is there such power as that of the Catholic priest? With the angels? With the Mother of God? Mary conceived Christ the Son of God in her womb and bore him in the manger at Bethlehem. Yes. But consider what happens at Mass. Does not the very same thing happen, so to speak, under the consecrating hands of the priest, at the moment of trans-substantiation (*bei der heiligen Wandlung*)? Beneath the forms of bread and wine Christ is truly, really and substantially present and, as it were, reborn. There at Bethlehem Mary bore the divine Child and wrapped Him in swaddling clothes; the priest does the same as he lays the Host on the Corporal. Once did Mary bring the divine Child into the world. But lo! the priest does this not once but hundreds and thousands of times as often as he celebrates. There in the manger was the divine Child, given to the world through Mary—little, passible, mortal. Here on the altar, beneath the hands of the priest, is Christ in his glory, impassible and immortal, as he sits in

Heaven at the right hand of God, triumphing gloriously, perfect in all respects. . . .

Do they make the Body, the Blood of the Lord merely present? No; they sacrifice (*sie opfern*); they offer the sacrifice to the heavenly Father. It is the same sacrifice which Christ made by shedding of blood (*blutiger Weise*) on Calvary, and in bloodless fashion (*unblutigerweise*) at the Last Supper. There the eternal High Priest, Jesus Christ, gave his flesh, his blood, his life to the heavenly Father as an offering; here in the Mass he does the same thing through his representative, the Catholic priest.

He has set priests in his place so that they may repeat (*fortsetzen*) the same sacrifice which he offered. To them has he transferred power over his sacred humanity; to them he has given the same power over his body. The Catholic priest not only can make him present on the altar and enclose him in the Tabernacle—to take him again and dispense him to the faithful; but the priest can also offer him, the incarnate Son of God the Father, as an unbloody sacrifice. Christ, the only-begotten Son of God the Father, through whom heaven and earth were made, who sustains the universe—he is here at the disposal of the Catholic priest (*ist dem katholischen Priester hierin zu Willen*). . . .[1]

Few Christians, surely, could read this document unmoved. It illustrates the piety of multitudes with moving eloquence. It also states with stark simplicity the issues which divide multitudes from them. Bracingly unambiguous itself, it evokes an unambiguous 'No' from those who see that the New Testament is irreconcilable with it. If this is what priesthood means, we have not so learned Christ.

[1] For the comment of Karl Holl, see p. 53 above. Heiler, *op. cit.* p. 226 gives a similar excerpt from a text-book by the Jesuit Karl Haggeney (Freiburg, 1916), used in Catholic seminaries.

CHAPTER XVIII

THE TOTALITARIAN STATE AND THE CROWN RIGHTS OF THE REDEEMER

I. PAGAN DEIFICATIONS OF THE STATE

A FRENCHMAN, who played a brave part in the underground resistance movement during the Second World War, recently remarked that freedom means hearing a sound at the door in the early hours and turning over to go to sleep again, knowing that it is not the Secret Police, but the milkman.

M. Georges Bidault was not giving a careful definition of freedom, of course; nor was he making a comprehensive survey of the complex issues raised by freedom of speech or freedom of association in modern society. He was merely illustrating, from the experience of thousands of men and women, the grievous menace to the human person in modern civilization. He was dramatizing the widespread repudiation of the very things which make man Man, by the modern mass-mentality. This totalitarian temper is more widespread than we like to admit. It is not confined behind an Iron Curtain. Absolutist political methods are advocated and practised in four continents. Moreover, civil liberties are gravely threatened in the 'free' world, where the cult of the paid informer, telephone tapping, the secret scrutiny of the mails, the increasing refusal of visas for entry and departure, recall totalitarian practices against which the free world was fighting desperately a decade ago.

Further, this totalitarian temper is, in some sense, religious. We should be living in an atmosphere of fantasy if we assumed that the only religious loyalties available to modern men are provided by those traditional faiths of which they are the natural heirs—notably Islam, Buddhism Hinduism, Judaism and Christianity. There are other faiths to which men give themselves. The *mystique* of racial destiny or imperial mission takes many forms, as the pages of de Gobineau, Dostoievsky or Kipling testify. Political ideologies evoke and sustain the devotion of the elect Party and, through it, of the disciplined multitude; either assuming an explicitly religious character, or using quasi-religious ritual forms and philosophies of history. Fascism, Nazism, Communism, Japanese *bushido* and Emperor cult are modern versions of the immemorial 'religious' secularism which would virtually deify the State or Society by giving it an absolute character. The omnicompetent State absorbs the sacred rights of the individual; it repudiates the unique status of the human person with cynical ruthlessness, prescribing not only how he is to live from the cradle to the grave, but how he is to think and what, in fact, he is to worship. Nationalism becomes the chief end of man. The parade-ground is its symbol; the ant-heap its working model. Right and wrong are no more than tiddly-winks for political opportunism to play with. Truth has no transcendent, absolute, meaning. Dr Gilbert Murray tells us that a little time ago he saw a letter from a cultivated and liberal-minded woman who had spent some years first in a Nazi and then in a Communist prison; she was kept without books until at last, by some special grace, a friend was allowed to send a few; among them a Thucydides. She read again the funeral oration of Pericles about Athens, and almost broke down. 'That was the sort of city that recalled the ideals of her youth; not like any city remaining in Europe as it now is.'

Thucydides himself was idealizing somewhat; and the great speech was primarily concerned with Athenian citizens rather than with their slaves, admittedly: we must be allowed to observe that no city in Europe today boasts a slave market like that for which Athens was celebrated. But this distinguished classical scholar and humanist, and the modern liberal philosophers whom he here represents, are properly shocked at our modern reversions to barbarism, and we share their sense of outrage. But something is lacking, nevertheless. Our liberal philosophers would be more convincing to many if they looked to Mount Zion as well as to Hellas, and learned from Hebrew prophets rather than from Greek philosophers something of the meaning of religious faith. For this is ultimately a religious issue. In E. M. Forster's *Two Cheers for Democracy* and in George Orwell's *Shooting an Elephant* (to name two of many modern liberal manifestos), there seems to be little recognition of the dimension of the transcendent and the eternal, coming down from heaven upon the plane of human history, like the plumbline of the prophet (Amos vii. 7–8):[1] what our Calvinist, Puritan or Covenanting forefathers knew as the Prerogatives of Christ the King.[2] When the Huguenots were besieged in St Quentin by the Spanish representatives of Hapsburg absolutism, an arrow was shot over the city wall into the market place, carrying a scornful demand for surrender. Coligny ordered it to be shot back again bearing the words: *Regem habemus* (we have a King).

Without a similar world-transcending faith, liberalism is

---

[1] Cf. Karl Barth's 'senkrecht von oben'.
[2] Covenanters' Memorial, Greyfriars, Edinburgh.

wistful and lost. It complains that a Hitler, a Stalin or any dictator typical of the modern age has no sense of the sanctity of individual personality. This is true. It is the most ghastly truth of our time. But if there be no living God, the sovereign Creator and Redeemer in whose image man is made, why should the individual take precedence over the mass; over Party or Nation or Race? Why should the ant be more important than the ant-heap? Take away faith in the living God who made man for himself, and who overarches the whole human scene in his transcendent sovereignty—and the special status of the individual is gone. That place of honour which liberal philosophy claims for him is his only because Christ died for him. To Lord Russell, presumably, and to other modern prophets of humaneness and common sense, this is merely the conventional language expected of professional exponents of religion, with their stale terminology of original sin and salvation by the grace of God. But we are recalling such language with a new interest and urgency today, because we are discovering, as Dr George MacLeod of the Iona Community once put it, that it is precisely in those countries where they care nothing for Christ's death that in a very short space of time they come to care nothing for a man's life. Worship Leviathan—the *Polizei-Staat, totaler-Staat*, single-party State—and the life of the individual man or woman soon becomes no life. To reinterpret the famous words of Hobbes in a sense not intended by their author, it becomes 'continual fear and danger of violent death: the life of man is solitary, poor, nasty, brutish and short'. It has become increasingly evident to us that the sacred right of the individual human person is a *sacred* right, but only because it presupposes dogmatic faith in a revelation from on high. The sanctity of the free personality of man is going to depend in the future, as it has done in the past, not on the so-called decencies of man, nor on the benevolent paternalism of the welfare state, nor on the tender mercies of private enterprise, nor on the visionary operations of inevitable progress, but on the vitality of supernatural religion: in short, on the vindication of the Crown Rights of the Redeemer in His Church. Protestants stand for the two ideas of supernatural religion and liberty: for these two ideas in combination: and for the historic conviction that in the long run you cannot have either alone. You must have both together, or neither; since God's service is perfect freedom, and since it is only in freedom that God can be truly served.

It has been contended that history is a cordial for drooping spirits. This is a dubious legacy from the liberal era, for it is equally true that history is a purge for complacent optimism. Yet we may probably learn something for our comfort from history here, since the totalitarian issue is not new and men of faith have had to face it often. This neo-paganism is obviously as old as paganism proper. It is pre-Christian and of great antiquity, though sturdy pagans down the Christian ages have never left it without witness. It looks back to the time when society, organized as clan, tribe, nation or race, is everywhere the essential unit of human life; and when religion depends on the society and subserves its interests. The Danish philosopher Höffding's definition of religion as the conservation of socially recognized values, though a bad and grovelling philosophy of religion, is not bad history; for in the ancient world the State (to use our modern term) virtually demanded the worship of the individual; and religious institutions found their main meaning and justification in their vital social function.

2. THE ISSUE IN CHRISTIAN HISTORY

Let us look at the world of classical antiquity; the thousand years from, say, 700 B.C. to A.D. 300. To us, the dominant motive there was secular; religion in the city-state five centuries before Christ was devotion to the city itself; in Pallas Athene the Athenian worshipped the incarnation of the society which made him what he was. Or let us look at the Semitic world which surrounded Israel in the age of the great prophets. Moloch and Melcarth personified the national ethos of the Semitic groups acknowledging them: religion provided sanctions for patriotism; the god was on the level of his people, representing and requiring no more than popular (or priestly) sentiment approved. Chemosh was little more than Moab's 'John Bull'. Those gods were tribal gods. Patriotism was not only *a* religion; it was *the* religion; sacred occasions symbolized and conveyed it. Or let us look at the Roman Empire, when Caesar Augustus was the incarnate 'genius' of the imperial system, and was worshipped as such. As in the worlds of Pericles and Alexander, so in the worlds of Cicero and Hadrian, the State claimed the pre-eminence and religion was merely one of its departments, the visible expression and guarantee of national stability. Indeed, religious recusancy was political disaffection, and a faith not sanctioned by law (*religio licita*) was treason. Caesar, in the extravagant language of the poet Martial to the Emperor Domitian, is *dominus et deus noster*; the ruler enjoys divine honours.

To understand the Christian martyrs of the third century of the Christian era we must imagine a modern reversion to paganism which would sum up an Englishman's religion in the formula 'For King and Country', which would cover the Table of the Lord with the Union Jack, and which would decree that the most sacred feast day in the calendar was not Christmas Day or Easter Day, but Empire Day. It was precisely that situation which sent Polycarp to the flames at Smyrna and Blandina to wild beasts at Lyons. These martyrdoms meant that Caesar worship and State absolutism were being challenged in the name of the Crown Rights of the Redeemer. The story, in Eusebius, of one Sanctus who was martyred for Christ's sake, helps us to understand why the Roman eagles went down before the Cross. To all examination before the Roman authorities Sanctus replied simply and unvaryingly 'I am a Christian'. 'This he confessed again and again', says the old historian, '*instead of name and city and race* and all else; and no other word did the heathen hear from his lips'. *Christianus sum*. I am a Christian.

That story, and many another like it, go far to explain why the religions of Israel, of the Hellenistic world and of Rome failed to capture the empire, whereas the Christian faith became conterminous with Western civilization itself in three centuries. The Church asserted the Crown Rights of the Redeemer. In principle, at least, it made no reservations on behalf of blood, nation or culture. It worshipped One who had 'made of one blood all nations of men for to dwell on the face of the earth; and who did send his blessed Son to preach peace to them that were afar off and to them that were nigh'. All loyalties were challenged and tested by this supreme loyalty. It was Christ who was to have the pre-eminence (Col. i. 18), not the Jewish Law and not Caesar's empire: not glories of our blood and state but the glory due to God alone.

Something, perhaps, may be said in favour of the intention to which this deification of the State gave expression. Christianity itself has never denied that the powers

that be are ordained by God (Rom. xiii. 1); that government is a divine gift to fallen humanity, and that, as a dyke
against the flood of anarchy, it is an aspect of the long-
suffering and the grace of God. Even tribal religion does
express the intimate bond between civilized life and the
faith which animates it: values admittedly precious are
thereby conserved: so far, at least, Höffding was right.
But this very excellence is its own fatality; for with the
downfall of the civilization goes the downfall of the religion; the bondwoman is cast out. Only religions which
have risen above nations and civilizations have attained to
historic permanence, for true religion demands primacy in
the life of the spirit. It must be an end in itself, or fade
away as that to which it is merely a means fades away.
A religion which merely serves socially recognized values
is not big enough for the centuries or for the race of men.
It deifies the earthly City (*civitas terrena*) instead of looking
for that City that hath foundations, whose builder and
maker is God. Its citizenship is on earth rather than in
heaven. It belongs to time rather than to eternity; and its
end is death.

'Thou hast conquered O Galilean.' Though this word
of the apostate emperor Julian is apocryphal, it is apt. As
the third century passes into the fourth, Christianity is on
the steps of the imperial throne, and with Constantine it is
seated crowned there. The religion of the martyrs becomes
the State religion; it has conquered indeed. A new chapter
of a thousand years opens.

This chapter from, say, A.D. 300 to 1300 is one which
soon begins to keep its left- and right-hand pages distinct,
so to speak. The story of Christendom is now to be two
stories rather than one, for the unwieldy empire soon
cracks and breaks into two halves, East and West: the one

pivoted on the new city of Constantinople, the other on the old city of Rome: in language, culture and ethos, the one Greek, the other Latin. The Church Catholic which is thus differentiated by geography, language, temperament and genius into two great branches—a cleavage which schism will later make fundamental—yields two histories rather than one from now on. We must look at them in turn.

In the Greek or Byzantine East where are the Redeemer's Crown Rights? It is easy to be deceived by the marked ecclesiastical flavour of the Byzantine story. Theology, if not religion, seems at first sight to be the master passion of society in the Eastern Empire. Dogma was the breath of life to the shopkeepers of Constantinople. Men took their seats on one side of the Circus or the other as a sign of their theological rather than of their political allegiance. The 'Blues' and 'Greens' of Constantinople (the Blue Shirts and Green Shirts of those days)[1] fought in the streets about the Trinity, rather than about economics; their coloured uniforms referred not to politics but to orthodoxy; like a notorious Arian emperor, they 'loved the ecclesiastical game'. In short, the Byzantine empire was by definition the Roman empire in its Christian form. Indeed, it was Christendom's bastion against Islam until 1453; and though the genius of Gibbon misled the nineteenth century into underestimating and disparaging it, the twentieth has been taught by J. B. Bury, Norman Baynes and others to realize something of its staying-power and greatness. Yet, in spite of this new appraisal of

---

[1] Cf. the *bianchi* and the *neri* (white shirts and black shirts) in Florence seven centuries later. Coloured shirts are far from being a twentieth-century invention.

the Byzantine achievement, the older impression of its sterility and ossification dies hard. And the reason is not far to seek. The Christian Church is the handmaid of the State in the Eastern Empire; the old tyranny yields place to a new, writ large; Caesaropapism. The head of the State virtually and actually controls the Church, even though he (or she) does not often use language as blatant as that attributed to the Arian emperor in the fourth century: 'My will is law.'[1] The Church is established and unfree. This absolutist theory of Roman sovereignty received its fullest expression and its most rigorous application at the hands of the emperor Justinian (527–65), whose fame rests on a twofold achievement. He was responsible for the definitive codification of Roman law, and for the building of the Church of the Holy Wisdom. Unlike St Peter's in Rome, the great basilica of St Sophia in Constantinople expresses and reaffirms an imperial supremacy over both Church and State which is absolute.[2] There is no clear differentiation between the things that are Caesar's and the things that are Christ's in this Byzantine 'erastianism'. And at last, in our own day, the Church of Holy Russia

[1] ὅτι ἐγώ βούλομαι τοῦτο κανών. It is the phrase put into the mouth of Constantius by Athanasius (*Hist. Arian.* xxxiii).

[2] The great authority of Baynes is against this unqualified interpretation, however. At the time of the Iconoclastic controversy (eighth to ninth century) the image-worshipping party insisted that the affairs of the Church were the concern of the clergy only. The emperor Leo VI made his brother Patriarch in an attempt to establish a precedent for complete imperial control of the Church. But, as Patriarch, his brother reproved and excommunicated him for adultery! The emperor thereupon made another attempt to appoint the Patriarch. Had this precedent been followed it would have meant Caesaropapism. But these two attempts were not repeated in the sequel. 'Men grew accustomed to think that in all moral issues...the Patriarch had undisputed rights above his master the emperor.' The very nicety of this balance illustrates not only the actual working of Byzantinism, but also the inherent complexity of the Church-State relationship in every age.

collapsed because it was virtually the Church of the Czars. It went down with the secular system with which it had so long been identified. The Redeemer's rights were not Crown rights.

The fortunes of the Church in the West were different. Gibbon has accustomed us to think of the decline and fall of the Roman Empire in the West when the Barbarians from the north came down upon it in the fourth and fifth centuries. And the Western Empire certainly declined and fell before marauding Huns and Vandals, conquering Goths and Franks. What, then, of the Church in the West, centred by an historic inevitability in Rome? If we are to understand the history of Western Christendom rightly, we must reckon with the curious paradox that the Roman Empire did not really fall. It lived on as the Roman Church. Roman Catholicism is the residuary legatee of Roman Imperialism, the Popes being the true successors of the Caesars. The imperial tradition of Rome cast its spell over the invading hordes from the barbarian north by becoming embodied in the Holy See which converted and civilized those hordes. What the eternal city could not retain by force of arms she held and preserved in the name of religion. The Papacy, as Troeltsch has well said, was 'the third act of the Roman drama'; it was the last creative achievement of an ancient civilization which had produced, first, a republic and, second, an empire. Even though Romulus Augustulus laid down the imperial dignity in A.D. 476, and there was no longer a Roman emperor in the West, the old Roman rule was not at an end. Indeed, its third phase had already opened. Half a century before, when old Rome was falling in ruin about him, Innocent I (402–17) had continued calmly to tell bishops in the West what the Apostolic See expected of them: and Leo the Great (440–61) made good the same precedent by enforcing ecclesiastical discipline in regions as far distant from one another as Thessalonica, Africa, Gaul and Spain. In the famous words of Hobbes, 'if a man consider the original of this great ecclesiastical dominion he will easily perceive that the Papacy is no other than the ghost of the deceased Roman Empire, sitting crowned upon the grave thereof. For so did the Papacy start up on a sudden out of the ruins of that heathen power.'

Are we to assume, then, that whereas Caesars were virtually Popes in the Byzantine East, Popes were virtually Caesars in the Latin West; and that the Church of the Middle Ages was a great political rather than a great religious institution? Protestants have sometimes quoted the pregnant sentence of Hobbes to support this assumption; and it was no less an historian than Professor Mandell Creighton (later Bishop of London) who contended that the Roman Church is the most complete expression of 'erastianism' 'since it is not a Church at all, but a State, in its organization; and the worst form of State—an autocracy'.[1]

Creighton was an authority on the history of the late-medieval Papacy, and his verdict is not untrue of medieval Catholicism in its decadence and decline during the greater part of the fifteenth century, when the Popes were hardly distinguishable from Renaissance princes, and have been a byword for unblushing worldliness ever since. Further, it has some support from the Catholicism of the past four centuries which, as we have seen, followed an ever-narrowing path of absolutism from the Council of Trent to 1870 and the present day. But how far is this

[1] *Life and Letters*, II, 375.

verdict true of medieval civilization proper; of the great popes, monks, friars, canonists, scholars and saints who built the cathedrals and abbeys of Europe and who, in what was surely an age of faith, made a noble and ever memorable attempt to realize the dream of a *respublica christiana*, God's 'right order' within the world?

Modern historians recognize that the second half of the eleventh century was one of the great turning-points in the history of Western Europe. What is so inadequately labelled as the Investiture Controversy was far more than a struggle between kings and popes over episcopal appointments. When the emperor Henry IV crossed the Alps to capitulate to Gregory VII, and stood in the snow outside the castle of Canossa asking for papal absolution, two opposed conceptions of the nature of Christian society were confronting one another. Canossa dramatized a spiritual crisis in the history of Western man. More than a highly dramatic episode heralding the partisan conflict of papalists and imperialists, it disclosed the fundamental meaning of the conflict: namely, the rival claims of Empire and Papacy to be the divinely approved instrument for the establishment of right order in human society.

The pope who thus flung down the gauntlet to the secular power is often remembered by his personal name of Hildebrand ('Hildebrandus papa'), rather than as Gregory VII, because his fiery personality dominated every act of his militant reforming policy, and breathed a personal note into the official letters which sought to make that policy effective. He brought the ardour of a crusader to the realization of his reforming ideal. It was the Hildebrandine ideal that the Church should be purged of its secular corruptions and entanglements (save, of course, when the Church wished to make use of the secular arm).

To this end the whole Western hierarchy—powerful prelates such as Hincmar of Rheims, for example—were explicitly subordinated to the papacy. Without papal approval and recognition, expressed through the bestowal of the *pallium*, no Western archbishop might validly exercise the functions of his office. But Gregory VII went further and so prepared the way for Innocent III and the papal empire over the whole Western world in the thirteenth century. He was not content to claim that the Church, thus centralized in the papacy, should be free from all secular control; he asserted the divine authority of the Church over secular governments and their temporal affairs, and twice excommunicated and deposed an emperor. Indeed, in his letter to Hermann of Metz[1] justifying the excommunication, and in the literary warfare between papal and imperial publicists of the twelfth and thirteenth centuries, the harsher views of St Augustine as to the demonic character of the State, received a new and dangerous emphasis.

The more fantastic statements and claims made in this famous letter were embarrassing to its recipient, a well-educated churchman who knew that Gregory's course was virtually unprecedented and revolutionary.[2] They help to explain why the Pope became an embarrassment to his own cause and party in the final phase of his pontificate from 1080 onwards. His letter to Germany about the election of a new anti-king, on the death of Rudolf of

---

[1] *Registrum Gregorii Septimi* (Jaffé), VIII, 21. It bears the title: 'Against those who are stupidly saying that the emperor cannot be excommunicated by the Roman pontiff' (*Contra illos qui stulte dicunt imperatorem excommunicari non posse a Romano pontifice*).

[2] Hermann's letters to the pope asking what he should say to people pestering him about the excommunication are evidence of his embarrassment. Had the reason for the papal action been obvious Hermann could have stated it.

Swabia,[1] is more important, perhaps, than the much-quoted letter to Hermann of Metz, for it clearly expresses the grounds on which the new theory of the papal supremacy over the empire is to be based. The oath which the king-elect must take is the regular feudal oath of allegiance which a vassal swears to his overlord; and there is no mistaking its meaning here. Indeed, the struggle for the freedom of the Church from secular control was now over; the equally important struggle for the freedom of the State from ecclesiastical control was about to begin. The immediate and urgent issue for the imperialist party was the vindication of the freedom of the Empire. And not only for the imperialist party. Medieval man—whether his politics, so to speak, were imperialist or papalist, Ghibelline or Guelph—believed that the Roman Empire was the Holy Roman Empire, and that the Emperor ruled by divine right. A merely secular understanding of the temporal order would have been entirely alien to the medieval mind. 'There is a divinity doth hedge a king.' Gregory's second excommunication and deposition of the Lord's anointed in 1080 was therefore gravely disquieting even to many of his own party; they felt that he had overreached the due limits of his power. It was noticeable that on recognizing Rudolf of Swabia in 1080 as the new ruler of Germany the Pope had made no mention of Italy. This suggested that the new Emperor was to be shorn of part of his patrimony; he was not to be the ruler of the lands south of the Alps as tradition required. Further, the Pope was now giving a

[1] *Registrum*, VIII, 26. This is the pope's letter of February 1081 to Bishop Altmann of Passau and Abbot William of Hirschau giving instructions about the election of a new anti-king to replace the anti-king Rudolf of Swabia, now dead. The Pope now takes for granted that it is he who decides who is lawful king in Germany. He adds the precise form of the oath which 'must be exacted' from the new king.

misleading account of what had happened at Canossa, saying that he did not restore Henry to kingship after granting him absolution there. But this was disingenuous at least, since the Pope had certainly recognized Henry as king for three years after Canossa. His own letters and other contemporary documents leave no doubt about the fact. Many facts suggest, indeed, that whereas in 1077 Gregory had acted with a magnanimous disregard of his own immediate interests,[1] and had restored the penitent sinner as befitted his priestly calling and responsibility—in 1080 he was no longer acting without bias and political motive. He had changed during those three years. The motive behind the second excommunication seems to have been political, since the contemporary documents give no hint of any ecclesiastical reason.

Probably the most remarkable and illuminating fact of all is that the whole papal Curia finally turned against their head. Thirteen cardinals, most of whom had been appointed by Gregory himself, deserted him; it is the most extraordinary fact in his whole career, and most lives of this pope omit it. Further, this was a wholesale official desertion: Peter the Chancellor, Theodinus the Archdeacon, John of the College of Cantors, John of the School of Cantors, Peter the Oblationarius, Poppo the head of the College of Regionarii (with their respective staffs), and even Cencius, head of the Judices and companion of Hildebrand's boyhood—all turned against and left their master. The only possible inference is that his unprecedented claims became intolerable at the last. In the following year he died at Ancona, saying: 'I have loved righteousness and hated iniquity; therefore I die in exile.' But

---

[1] Bismarck's 'We will not go to Canossa' showed that he misunderstood what happened there.

the men of his own household, his closest entourage, evidently interpreted his career differently. Papalists and imperialists alike could not dispute the fundamental presupposition of the age, that kings and emperors were ordained of God and that the Hildebrandine claims disturbed the proper parallelism and balance of the medieval order, and were dangerously revolutionary. In the words of John of Jandun:[1] *Potestas imperialis est immediate a Deo non a Papa* (the powers of the emperor derive immediately from God; not from the Pope).

One can understand the delight of Ulrich von Hutten who, when rummaging among old and forgotten manuscripts at Fulda monastery in 1519, two years after the nailing up of Luther's ninety-five theses, found the *De Unitate Ecclesiae Conservanda*, covered with dust, but with its ancient eleventh-century script still legible. Few literary finds have fitted into contemporary events so opportunely. In sending the manuscript to Scheffer of Mainz to be printed, Hutten acted as a politician rather than an antiquary. He saw that this eleventh-century treatise had contemporary as well as historic value: it presented the emperor Henry IV in a new light: it exposed the fables in support of papal authority against which the Reformers were again beginning to fight; and it made excellent propaganda at the court of the emperor Charles V, whose attitude to the Reformation at this early stage was not yet defined.

This famous treatise written between the years 1090 and 1093[2] is perhaps the best representative of the

---

[1] Imperialist writer of the early fourteenth century; contemporary of the better known Marsiglio of Padua.

[2] Its authorship is usually ascribed to Waltram of Naumburg, but this is doubtful. See the preface to W. Schwenkenbecher's critical edition (*Scriptores Rerum Germanicarum*, Hanover, 1883).

controversial literature produced on the imperial side in the eleventh century; it is one of the most famous defences of the Empire against the claims made by the Hildebrandine or papalist party after 1080. It challenges Gregory's fully developed ideal—the complete sovereignty of the spiritual over the temporal in the affairs of men. Gregory's final view of the world was completely theocratic; the Pope, as the successor of the blessed Peter, and the heir of his tremendous powers, is supreme over all temporal rulers as his feudatories. And as the papal letter to Hermann of Metz is the most definite and fullest expression of this Hildebrandine claim, it is not surprising that the protagonists of the Empire concentrated their attack upon it. Indeed, the first book of the *De Unitate Ecclesiae Conservanda* is devoted to answering the arguments in the letter to Hermann. Other contemporary writers on the imperial side may have been more convincing to the plain man: Petrus Crassus, for example, in his *Defensio Henrici Regis*. He had studied Justinian, and took his stand on Law, asserting the hereditary right of princes against the papalist contention that imperial right rested on election only. Again the very intransigeance of the controversial method of the imperialist bishop, Guy of Osnabrück, doubtless had its strong appeal when historical arguments, so dear to the polemics of the period, could be a wildly inaccurate basis for partisan propaganda. Guy deals roughly with the genuine dilemma caused by the rule of an evil king. Whereas Petrus Crassus, Wenrich of Trier and 'Waltram' agree that the Church must suffer such evil patiently, using no sword but that of the Spirit, Guy of Osnabrück denies that even the sword of the Spirit may be used against the Lord's anointed king, whose royal power is without limits: it is hereditary and absolute.

'Waltram's' discussion moves on a higher level. He has the scholarship, the historical sense and the dialectical restraint which many of his contemporaries lack. Further, though he appeals effectively to history, his argument is mainly scriptural and theological. He had evidently read St Augustine; and as the papalist party was now looking back to St Augustine's *De Civitate Dei* in justification of its polemic against the state and all temporal power, we may fittingly conclude our discussion of this momentous crisis in the eleventh century, by asking what effect the formative thought of the great Augustine had upon it and its later developments.

St Augustine's philosophy of human history, which matured from A.D. 412 to 426 in his slowly written pages *Concerning the City of God*, was based on the old contrast between two societies or cities (*civitates*); an earthly and a heavenly; the *civitas terrena* and the *civitas coelestis*. This mysterious and woeful contrast had originated in the pre-temporal, pre-mundane order, with the revolt of Lucifer and the angels. Indeed, before Augustine, Tyconius had expressed the contrast as that between the *civitas dei* and the *civitas diaboli*. With the fall of Adam this contrast, which had originated in the eternal angelic world, was transferred to our earthly world. Self-love, which went so far as to despise God, created the *civitas terrena*; whereas the love of God which went so far as to despise self, created the *civitas coelestis*.[1] The earthly society or city goes back to Cain the fratricide (Gen. iv. 17); the heavenly city to Abel. In subsequent human history, which Augustine divided into six stages from the Flood to the Second Advent, these two

---

[1] fecerunt civitates duas amores duo, terrenam scilicet amor sui usque ad contemptum dei, coelestem vero amor dei usque ad contemptum sui (*De Civ. Dei*, XIV, 28).

civitates mingle: they are mutually involved:[1] only at the end of the world will they be separated (cf. Matt. xiii. 24–30), the one to reign eternally with God, the other to endure eternal punishment with the devil.[2] What, then, is St Augustine's view of the *civitas terrena*? And how far is it true to say that in the contrast between *civitas terrena* and *civitas dei* he sees the essential contrast between State and Church?

The two pre-eminent representations of the *civitas terrena* for Augustine were Babylon (the first Rome, so to speak), and Rome (a second Babylon).[3] Indeed, as his purpose was apologetic, and as he was deliberately defending 'the most glorious city of God' against its detractors—the protagonists of a dying paganism who sought to make the Christian Church answerable for the woes of the time—he saw in the pagan Roman empire the supreme example of the *civitas terrena*. For such a State presupposes that stark duality of rulers and ruled which is both the result of sin and the machinery for dealing with it. Indeed, in the struggle of self-seeking with self-seeking, every man being for himself, society would be nothing else than a vast freebootery (*magnum latrocinium*) if the ruthless demonic power of the State did not aim at a relative good—namely the useful good of stability and peace (*pax terrena*). There is honour even among thieves, if only for utilitarian reasons. And even the citizens of the *civitas dei*, whose lives are interwoven with that of the *civitas terrena*, have an interest in this 'peace of Babel', and a proper regard for human laws which safeguard it. Thus, even though Augustine

[1] perplexae quodammodo invicemque permixtae (*De Civ. Dei*, XI, 1).

[2] una praedestinata est in aeternum regnare cum deo, altera aeternum supplicium subire cum diabolo (*ibid.* XV, 1).

[3] Babylonia quasi prima Roma...Roma quasi secunda Babylonia (*ibid.* XVIII, 2).

emphasized the inherent sinfulness of the secular political order with occasional harshness, he always admitted that at least the Law of Nature was germinally present in it: its very interest in the preservation of peace through law and order was a germinal recognition that peace may not be had or preserved without righteousness.[1] A more dubious, not to say disastrous, doctrine, which Augustine developed in his controversy with the Donatists, was that the State, albeit a *magnum latrocinium*, ought to place its services at the disposal of the Church; and that the sin-tainted State is in some sense sanctified by so doing.

It is but a step from this doctrine that the Church may make use of the 'secular arm', to the doctrine explicitly formulated from Hildebrand onwards that the authority of the Church extends over and should control the whole temporal realm. In the heat of conflict the enunciation of these doctrines went far beyond anything in Augustine. Indeed, Aquinas virtually disallowed their excesses by reverting to a moderate position much nearer to that of the *de Civitate Dei*. Aquinas recognized (and he was writing not long after the pontificate of Innocent III had made the Pope the ruler of the Western World) that the State had an independent basis in God, the giver of all power, and in the Law of Nature. The great Schoolman claimed, of course, that the State should be subordinate to the Church, at least in all matters pertaining to Salvation; and that the Church alone could determine, of course, just what matters do pertain to salvation. But apart from this comprehensive

[1] Augustine adds, of course, that *true* righteousness is only made possible through that true knowledge of God which is possessed by the *civitas Dei*. Without that knowledge, so called 'virtues' are *vitia potius quam virtutes* (vices rather than virtues). Hence the apocryphal epigram, wrongly attributed to Augustine, that the virtues of pagans are only splendid vices (*virtutes gentium splendida vitia*).

proviso, Aquinas recognized that the State is (almost) as independent of the Church as the Church is of the State.

Thus, the close of the eleventh century marks one of the great turning points in the history of the west. Religion is to be related to life, not by repudiating a monasticism which withdraws from secular life (far from it), but by an ecclesiastical control of that life in all its ranges, in the name of Christ the King.[1] In an age still rude, brutal and barely Christian, Western Catholicism confronted the secular power with the Crown Rights of the Redeemer in his Church. Those rights came to be expressed, as we have seen, in terms of canon law, hierarchical organization and temporal power; but they were deemed to be the rights of Christ. The Church was Christ's Church and the Bishop of Rome was his vicar. Western Catholicism reminded emperors and kings that there are aspects of human life which belong to Christ and which can never belong to Caesar. It asserted the reality and supremacy of the spiritual order in this naughty world. It met mailed fist with the great word from Matt. xvi. 18: 'upon this rock I will build my church; and the gates of hell shall not prevail against it.' It turned from the things of which bare reason is the assessor to revelation and sacrament, 'where faith prevails and love adores'.[2] In no unreal sense some of the great medieval popes might be called the first Free Churchmen, in that they did vindicate the transcendent reality and freedom of supernatural religion. In the name of the Redeemer they did battle with society still barbarian and half pagan in its gross sensuality and violence; they quenched the slumbering fires of paganism in the waters of baptism, and in the name of the Redeemer laid claim to

[1] The *supernus rex* of the *civitas coelestis* (Aug. *De Civ. Dei*, xi, 1).
[2] See p. 73, above.

the *whole* of human life from the cradle to the grave—and beyond the grave.

That this papal Church itself became rich and worldly, fat and tyrannical, no informed person would deny. That it sometimes forgot the rights of Christ and appropriated them to itself in insolent pride is notorious and incontestable. It described that mounting and descending curve made familiar by medieval monasticism itself—vision, devotion, greatness, degeneracy, decay. And at length, in the name of reform and evangelical freedom, its rule was refused by multitudes and, for good and ill, modern history was born. Yet, in spite of its high clerical and hierarchical pattern, it is the high Churchmanship of this medieval achievement in the West which modern Protestants cannot afford to forget, whether they represent State Churches or Free Churches. For a Hildebrand, an Anselm and an Aquinas (as for Calvin, Isaac Watts and Thomas Chalmers in later generations) the Church's one foundation was Jesus Christ, her Lord. The Bride belonged to the Bridegroom alone.[1] These men steadily refused to allow that Christ's holy religion could ever become a department of state, 'a mere Portfolio of Public Worship'. With the ultimate fate of Byzantinism before our eyes we see what they saved us from, in the West, and the debt we owe them.

So much, then, for the second stage of our survey; the thousand years of medievalism. We come to the latest stage by asking what happened to this high conception of the Church at the Reformation.

---

[1] The *civitas dei* is *sponsa Christi* (Aug. *De Civ. Dei*, xv, 22).

3. CHURCH AND STATE WITHIN THE
PROTESTANT TRADITION

Fifteenth-century history is notoriously complex; it is concerned with the close of the so-called Middle Ages and the beginnings of the modern world. Professor T. F. Tout used to say that we cannot yet understand it because it is too difficult; a judgement equally true of the age of the Reformation. Certainly the fifteenth century is no mere end of an era; where the great mists lie the great rivers spring.

The late medieval story of England or France is relatively straightforward. Feudal anarchy is giving place to national unity; after the Wars of the Roses come the Tudors and the 'totalitarian' State of Queen Elizabeth; out of the anarchy of the Hundred Years War in France come the nationalist, Joan of Arc, and the rule of a very able king, Louis XI; the great fiefs are slowly absorbed by the Crown; there are no longer to be any lumps in the national porridge. History in these two modern nations will be that of the *first* estate for some time to come.

But a reverse process, a process of disruption, takes place in Germany and Italy and its after-effects are still with us. At the close of the Middle Ages Germany has little unity; it has gradually disintegrated into fragments which make its map look like a Byzantine mosaic; the great fiefs, so far from being absorbed by the Crown, themselves develop into sovereign independent states with dependent satellites. German history is therefore that of the *second* estate, the territorial nobility; a fact of far-reaching import, especially for the history of the Reformation. Lutheranism has always tended to be conservative and erastian; the territorial prince was too much even for Martin Luther.

The Italian story is similar, save that here a multiplicity of sovereign independent states arises out of municipal rather than feudal units, out of towns rather than territories; Italian history is a history of the *third* estate. Here as in Germany, the central power being either weak or non-existent, other forces seize their opportunity. Whereas in Germany it was the territorial nobility which absorbed the cities, in Italy it was the city which absorbed surrounding territory and finally became a monarchy. The German emperors, Maximilian and Charles V, could not weld diversity into a unity; and in Italy, neither Gian Galeazzo Visconti nor the Medici, neither the Popes nor any of the great Condottieri, could make an Italian nation. It is not too much to say that just as National Socialism, in our day, was an attempt to carry on Bismarck's policy of welding together territorial traditions represented by the great houses of Hapsburg, Hohenzollern, Wettin and Wittelsbach; so in Italy the very violence of the Fascist or corporative reaction against the old disintegration and atomism was the measure of difficulties still to be overcome there. In fifteenth-century Italy these difficulties are very plain. Aristotle had no greater variety of city-states to study when he wrote the *Politics*. Compare, for example, Venice with Genoa; Florence with Siena or Lucca; old-world, rural, feudal Savoy with the 'modern', urban despotism at Milan; an hereditary, military rule in Naples with an elective régime of priests in Rome. It is as a wonderful field of political morphology that it is still a fruitful source of the difficulties, not only of historians, but of modern politicians.

In short, this period of history mirrors the abiding problem of political science; namely, how to secure and encourage individual liberty without fostering disruption and anarchy. German historians, naturally enough, have come to different judgements about so formative an age. They fall roughly into three schools. The Prussian school regards the decline of the monarchy as a disaster; as a result there was no true national life; and that 'Teutonic shrinkage' took place whereby two large groups of Teutonic blood were permanently alienated from the German Empire: the Netherlands, because of an excessive development of feudalism; and Switzerland, because of the growth of republicanism. A second school champions the towns in the momentous three-cornered struggle between them, the monarchy and the nobility; the decay of townlife deprived Germany of commerce, stunted its intellectual interests and handed it over to militarism. There is a third or optimistic school which contends that history justifies itself; infinite variety developing in different directions was a good thing, making the development of individual ability possible.

It is interesting to note that similar views were held contemporaneously in Italy. Machiavelli is the champion of Italian unity and of 'totalitarianism'; Guicciardini is a liberal, holding that unity is too dearly bought at the price of provincial, local and individual interests. He would hardly have been found shouting *'Viva il Duce'* in the twentieth century.

It is against this general background that we have to understand the issue of Church and State in the era of the Reformation. As we have already seen, the rebellion which Luther found himself launching—against his intention and his deeply conservative instincts—helped to destroy the unity of the traditional medieval system. The unity of Christendom as a whole had already been disrupted by the formal schism of Constantinople and Rome four centuries earlier. The medieval structure in the West, too, had been ominously cracking and disintegrating for over a century, and parts of it now fell down. Some new structure was necessary, therefore, within which men and nations might live in safety. Some new and positive polity for Church and State became an urgent need, and kings and magistrates proceeded to exploit that need by extending their secular authority to the ecclesiastical sphere which, in the Middle Ages, had been conterminous with, yet independent of, the civil sphere. Thus nationalism, in the sense of state absolutism, was born, and Protestantism took the form of established or state churches in almost every country where it triumphed. The Tudor Henry VIII was no exceptional phenomenon in that age of nascent erastianism. Machiavelli's 'Prince' everywhere put himself forward as the supreme head of society, and the divine right of popes gave place to the divine right of kings. The Middle Ages, wherein the Roman Church had successfully claimed to exist as a separate order within the State, and even to dominate the State—were now at an end.

What then, was Luther's constructive attitude to this menace, the state control of evangelical religion? Did he regard it as a menace? Much research is still being done on his own attitude to this *landesherrliche Kirchenregiment*[1] as distinct from the attitude of later Lutheranism, which first appears with Melanchthon.[2] The crucial issue is whether the *Staatskirchentum* of later Lutheranism corresponded to Luther's own ideal. We may say with confidence that it did not. Yet the issue is complex. From the beginning,

[1] I.e. rule of the Church by the territorial prince.
[2] See F. Hildebrandt, *Melanchthon, Alien or Ally?* (Cambridge, 1946), pp. 55–77. Also K. Holl, *op. cit.* I, 326–80.

Luther's mind struggled with two controlling principles; here as elsewhere he thought and lived in terms of paradox. For the clearer guidance of the reader the discussion of the issue is first summarized in the following scheme:

A. Luther is at pains to establish two scriptural principles:

(i) The divine sanction of civil government, and its independence of all clerical tutelage or control.

(ii) The limits of this power, which may be exercised only over the bodies and goods of men, not in the domain of conscience, where man is answerable only to God.

B. Hence the title of the treatise which he devotes to this issue in January 1523: *Of Civil Authority, and of the Limits of the obedience owed to it*. Written at the request of Duke John of Saxony, it develops ideas already expressed in the *Address to the Nobility*, and in the exposition of the fourth commandment in the *Sermon on Good Works* (March 1520), where Luther's characteristic paternalism supports a fourfold obedience to authority.

The treatise fights on three fronts; it repudiates three distinct views of the proper relation between State and Church:

(i) The medieval, Roman view. Luther denies that the State, as the 'secular arm' of the church, has a duty to undertake religious persecution or coercion.

(ii) The 'Machiavellian' view. He denies that Christian men may be persecuted as such by the civil power for reasons of state.

(iii) The 'anarchist' view of Christian idealism and pacifism. He denies the 'anabaptist' thesis that because the Gospel forbids resistance to evil, the Christian State may not use force in the name of Law.

C. Luther distinguishes between

(i) Natural society—which, because of sin, cannot subsist without the coercive sanctions of police force and sword.

(ii) The religious sphere—where the Word is the only agency which may rightly be employed.

D. Luther thus anticipates some of the living issues of our own time. It is doubtful whether he also anticipates those erastian elements in historic Lutheranism which are now criticized and disavowed.

In Luther's letter dedicating his treatise of January 1523 to John, Duke of Saxony, the general problem of Church and State emerges from a particular problem which has always disturbed the consciences of Christian men: how may the right of the temporal power to use the sword be reconciled with Matt. v. 39?

Numerous souls are disturbed by the words of Christ: But I say unto you that ye resist not evil; but whosoever shall smite thee on thy right cheek turn to him the other also. And if any man will sue thee at the law and take away thy coat, let him have thy cloak also. On the basis of these words the prince Volusian objected to St Augustine that Christian doctrine allows a bad man to do evil, and is therefore incompatible with the exercise of temporal power. The scholastic doctors saw the difficulty and, in order to avoid denying to ruling princes a Christian character, they declared that this word of Christ was not a precept for all but a counsel addressed to those who aim at perfection.

Luther had already challenged this old scholastic distinction between gospel precepts and gospel counsels, affirming that all Christ's words are valid and obligatory for all.[1] This meant, however, that for the prince or magistrate (or hangman!) who genuinely desired to be a believing Christian, the moral problem of knowing whether his governmental function was compatible with profession of the Christian faith, appeared in all its notorious gravity. 'I hope to be able to show to princes and magistrates', says Luther, 'that they may remain Christian, and that

---

[1] See above, p. 108.

Christ may remain the supreme authority without transforming the commandments of Christ into mere counsels.'

As Luther wrestles with this problem of the power of the State in relation to the Gospel of redeeming love, he quotes the familiar texts, Rom. xiii. 1 f.; I Peter. ii. 13 f.; the counter-texts, Matt. v. 39, 44; Rom. xii. 9; I Pet. iii. 9; and there is an astonishing modernity about his way of honestly stating and facing, one after another, the difficulties so familiar to us who face them four centuries later. But it is important to notice that his attitude, in two important respects, is essentially medieval rather than modern: here his thought is nearer to Aquinas than to Calvin.

In the first place, it would be an anachronism to expect Luther to use the words 'state' or 'society' in the modern sense of these terms. We have already observed that the history of Germany (of Middle and North Germany, at any rate) was to be that of the second estate, the nobility, for a long time to come. There was no unified state or nation in the modern sense, but a large number and variety of political powers or sovereignties,[1] overarched by an imperial sovereignty which was often limited by circumstances, and nominal rather than effective. When Luther struggles with the immemorial problem of Church and State, therefore, it is not surprising that he fixes his attention on the dominant factor constituting society in general as he knows it: namely, the nobility, or governing aristocracy (*Obrigkeit*). His vast and astonishing assumptions as to the divine right of the nobility to rule, cannot be rightly understood unless this is remembered. Luther was a reformer, but a reluctant rebel; he was neither egalitarian

[1] After the Thirty Years War, Germany was made up of more than three hundred sovereignties.

nor revolutionary in his thought about society. Like Calvin, he mistrusted the multitude, and had no wish to overturn existing social institutions: and as for wishing to do so with the help of the rude fist of Mr Everybody (*Herr Omnes*), the thought horrified him. And, in any case, he believed that, given free course, the Gospel would pioneer its own victorious way. Revolution is never right, therefore. It is the work of the devil. Carlstadt and his followers who were menacing Wittenberg in 1522 with revolutionary iconoclasm in the name of a lay-Christian puritanism, were—from Luther's viewpoint—presuming to exercise an authority and an office which belonged not to them, but to the Christian nobility alone. The princes alone have the right and duty, as Christians, to take effective action for the common good of Christendom. That is why, in 1520, Luther had addressed his reforming manifesto, neither to the emperor nor to 'the people', but to 'the Christian Nobility of the German Nation'; calling upon them to oppose and reform the disorders within the Church.

In the second place, Luther is medieval in his attitude to natural law. The authority behind his appeal to the territorial prince is not only Scripture ('the powers that be are ordained of God'), but the law of nature, written on the very heart of man at the creation, and having a divine sanction. The divine sanction of law extends beyond the Decalogue; it covers those forms or institutions which are a permanent fact of human society—marriage, the family, the principle of parental authority, *and the principle of princely authority*. For princely rule (*Obrigkeit*) corresponds in civil society to the position of the father in a family. The sanctions of natural law give the same honour and obedience to the territorial prince as is given to parents on the basis of the Fourth Commandment. In the name of natural law princes may demand from their subjects reverence, honour, various forms of service, taxes and even the sacrifice of life itself; on this presupposition, indeed, the prince proceeds against thieves, murderers and rebels with the sword. 'Fair enough', we may say; 'the territorial prince is the embodiment of law and justice in the sixteenth century.' But Luther goes further in his reliance on the *lex naturalis*. He assumes that it legitimizes the entire agrarian structure of medieval society, as being the very ordinance of God. He brands any attempt to disturb this order as revolutionary, and therefore as a crime legitimately punishable with death. This backward-looking view had, as we shall see, important consequences for Lutheranism in the future. The basic assumption here —the rigid stratification of social ranks and functions, and the almost religious respect due to the ruling class—is thoroughly medieval.

But in spite of all this, Luther has nevertheless broken with the most fundamental of medieval assumptions in his new concept of clerical status and ecclesiastical power. For him, the true power of the Church consists only in the proclamation of the Word; the Church is 'allowed of God to be put in trust with the Gospel'; its sufficient and only privilege is to witness to God's redeeming grace. And even this is no longer a *privilegium cleri*; it is the privilege and duty of all believers.

Now the practical outcome of Luther's thoroughly medieval attitude towards the nobility, and of his thoroughly non-medieval attitude towards the clergy, was a new and non-medieval extension of the responsibilities and powers of the nobility. He not only asserts (with medieval imperialists) the divine sanction of civil government, and (with Marsiglio of Padua, John of Jandun and the French publicists of the fourteenth century) the independence of that government from priestly tutelage and all ecclesiastical control: he goes further. In certain situations—when, for example, the ecclesiastical situation cries out for reform or administrative action—the territorial nobility has the right and the duty to take that action. Luther always boasted, indeed, that he had established better than anyone else the divine right of civil authority.[1]

The prince's function is one of governance, coercion and restraint because of sin. Ideally the Christian man and the Christian community have no need of rules and laws, and a ruling *Obrigkeit* to enforce them, for 'if all the world were genuinely Christian, king, prince, lord, law and sword would be neither necessary nor of any use'. All men would be taught by the Spirit in the heart, and would love the neighbour and do wrong to none. This would happen spontaneously and not in obedience to an elaborate code of regulations. Quoting I Tim. i. 9 Luther says: 'You don't *order* a good tree to bear good fruit; it bears fruit appropriate to its kind quite naturally, without instructions or orders. One would be a lunatic to write a book full of laws and precepts intended to instruct an apple tree that it should bear apples and not thorns.' In theory, therefore, we ought to distinguish between the sphere of sin where force operates in the name of law; and the inner life of evangelical freedom where love operates in the name of grace. And, in principle, that is what Luther does. He attributes totally different functions to the 'State' and to the 'Word of God', and allows no confusion between them. The State is and ought to be a coercive, restraining and

[1] *WA*, xix, 625.

punitive power, but its competence does not extend to the domain of conscience. Alongside of it, therefore (though necessarily within the framework of human society where state action maintains internal order and external peace with the sword) the Spirit of God operates through the instrumentality of the Word, acting upon the consciences of men, regenerating them, and progressively sanctifying them. And this parallel operation of the Spirit takes place in a sphere which is reserved to the Spirit alone. No other authority—not even the paternalist authority of the prince —may take precedence of it.

Thus Luther's paternalism is by no means absolute; it is explicitly and genuinely qualified. Expounding the Fourth Commandment he says that we ought to honour father and mother, not only in outward semblance but with submissive obedience, *so long as they do not require or command anything contrary to the first three commandments.* 'Where parents are so mad as to bring up their children only for this world, the children ought resolutely to resist them.' We must obey God rather than parents! And Luther includes here, as he does in his *Catechisms*, not only parents but all those who are divinely invested with any authority. The prince rules under God. His authority is neither absolute nor arbitrary. It is his duty to respect the conscience of his subjects. Luther goes so far here as to justify, on this basis, the subject's right of resistance—passive resistance. An individual may refuse obedience to the civil authorities if they should seek to extend to the sphere of conscience a coercive power which is limited to the sphere of bodies and goods. Luther thus justifies conscientious objection and passive resistance on the basis of the Word of God. He himself exercised this right before the highest representatives of civil authority at Worms.

Does this imply, then, the complete separation of Church from State? Hardly. Indeed, one may answer this question with another. Is complete separation possible or even conceivable? The Church is visible, within any State, as a large number of parishes or religious groups, made up of people who are at once Christian in the authentic, ideal sense, and Christian in the empirical sense: that is, they are partial Christians who, inasmuch as they are still prone to evil, are still in need of legal restraint. Living in the world as he must do, the Christian is, in reality, never entirely purified from all sin and never a Christian in the authentic sense. He therefore remains subject to the salutary discipline of the State and to the prince's brisk use of 'the sword'. He is subject to the Law which, by definition, is common in its operation. Luther denies to the State the right to intervene in purely religious issues; the second half of his treatise is devoted to the exposition and the defence of definite limits to state action. But, on the other hand, he defends with obvious justice the intervention of the State whenever members of the church visible, isolated or in groups, commit offences against the laws which necessarily control natural society. It is obvious, therefore, that this proper insistence on the equality of all men (Christians as well as non-Christians, priests as well as laymen) before the Law did not mean the control of the Church by the State. What Luther is saying, in accordance with his paternalist presuppositions, is that the prince, in his capacity as 'elder brother' or 'eminent member' of the religious community—*but not in his capacity as the representative and executor of temporal power*—should help to organize the religious community, so that the ministry of the Word may be maintained.

What, then, of the Christian idealism, already discernible

among the Anabaptists, who challenged the right of the Christian state to use force for the repression of evil, and preached absolute non-resistance? The problem, and Luther's answer to it, is not unfamiliar to a twentieth-century world tortured by the plain incompatibility of Christianity and hydrogen bombs.

If anyone wanted to govern the world in accordance with the Gospel, and to suppress law and the sword, claiming that today we have to do with Christians to whom the Gospel forbids both—I ask you, dear heart, what would such an one do? He would break the chains of the wild beasts, who would tear all comers to pieces; and he would still require us to consider these wild beasts as his very good, tame flock. Yes. And my wounds would soon teach me what to think of this. Thus the bad people, in the name of Christian liberty, would give themselves up to every kind of excess, and would claim to be Christians exempt from all law and not subject to any sword. We already hear fools talking thus. This is what you should say to them in reply. 'It is perfectly true that Christians do not need law and sword for themselves, and are not subject thereto' (i.e because they are subject to the Holy Spirit). But before wanting to govern the world in accordance with the Gospel, busy yourself first of all with giving us a world where there would be no longer anyone but true Christians. You won't succeed, however. For the world and the mass of mankind, are and remain refractory to the Spirit of Christ, even though all have been baptized and bear the name of Christian. True Christians are a minority within the mass. The world's nature resists all attempts to govern the world in accordance with Christian principles. One can't even govern a single country thus, or a group however small in numbers; for the bad people always far outnumber the good. To try to govern a country or the whole world with the help of the Gospel, would be as sensible as enclosing in the same farm yard, wolves, lions, eagles and sheep, and saying to them: 'Now, be very good, live peaceably, feed together; the gates are open, the grass is abundant and you have nothing to fear either from dogs or from blows of the cudgel.' The sheep would be peaceful enough, and would accept such peaceable governance. But they would not live very long....

It is the statesman's dilemma, and it is agonizingly real; we who are, or have been, or are about to be, pacifists, are impaled upon its horns, just as he is.

Luther is sensitively aware of the irresolvable complexity of the issue. Carefully and fairly he sets out objections and counter objections in detail, and in the third part of his treatise, where he deals with 'The Christian Prince', he subjects the traditional concept of the 'just war' (of which modern man still makes use) to close scrutiny. 'I declare', he says, 'that a vassal ought never to declare war on his overlord, the king or the emperor, but should submit rather to injustice; for to resist authority with armed force is illegitimate.' He also argues that a prince ought to concern himself less with a wrong which has been done to him by an equal than with the evils which he would provoke in asserting his right and redressing the wrong by force of arms. 'May one expose women to widowhood and make children orphans to revenge an insult or a wrong?' Luther thinks constantly of people rather than of policy, and his thought is pervaded with considerations of equity, wisdom and common sense. He is no doctrinaire theorist. Indeed, he brought these general principles to bear in 1525 when the peasants, who were being incited by 'agitators' to revolt, asked him for counsel. He counselled submission. One's Christian right teaches submission to legitimate authority. When, in spite of these warning (and disappointing) counsels, the peasants did resort to revolt, Luther approved of its savage repression, using language which surely belied his general principles. Critics of Luther here have all done the same, in war-time. But, however inconsistently, Luther passed severe judgement on the horrible excesses committed by the princes against the defeated and disarmed peasantry.[1]

But what of an 'unjust war'? 'Are the people obliged to follow their prince if he begins such a war? No. For no one is obliged to perpetrate an injustice. In such case we must obey God, who demands justice, rather than men, in accordance with Acts. v. 29. But what if his subjects are uncertain as to their prince's good right? If in spite of all their efforts, they have failed to be well informed as to the issues, they may follow their prince without compromising their souls' salvation. . . .' The cynic's smile here will be understandable; and all that Luther can do is to conclude with the essential thing, which is nevertheless a counsel of perfection; namely, that 'a prince should bear himself as a Christian before God, submitting to Him with entire trust and asking for the necessary wisdom to govern well, as did Solomon (I Kings iii. 9) '.

In 1526, at the request of an army officer, Luther devoted a special treatise to the problem of the Christian and war, entitled 'Can a soldier be saved?'[2] Here he repeats many of his previous arguments, recalling Luke iii. 14, Acts x. 34 ff. (as Calvin was to do later), and insisting that God alone is and will be the ultimate judge. He declares again that defence against the attack of an equal is legitimate, and that in a defensive war an army may fight with good conscience. He distinguishes between this legitimate defensive war and war undertaken for the love of war itself, or for the sake of conquest. The prince who embarks on such a war is 'a pagan and even a madman'. The aggressor is always in the wrong. God will resist him,

[1] See *WA*, xviii, 279 ff., 344 ff., 375 ff.   [2] *WA*, xix, 616 ff.

and will make him know that 'beyond the mountains there are also men with mailed fists'. When the intention of a prince is plainly evil his subjects will refuse him obedience, for they could not follow him with a good conscience. Luther here quotes Matt. xix. 29, and agrees that as Christ's disciples may have on occasion to abandon father and mother for his sake, so they may have to abandon their prince. But where his policy is no more than dubious he may have the benefit of the doubt since his subjects' love will ensure that they give him at least their provisional loyalty.

Is it realism or pathetic *naïveté* or both which here inform Luther's heroic attempt to relate the Gospel to the savage cynicism of power politics? One glance at contemporary records and memoirs[1] suffices to show why he felt that he had no option but to defend the stern coercions of prison, rack[2] and gallows in the interests of executive justice. Sixteenth-century Germany was no Garden of Eden; and Luther knew that in this fallen world-order natural society cannot subsist without the constraints of force in all their demonic ruthlessness. But there is something unreal about his ingenuous plea that the conscience of the ordinary peasant or citizen might be safeguarded by his refusal of obedience, if his prince decided on an unjust war of aggression or a dubiously just war of defence. Contemporary society did not think of Albert Achilles of Brandenburg (ob. 1499) as the *enfant terrible* of his time because he remarked with a guffaw that 'incendiarism is the ornament of war, as the Magnificat is of Vespers'. Given such

---

[1] See, for example, *Social Germany in Luther's Time, Being the Memoirs of Bartholomew Sastrow*, translated by A. D. Vandam with an introduction by H. A. L. Fisher (Archibald Constable, London, 1902).

[2] The prince's 'sword' was a euphemism for this, and much else.

a typical 'prince' as this, Luther's general argument may appear pathetically naïve. Indeed, many feel that he had much to learn from the detested and vilified Anabaptists, whose tiresome offence it was to believe that religion without social justice is a blasphemous sham, and that true religious reform necessarily includes genuine social betterment for the poor and disinherited. Luther's wild attacks upon them look suspiciously like an embarrassed awareness that their pacifism and social idealism were part of the implicit logic of the New Testament itself. Much that has been written about Protestantism's 'bourgeois' ethic is untrue of Protestantism before 1660, and equally true of Catholicism and Protestantism after 1660; but it is undeniable that Lutheranism and Calvinism have been, on the whole, movements of the middle-class bourgeoisie, and that Lutheranism had more appeal for grand-ducal politicians and prosperous burghers than for the poor and the oppressed who were expected to remain content with the lowly station in life to which it had pleased divine providence to call them. It is hardly strange that Anabaptists were rarely converted to Lutheranism or to Zwinglianism.

But Luther's sense of the theological principles governing the relation of religion to life as it really is, is not easily discredited. He holds firmly to both truths which constitute his paradox. And unless international politics must always ultimately be power-politics, involving mere questions of political expediency rather than high questions of moral law, Luther's general principles stand, even though he might have learned much from Anabaptists about their further implications. Luther cannot be made responsible for the dull subjection to state control in which German Lutheranism came willingly to acquiesce. If there be a villain of the piece, it is Melanchthon. In remaining willingly subject to civil authority so long as that authority did not overstep its scriptural limits, later Lutheranism was giving effect to Luther's own principles. But it seems true that protestants in Lutheran territories in Germany grew so accustomed, generation after generation, to the dangerous advantages which they enjoyed in having their evangelical faith protected by the civil authorities, that they grew insensibly unaccustomed to challenge or resist authority on grounds of conscience; and so became inured to their complete subordination to the State and to the established political order. In this way the power of the State becomes an end in itself, and the prime duty of the (Christian) statesman is to watch over the *sacro egoismo* which the twentieth century calls totalitarianism. Luther did contest this claim of the State to have no other duty than to assure and conserve its own power. Those who came after him were at least less vigilant. It is Roman Catholicism and the Churches of the sect-type which have expressed the proper Christian reaction against this erastian State Churchmanship. Heiler rightly argues that erastianism grievously menaces the essential oneness and independence of the Church of Christ's Body. He adds, rightly, that the rise of the modern Papacy means nothing less than the saving of the Church's catholicity.[1]

To sum up: it seems that circumstances proved too strong for the author of *The Liberty of the Christian Man*, even during his own lifetime. Not only Melanchthon and later German Lutherans, but the great Reformer himself

---

[1] *Katholizismus*, p. 342. See also a very illuminating page by the Lutheran theologian Otto Piper in his *Recent Developments in German Protestantism* (S.C.M. 1934), p. 53.

began to swim with the political current which was everywhere bringing the absolute ruler to port, and to acquiesce in the political opportunism of his princely protectors. The prophet who began by proclaiming the priesthood of all believers at last found himself virtually exalting the temporal prince as *summus episcopus* or as *membrum praecipuum ecclesiae*, which to an English Free Churchman sounds ominously like 'supreme head of the Church'. Luther had certainly not intended a state absolutism which would subordinate the Gospel to political expediency, even though this did become a characteristic of later Lutheranism. Yet he had to take his territorialist Germany as he found it; and as he became increasingly intolerant of 'extremists', his invitation to the secular power to control the organization of the Church was almost inevitable. The initial Reformation concept of the Church as a spiritual reality based on the Word of God alone was virtually abandoned; a fact which comments eloquently on much subsequent German history.

Just over twenty years ago a few Lutheran pastors bravely nailed a protest against Hitler's omnicompetent Reich on Luther's church-door at Wittenberg. It was the proper gesture, expressing as it did the fine witness of the Lutheran Confessional Church against Nazism. But might they not, with as much historical propriety, have laid their protest *at* his door? It is a nice question; and hard to answer simply. Luther was a very great man, the greatest figure in the Protestant tradition, a religious genius such as appears but rarely in the human story. But he failed to assert triumphantly the Crown Rights of the Redeemer in His Church; and it was just there that his great younger contemporary, John Calvin, succeeded. The Reformers knew little of religious toleration in the modern sense. They did not fight for the freedom of the

individual to think and worship as he pleased. They fought
for the freedom of Christ's Church from priestly and
secular tyranny. Yet it was Calvin rather than Luther who
inspired the revolt of the Reformation Church against the
Reformation State, and who taught Puritans, Covenanters,
Gueux and Huguenots to vindicate the Crown Rights of
Christ the King.

Calvin does not differ from Luther in essentials here. He
hesitates to admit any control by the State over the
spiritual life of man, and is a little self-excusing therefore
when he claims that the State should protect true religion
by watching over both tables of the Law. He affirms the
duty of the subject to obey his prince, since civil law presupposes that law of God which is its final sanction. Yet
the famous Epistle Dedicatory to King Francis, with
which Calvin's *Institutio* opens, clearly implies that the
divine right of kings is always qualified and limited by that
divine right to the obedience of men's souls which is
unlimited and final.[1] In the last issue we must always obey
God rather than men.

For this reason indeed, Calvin's thought about the State
strongly rejects those political theories of the Renaissance
which would have given a purely secular foundation to the
State, and to the right of the monarch. For Calvin, any
secular power which vies, so to speak, with God is guilty
of *lèse-majesté*, treason against Him who is the sole source of
all power. The right possessed by all worldly power is
always derivative: it is from God. The ruler is no more
than a steward, an official responsible to Him that sitteth
upon the throne. Indeed, though Calvin had no enthusiasm for popular sovereignty in the modern democratic

---

[1] Cf. Tertullian, 'deum non consulem timentes' (*Apol.* XLV). And Filmer,
'Cardinal Bellarmine and Mr Calvin both look asquint this way' (*Patriarcha*, I).

sense, he could attack monarchy with devastating acuteness
and power. In doing so he wrote as a prophet rather than
as a political theorist; the issue was one of religion and it
touched the deepest things by which he lived. He always
saw the king as, in some sense, the rival of God and he is
already prophetically aware that the Crown Rights of the
Redeemer will be challenged by the Divine Right of Kings.
In all Calvin's political thinking, therefore, the idea of
libertas played an increasingly decisive role. For him the
word had a twofold meaning. Primarily it meant the free
and sovereign lordship of God and the absolute validity of
his laws. But it also meant, inferentially and ultimately,
the solemn right and responsibility of the people to choose
by vote the bearer or instrument of that divine governance.[1]
Calvin affirms the sovereignty of the prince and the duty of
submission to him; but he always limits this duty by reference to the sovereign right of God over men's souls. He
is constantly thinking of the situation which might befall
French protestants if their king should refuse to allow free
course to the preaching and hearing of the Word. In such a
situation the individual believer would have no option but
to resist, albeit passively, and to risk martyrdom.

History provides two well-known and vivid illustrations
of this principle of passive resistance (which was enlarged
to include active resistance by Calvinist advocates of
tyrannicide in later decades).[2] The first is the sentence addressed by Beza to the King of Navarre after the massacre
of Vassy: 'Sire, it is in truth the lot of the Church of God
in whose name I speak, to suffer blows and not to return

[1] This comes out in Calvin's Sermons and Commentaries, and it includes
the magistracy.

[2] Here, again, Rome and Geneva—Jesuits and Calvinists—had a certain
kinship in their polar oppositeness. Mariana and Suarez match Hotman
and Buchanan in their advocacy and justification of tyrannicide.

them. Yet I also take leave to remind you that she is an anvil which has employed many hammers.' The second is equally memorable and more astonishing. Preaching in 1596 before James VI of Scotland, who was to become James I of England seven years later, Andrew Melville said: 'There are two kings and two kingdoms in Scotland; there is King James the head of the Commonwealth, and there is Christ Jesus the King of the Church, whose subject King James VI is, and of whose Kingdom he is not a king nor a lord nor a head; but a member.'

How does this historic issue appear to modern men? For the freemen of the evangelical tradition a state-church is, strictly speaking, a contradiction. The liberty which God's freemen claim is not a synonym for licence, an excuse for theological and ecclesiastical anarchy, but the freedom of Christ's Church from all alien control, notably that of the State. By asserting the Redeemer's Crown Rights, separatists in England, in the United States of America and elsewhere have carried a constitutive principle of the Reformation to its logical conclusion. In the United States, moreover, the dichotomy between Church and State is so explicit and thoroughgoing that the phrase 'a wall of separation' is sometimes used; it is a phrase which gives point to Lord Bryce's observation that 'of all the differences between the Old World and the New, the separation between Church and State is perhaps the most salient'. And it is now a matter for anxious discussion among discerning people in the United States that a judgement of the Supreme Court is even more explicit: 'We have staked the very existence of our country on the faith that complete separation between the State and religion is best for the State and best for religion.'

Thoughtful people are aware of an inescapable tension here, however. Free Churchmen (to use an English term) are not anarchists; that is, they are not opposed to the State as such. Like Burke, they emphasize the positive character and function of the State as the gift and the ordinance of God. They do not pretend, of course, that the distinction between the things that are Caesar's and the things that are Christ's is ever easy to draw. Indeed, the immemorial problem of Church and State is perhaps the supreme illustration of the tragic tension between the eternal and the temporal out of which man cannot escape. The fact is that the Reformers asked questions about freedom which have not ceased to be asked; we still fail to answer them effectively. And one such question, now urgent, is this: how is the freedom of the Christian man related to society? Protestantism asserted the sacred right of freedom in religion, as something higher than life itself. But Protestantism also had a new sense of the sacredness of civil society. As we have already noticed, its great doctrine of the Calling meant that *all* life was now recognized as, in some sense, sacred, and not only the monastic life of the cloister to which the word 'religious' had hitherto been confined. How, then, is man to reconcile these two sanctities—that of individual freedom, and that of the social order? Each has rights as well as duties. Indeed, the reconciliation of these two expressions of the sacred must always be the highest task of a freedom which would exalt not only the individual man but also his relationships. Civil society itself is, essentially, a religious order: this, too, is an aspect of God's grace.

The Reformers were not unaware of this. They had no illusions, of course, about the demonic character of the State and its institutions. But though necessarily tainted and corrupted with the original sin of which it is both the result and the expression, the State is nevertheless God's permitted remedy for sin; and as such it possesses a relative validity and sanctity. As a dyke against the flood of human lawlessness it is one of the effective signs of God's patience; it is his gracious gift to fallen man. The state-church principle was thus an attempt to embody the sacredness of the *whole* of life. It may not be arbitrarily dismissed as the abomination of desolation standing where it ought not— namely, erastianism.

Erastianism may be defined as the supremacy of the State in ecclesiastical causes. The term originated historically with the fact that one Thomas Erastus (1524–83), a German-Swiss theologian, wrote a treatise on excommunication in 1568, to show that any wrongdoing by Christians is the concern of the State, and should be punished by the State, and not by the clerical hierarchy in the courts of the Church. But erastianism has come to have the wider connotation of the control of religion itself by the State, the history of which we have been discussing in this chapter.

We ought to remember that this derogatory term may narrow our view of the sixteenth-century achievement unwarrantably. If there be some truth in the charge that the era of the Reformation witnessed the secularization of the Church, it is equally true that it witnessed the promotion of the State to its rightful place in the divine order. The very dangerous claim that a reigning sovereign is *eo ipso* the supreme head or governor of the Church, so far as the law of Christ allows, is not the only illustration of what was happening. The State begins to assume new responsibilities for the care of the poor, and for the fostering of learning. Civilians supersede canonists in the administration of law. Justices of the Peace sit as assessors with

Bishops to try offences against the Acts of Uniformity. Along with local priests they control the government of the local parish. Indeed, the rise of the new nationalism itself meant the subordination of private to public interests. It suppressed 'the overmighty subject'; it 'bridled stout noblemen'; it substituted for a corrupt and impotent jury-system the undoubted blessing (by comparison) of the Court of Star Chamber. It meant the end of the anarchy which had become an ignoble caricature of the feudal system: 'the oppressor's wrong, the proud man's contumely' which had ravaged fifteenth-century England with the Wars of the Roses, and fifteenth-century France with wars between Burgundians and Armagnacs.

The subordination of private to public interest. We should remember that the Church-State of Reformation England not only deprived 'criminous clerks' of the much abused 'benefit of clergy'; it also deprived the sturdy malefactor of that scandalous protection from justice which the livery of a great lord gave him throughout the fifteenth century.[1] In all this, the new State was vindicating nothing less than moral and even religious principles. It, too, was seeking to relate religion to life, even though its religious vision was often limited by worldly considerations, and its motives were sometimes dubious. In short, the rise of nationalism throughout Europe at the close of the Middle Ages may be rightly regarded as a victory of the unitary over the federalist conception of human society. Order, rather than disorder, was the watchword. The triumph of centralized government throughout the world

[1] See Plummer's edition of Fortescue's *Governance of England*, with its picture of the lawless power of the Duke of Suffolk, who made laws as the whim took him, brought low those whom he disliked and made great ones of his favourites (*qui leges pro suo arbitratu dixit...suppressit quos odivit et quos amavit erexit*).

of Western civilization was, in some sense, a moral triumph. Against the background of fifteenth-century disintegration and anarchy, it was 'totalitarianism' at its best.

And here a further contrast between Luther and Calvin emerges. Luther tended to consider the repression of evil as the sole function of the State. If he toyed with a more positive and constructive concept of the State and its mission in his earlier period—the ideal of a *Kulturstaat* fostered by the paternal power of the prince—the vision faded somewhat from 1526 onwards. Calvin, on the other hand, had a much loftier conception of what the State might be and do. According to him, even the most perfect society stands permanently in need of organization. Even in the Messianic Kingdom itself, there will be governance! Calvin is more willing, therefore, to maintain on the new evangelical basis of Protestantism the older permeation of the State by the Church which was a distinctive mark of medieval Catholicism. As we have noticed in an earlier chapter on the role of the Church in the world, Calvin's new presbyter will play as positive and active a role in the life of the State as did old priest.

Have modern men anything to learn from all this? We recognize of course that a merely national Christianity would not be Christianity. It would contradict itself. It would lack that catholicity which transcends narrower, albeit precious, loyalties because its character is absolute and universal. 'God is not an Englishman ten feet high': this was the quiet rebuke which an Indian mystic addressed to the bustling missionary who had not realized how prone we are to make God in our own image. 'You give us for Christ a sahib booted and spurred with fork and spoon from Birmingham.' This from a young Hindu. Grossly unfair as a generalization, it had enough truth in it, nevertheless, to explain why some forms of missionary enterprise have deserved their failure. To anyone who has been made aware of the light of the knowledge of the glory of God in the face of Jesus Christ, nationalism is not religion.

But, on the other hand, we men and women of this collectivist modern age have a new sense of the organic unity of human life and we are, perhaps, less sure than were our fathers of fifty years ago that Disestablishment would be an unmixed blessing. The events of our time which have intensified our traditional horror of erastianism have been a warning, too, against the frightful menace of the purely secular State, and of the national irreligion which it fosters.

The problem of Church and State is notoriously difficult, as all who are at all sensitive to its complexity will bear witness. It is probably insoluble here on earth where the redeemed of the Lord are still in the body, still subject to vanity and corruption. One thing is certain, however. The intrinsic difficulty of the problem is aggravated by our divisions. If the Church in which we believe *were* 'one, holy, catholic and apostolic', its formal recognition by the several States within Christendom as their national church would have all the advantages and few if any of the disadvantages of state establishments of religion. In the oecumenical movement the Protestant tradition now finds its greatest opportunity. The Sibylline books are offered to us. . . .

CHAPTER XIX

SECTARIAN DIVISION AND THE OECUMENICAL MOVEMENT

Now I beseech you, brethren, by the name of our Lord Jesus Christ, that ye all speak the same thing, and that there be no divisions among you; but that ye be perfectly joined together in the same mind and in the same judgment. For it hath been declared unto me of you, my brethren,...that there are contentions among you....Is Christ divided?   I COR. i. 10–13

The inner and essential unity of the Church lies in the fact that it is the body of Christ: this unity has been a reality from the beginning, and will be for ever. But it may be questioned whether this inner unity has ever been matched by any outward uniformity of doctrine, liturgy or organization....In our own day we are accustomed to the existence of many different Churches all claiming to be the true Church, and some of them claiming to be the only true Church. Along with many others I should take the view that most of those who make the former claim are probably right, and that all who make the latter are certainly wrong.   T. W. MANSON

THE history of the Christian religion begins indisputably on the note of unity; 'the multitude of them that believed were of one heart and of one soul' (Acts iv. 32). Even the mutual indwelling of Christ and the individual Christian (Gal. ii. 20) was more than a private spiritual experience; it was inseparable from the unity of individual believers with one another in the Church (John xvii. 20–1). Christian experience apart from Christian unity was as unthinkable for St Paul and St John as it was four centuries later for St Augustine, who argued that only in the unity of the Church can Christian charity be safeguarded, and that he who does not love that unity is a stranger to the love of God.[1]

[1] Cf. I Cor. i. 10; xii. 12–27; Rom. xii. 5; Eph. iv. 3–16; *C. Litt. Pet.* ii. 272; *De Bapt.* iii. 21.

But Christendom has long been sick of the palsy of disunion. Can she take up her bed and walk?

I. CHRISTIAN DISUNION AS OLD AS CHRISTIANITY

The oecumenical movement of the twentieth century is usually considered against the background of the Christian disunion which is so marked a feature of the Protestant tradition. This is both inevitable and fitting. But it is also fitting to remember that Christian disunion is not a failing peculiar to Protestantism; and that schism has not been the unenviable monopoly of a few sects. Christian disunion is almost as old as Christianity itself. From the moment when Paul 'withstood Peter to the face' (Gal. ii. 11) the ugly possibility of schism showed itself, and it soon became a reality at Corinth and elsewhere. The word translated as 'divisions' in I Cor. i. 10 is σχίσματα, schisms. The word is plural because there were four. And though those apostles and saints, Peter and Paul, managed to keep the unity of the Spirit in the bond of peace, their contemporaries and their successors down the centuries did not. The seamless robe early became a coat of many colours.

It is true that nearly two hundred years after Paul's friendly but firm exchanges with Peter and others, the Latin theologian Tertullian could write in his famous *Apology*: 'See how these Christians love one another', quoting this as the verdict of the pagan world. This is deeply moving and deservedly famous. But Tertullian was a barrister with something of the professional unscrupulousness of the brilliant advocate about him. He was 'a bonny fighter' if ever there was one. His controversial attacks on his fellow Christians reveal a power of abuse

314

which has rarely been surpassed. The venom of his attack on the evangelical heretic Marcion illustrates the *odium theologicum* which was already abroad in Christendom, and anticipates the hatred of Catholic bishops for one another during the christological battles of the fourth and fifth centuries, and of Protestant theologians for one another during the eucharistic controversies of the sixteenth. Indeed, it is ironical that the great Tertullian himself became a heretic in a later phase of his stormy career; he himself encouraged disunion by joining the Montanists. And in his final phase he quarrelled with and left them, setting up, if St Augustine may be believed (*de haeresibus*, LXXXVI), as a 'Tertullianist'. That is, he became, like Ephraim of old, 'a wild ass alone by himself'; so that his rhetorical flourish about the unity and mutual love of Catholic Christians was no more supported by contemporary evidence than we were when we last sang with our customary gusto

> We are not divided,
> All one Body we;
> One in hope and doctrine,
> One in charity.

Strifes, divisions, heresy-charges, schisms, excommunications, exilings, crusades against 'heretics' or 'schismatics', reformations without tarrying for any, wholesale massacre, the axe, the rack, the stake—all this has been the recurrent feature of a story which has been glorious and wonderful in other respects.

The disunion of the great sees of the near East in the fifth century—Alexandria, Antioch and Constantinople—drove from the Orthodox Church the majority of Christian Syrians, Copts, Ethiopians, Persians and Armenians: and these Nestorian and Monophysite schisms helped to ensure the ultimate triumph of Islam. The relations of these great episcopal sees with one another and with Rome were largely those of jealous rivalry for prestige, power and primacy. It is the familiar human story of power politics rather than of oecumenical unity. From the fifth century onwards the Bishop of Rome begins to claim jurisdiction over all other Churches. Already in 378 Damasus claims control over Illyricum, appointing the Bishop of Thessalonica as his 'vicar'. At the General Council of 381 primacy in the East is awarded to Constantinople however, and at Chalcedon in 451 the famous twenty-eighth canon pronounces Rome and Constantinople equal (τὰ ἴσα πρεσβεῖα). But Rome affected to treat the canon as invalid, and the East blandly ignored the absence of Leo's signature.[1] And here we cannot help adding that the occasional manipulation of the official documentary decisions of these General Councils—through additions, omissions or forgery—is a strange comment on the doctrine that the deliberations and decisions of the holy fathers were the work of the Holy Ghost.

The rivalry between the Eastern and Western branches of Christendom continued, each claiming (presumably) to illustrate and embody what Cardinal Manning was to call 'the temporal mission of the Holy Ghost'. The final break came in 1054, ostensibly over unleavened bread, clerical marriage and clerical beards, but in fact because the oldest sees in Christendom still declined to admit the claim of the Bishop of Rome to exercise a controlling jurisdiction over them. In that year Leo IX excommunicated Caerularius of Constantinople, 'wrongly called a Patriarch' (*abusive dictum patriarchum*),[2] and the long-standing rivalry became

---

[1] The protest of Leo I is found in *Ep.* 104 *ad Marcianum Augustum*.

[2] The Bull refers more than once to this unforgiveable offence: *se adhuc scribit oecumenicum patriarcham*. The Bishop of Rome could bear no rival near the throne.

a disastrous and permanent division. And what Eastern Christians had done in the eleventh century, Western Christians were to do in the sixteenth. The ancient Roman desire to rule had thus provoked two huge breaches in the unity of the One Body. And just as Eastern Orthodox Christendom, which thus vindicated its right to be itself, had itself been divided over orthodox doctrine and rent by schism, so too Protestant Christendom, though successful in throwing off the yoke of Rome, did not avoid its own further divisions and subdivisions. In short, Christian disunion has been a dominant fact of Christian experience for nineteen centuries: it did not begin with Protestantism.

2. THE OECUMENICAL VISION OF THE TWENTIETH CENTURY

In this twentieth century the tide seems to have turned. Christians who have long been divided confessionally or denominationally are coming together. The twentieth century has witnessed a reaction against such Christian disunion in Canada, in Scotland, in South India, in China, in English Methodism. Further, the International Missionary Council and now the World Council of Churches are illustrations and effective vehicles of this movement towards oecumenical unity. Some have rashly hailed the oecumenical movement as the great new Christian fact of our time: and though this enthusiastic judgement is a little facile and may prove to be premature, there seem to be at least three main reasons which justify our taking it seriously.

The first is theological. In our day we have become newly aware of the indisputable oneness of the Church of Christ. If one thing is clear from modern theological work in different communions and in many countries, it is that 'the governing idea in the New Testament is that of the Church, a unique society, constituted by the act of God in history'.[1] The distinctive feature of biblical religion, in contrast to platonizing philosophies of redemption, is that God is known for what he is by what he has done and does in historic time. The Scriptures praise him for his mighty *acts*. The Gospel proclaims something given and done objectively in history; the redemptive action of the living God.

To what end? The answer of the whole Bible is that the living God has acted decisively, and with a proleptic assurance of final victory and glory, in order to make for himself a people—the People of God. In witness to this the Scriptures point to the divine process of redemption at work: the deliverance of God's people from bondage, of which the Exodus is one effective sign and the return from exile in Babylon another: further, a covenant-relationship with them, of which Sinai is the prototype; a covenant so close and inescapable that it is expressed in terms of relationships which are integral to our very existence as men, and are no artificial or temporary constructions of human caprice. The covenant relation at Sinai means what it comes to mean; namely that Israel, the people of God, is bound to God as a son is to his father, as wife is to husband, or as a nation is to its king. Such relationships are permanent and indissoluble; and God's covenant with his people (ultimately with *all* people—the Israel of God being meaningless unless it is universal) is so described because it cannot fail. This Covenant is no pagan bargain which man proposes to make with God; it is the result of the gracious and unceasing initiative whereby the Holy

[1] C. H. Dodd.

One will redeem his people Israel. Though man's rebellious estrangement from the God who made him is the meaning and result of sin; and though sinful human history is in one sense, separate from him who is of purer eyes than to behold iniquity—man and his history are nevertheless inseparable from God's sovereign providence and grace. He is Judge and Redeemer.

The prophets, who knew that human history is the workshop of the divine action, and who saw the results of man's sinful pride working themselves out as the wrath of God which is revealed against all unrighteousness, also knew the yearning love of God in his covenanted promises, and looked for the day of the Lord which should be light and not darkness. But they never announced that this day had dawned; their present experience of a redemptive process at work in their world always pointed beyond itself: it awaited its consummation in the fullness of time.

The scriptures bear witness, therefore, to an Event which brings this *praeparatio evangelica* to its decisive climax, making all things new for ever. That Event is Jesus Christ, the Incarnate Word of God, crucified and risen from the dead. The Old Testament cannot satisfy us, since we have seen something which its prophets and kings desired in vain to see, as they waited for the consolation of Israel. We look back to that day of the Lord to which the prophets were always looking forward; when out of the very depths of a human situation where sin was judged with absolute finality, the redeeming love of God was made manifest, with power and great glory.

In Christ the kingdom of God becomes a reality on earth. The covenant between God and man is at last perfectly realized, not as an abstract ideal but as a concrete fact; not as glory to be revealed at the end of the ages but as the powers of the age to come manifested in an actual human life, which bodies forth all that human life is meant to be according to the purpose of God. Here the Word of God is incarnate; speaking about eternity by confronting men with it; convicting men of sin by being its spotless mirror; overthrowing the powers of darkness by entering of set purpose into their power; bringing life and immortality to light by tasting death for every man.

Thus, the more we appeal to the New Testament in justification of historic Protestantism, the less can we escape from the New Testament concept of the Church. Those who appeal to Caesar must accept his verdict. Modern biblical theology is not without its wilder vagaries and fantasies, but it is driving us back to the concept of the Church as integral to the Gospel of our redemption. Modern Protestantism is at last rediscovering that the doctrine of the Church—interest in which is again widespread—is no theological 'extra', a luxury for those who have a taste for ecclesiastical needlework, gothic architecture or the minutiae of liturgical tradition; and which may therefore be safely left to art specialists, monks and pious ladies. We are rediscovering a theological truth of the utmost practical significance when we reaffirm with Roman and Genevan, with Jesuit and Covenanter, with Greek Orthodox and Methodist—that so far from the Church's being a decorative appendage to Christianity, the Church *is* Christianity; and that the faith without community, the fellowship of the One Body, would be a contradiction in terms. Hence, the position in which the Church finds itself today compels Christians to think again about Christian unity. The Church is again in the forefront of dogmatic interest, and the oecumenical movement is one inevitable result of this.

The second reason became clear and cogent on the mission-field where traditional sectarian differences are often meaningless and irrelevant. As a shrewd Indian proverb puts it—'the enmity between first cousins is the hardest to eradicate'. Some of us first heard this proverb from the lips of Azariah, Bishop of Dornakal, at the Edinburgh conference of August 1937, when he was making an impassioned appeal for Christian unity. Delegates from Christian Churches throughout the world, except the Roman, were listening to him; none of them could have listened unmoved. His speech was one more reminder that the divisions of the older Churches in Christendom are not a domestic affair peculiar to the West: they perpetuate themselves with tragic irrelevance in India and on the North China plain; in Africa and the islands of the Pacific. Like old wounds which refuse to heal, they poison every part of the Body of Christ. Ideally, of course, schism cannot be justified: it breaks the visible unity of the One Body: it is one of the evils between which Christian men have sometimes felt compelled to make their tragic choice in this fallen world-order. But schism innocently adopted by the young, indigenous Churches of the East lacks even that dubious pragmatic justification at the bar of history. It is imported, alien and artificial. It does not spring out of the dissidences of a past which Western memories cannot forget and which Western consciences may not belittle. The divisions between, say, Methodists and Anglicans, Presbyterians and Baptists, in China or Syria or Madagascar, may not be merely 'unhappy': if they are casually taken for granted as a natural and permanent feature of world Christianity, they are inherently blasphemous.

Bishop Azariah urged, therefore, that a great campaign of education had to be undertaken in the older Churches of Christendom (how right he was!), if union schemes were to come to anything. The poignant climax of his appeal was unforgettable: 'the problem is one of life and death to us; do not give your aid to keep us separated.' It was the Man from Macedonia (Acts xvi. 9) in a new and ironic role. 'Come over and help us. Do not hinder us by your help.'

The next oecumenical conference of the Christian Churches met at Tambaram, Madras, not many months after Edinburgh. Western delegates to that conference reported one unforgettable experience there; the almost monotonous persistence with which delegates from the younger Churches repudiated denominationalism and demanded Church unity. They reminded delegates from Europe and the United States of America that in communities where there is always the dead weight of millions of non-Christians, the traditional sectarian divisions of Christian history may mean nothing less than disaster.

In short, the missionary problems created by the divisions among Christians are real and ineluctable. At every point, it is alleged, these divisions blunt the appeal of the Gospel, especially to the adherents of other religious faiths. Christian witness cannot be impressive, and Christian evangelism cannot be truly effective, unless Christians act unitedly. Indeed, it is universally recognized that 'the modern movement of Christian missions has been at almost every point the direct progenitor of the contemporary movement for Christian unity' (H. P. Van Dusen).

The third reason, closely bound up with the second, is strategic and practical. Can evangelism by divided forces be effective against the gigantic secular forces of the modern world? When Bishop Azariah described the

Church in India as face to face with giant non-Christian forces, he might have been making a prophetic comment on our own immediate situation. For we see the Christian Church everywhere fighting for its very life against secularism, if not downright paganism; and losing ground. If this should be interpreted merely as a *cri de cœur* from one of Protestantism's 'unhappy' divisions, it is worth recalling that in 1951 a French archbishop was reported as saying that no more than four million souls have any connexion with the Catholic Church in his country. He may have been incorrectly or inadequately reported, but one suspects that corresponding statistics for other parts of Europe and for Great Britain would not be very different. And even thronged churches and religious gatherings in the United States and Canada do not blind discerning people there to the same secularist trend.

The Christian tradition itself is being gravely menaced in at least two ways: it is being undermined by the secular humanism which assumes that modern man may retain Christian values without troubling to confess and practice the Christian faith: it is also being subtly undermined by the heresy, widespread in the English-speaking world, which virtually makes the institutions and assumptions of democracy into a religious faith, or into a substitute for religious faith. But, like patriotism, democracy is not enough. It is certainly not a self-sufficient philosophy of life.[1] And it has nothing at all to say about death; no political philosophy has or can have. Any word about the mystery of our mortality must come by 'revelation'. It must be 'from the beyond', and be received by faith. Further, any relevant word about the most urgent issue of our time, man's estrangement from his fellow-man, must

[1] See p. 14 above, and note.

be a transcendent word of judgement and reconciliation—
that redemptive forgiveness which will reconcile man to his
brother because it has first reconciled him to God. Man's
deep and enduring need is a Gospel, from God Himself.

But—and this is the urgent question for divided Christians here—'how can we persuade an incredulous world
that we have the secret of that unity which overleaps all
barriers of religious or cultural inheritance, of economic
status or of sex itself, so that we become one man in Christ
Jesus, if we present to that world the appearance of com-
peting sects?' That is Archbishop William Temple.[1] He
constantly reminded us that as there is but one Head of the
Church, so there is and can be but one Body. Our divisions
do not destroy the indestructible fact of its oneness. We
have, therefore, to manifest the existing oneness of the
people of God. This truth has been powerfully and acutely
expounded in Professor T. W. Manson's important book
The Church's Ministry. The message to the Churches of the
World from the recent oecumenical conference at Lund
reminds us, further, that the depth and pain of our divisions have to be measured by this our existing unity in the
headship of Christ, which is real, fundamental and inescapable. The message proceeds to ask whether we are
showing sufficient eagerness to enter into conversations
with churches other than our own, and whether we should
not act together in all matters except those in which deep
differences of conviction compel us still to act separately.
For our present-day interest in reunion, so fashionable in
certain limited circles, so well-intentioned and leisurely,
seems almost blind to the urgency of the whole situation.
We underestimate and even ignore the growing secularism,

[1] In his Presidential Address to the Upper and Lower Houses of the
Convocation of Canterbury, 25 May 1943.

already referred to, in traditionally Christian countries. The widespread decay of the classic faith of Christendom is a revolutionary modern phenomenon, the scope and implication of which we cannot yet measure, but which is probably without parallel in the Christian history of the past ten centuries. It is handwriting on the wall such as Christendom has not seen for a very long time past, and it raises issues which are uniquely urgent. If this be disputed on the ground that the forces of open secularism are still relatively insignificant, we may reflect that the open enemies of Christ are perhaps less dangerous than the nominal Christianity of the indifferent multitudes, that discreet, respectable and private godlessness which betrays Christ by ignoring him and which, though it does not openly deny the Faith, can hardly be said to profess it. But serious and informed people will not take very seriously the contention, often glibly made, that the differences of religious and theological principle presupposed by our Christian divisions are relatively insignificant when compared with the differences between our common faith and a blatant irreligion which menaces it. This glib 'liberalism' betrays a frivolous attitude to what religious faith really is in the full dimension of its passion and commitment.

Indeed, this seeming enlightenment which would tolerate conflicting beliefs indiscriminately, so long as we all remain 'Christian', is not only muddle-headed; it masks the indifference which Pope Gregory XVI rightly branded as poisonous.[1] And it carries its own warning. We shall not solve the urgent problem of Christian disunion with any easy repudiation of the particular ecclesiastical loyalties by which we live. It should be no part of oecumenical tactics to contend that our traditional

[1] See above, p. 237.

325

differences are ultimately unimportant and meaningless. Our fathers risked the evil of schism for something more than a shibboleth: and it is for something more than unimportant details that we perpetuate it, whether we be of Rome or Constantinople, of Canterbury or Geneva. It is one thing to say that the shocking divisiveness of modern Christendom is artificial or stupid, and to add that it has no modern justification other than that of custom and tradition. Such sentimentality must speak for itself. But it is quite another thing to belittle classic controversies over great and abiding issues of principle, wherein men and women 'resisted unto blood', and to say that they were trifling and indefensible. Our real problems are rooted in history, and they will not be solved by flippancy.

Here the common experience of delegates to the great conferences held during this century at Edinburgh, Jerusalem, Stockholm, Madras, Amsterdam and Evanston, is instructive. Those delegates received a deep and rich experience of the Church Universal; a new understanding of catholicity. But it grew out of the concrete and particular church-loyalty in which each Christian man and woman there was rooted. Just as universals are necessarily given to us in terms of particulars, so the Church Universal is mediated through the tradition, the local habitation and the name, which we know and understand and love. It may be no more (and no less) than St Michael's or Zion or the Holy Innocents at the corner of the street, but it is nevertheless the place where God himself has made the place of his feet glorious. The *undenominational* Church, which Principal William Robinson has described as the most dreaded enemy of Christianity, and offspring of the 'Protestant underworld',[1] is like the undenominational

[1] *The Shattered Cross* (Berean Press, 1945), p. 7.

teaching of religion: obviously undesirable, it is, in effect, impossible; and because that which attaches a man to no denomination detaches him from all, the undenominational church ends by fading away or by adding a new denomination to the denominationalism which it loftily repudiates.

'When I mention religion', said the parson in *Tom Jones*, 'I mean the Christian Religion; and not only the Christian Religion but the Protestant Religion; and not only the Protestant Religion but the Church of England.' Whatever we may think of its defects, Parson Thwackum's famous pronouncement has several merits. Whatever we may think of his conclusion, and of the almost truculent confidence with which he reaches it, we cannot mistake his meaning. Plainly enough, here is no anxious appeal for ambiguity, no peculiar and private piety, certainly no hesitating agnosticism. The man is not advocating a vague and inoffensive religiosity to suit all tastes; indeed, he is not advocating anything, but pointing to something definite which he himself knows, and which has all the concreteness of history in it. As a Christian he has received something; he shares in something given, something handed down to believing multitudes and to himself across the tragedy and corruption of the human centuries. His bigotry may be indefensible, but his stand for objective fact is not. He will have nothing to do with the easy suggestion that all religions are but aspects of one and the same religion. And he is right. For such a contention is palpably false to historical and evangelical fact.

Granted that it is only the great vision of the Church Universal—One, Holy, and Apostolic—which tests and deepens such denominational loyalties; still, the complementary truth may not be forgotten, that the great whole is made up of these several parts. Thwackum was not wrong, therefore, in what he asserted; such a man is usually wrong in his denials; and this dual aspect of our religious loyalties is the measure of the tough difficulties which lie ahead of the oecumenical movement. Perhaps the desired synthesis may be reached only in terms of thesis and antithesis, set out by John Henry Newman and Oliver Cromwell respectively. 'Depend upon it', said Newman, 'the strength of any party lies in its loyalty to its first principles.' Said Cromwell to the Presbyterians of Scotland: 'I beseech you in the bowels of Christ, think it possible you may be mistaken.' The problem will be worthily and effectively solved only in terms of that polarity. That is, if the different denominations have had, as they cannot but believe, an historic meaning within the purpose of God, they must consciously rediscover and reaffirm it, not in order to standardize and perpetuate their past, but in order to learn in humility how that past may contribute to the rediscovered unity of the One Body. It is all very well to say that the fundamental unity of Christians is their unity in Christ. That is too obvious and general a truth (God forgive us) to be of much value in solving our very concrete problem. The formula is too general. There will be almost as many interpretations of it as there are individuals making their appeal to it.

Here we are at the old impasse. The crucial issue at every oecumenical conference is the nature of the Christian Church.

3. ECCLESIOLOGY AND CHRISTOLOGY

Since the momentous missionary conference met at Edinburgh in 1910 under the presidency of Bishop Brent, great oecumenical conferences have been meeting at intervals. But they seem to have been shy, as yet, of raising that fundamental issue which the oecumenical movement has to face if it is to get anywhere: namely, the nature of the Christian Church. There have been permanently valuable discussions of 'faith and order', and of 'life and work'. There have been friendly and frank exchanges over those traditionally divisive issues, the Ministry and the Sacraments. But sooner or later Christians at present divided will have to reach an agreed doctrine of the Church if they are to throw down their confessional boundaries and to become corporately united. Is there reasonable hope that a Christendom in earnest about reunion would be able to do this? If so, further difficulties—notably the very real issue between those for whom the episcopate is of the *esse* of the Church, and those for whom it is not—should not be insuperable.

Informed Christians are aware that this ecclesiological problem is closely bound up with the christological. As the Body of Christ, the Church is the extension of the Incarnation. Indeed, doctrines of the Church, its Sacraments and its Ministry may be classified in an illuminating way along lines which recall the christological debates of Christian history. What do those debates mean, and how can they help us?

The central theological issue, which we can neither evade nor ignore nor solve, is the abiding issue of Christology. Sin being what it is—our rebellious alienation from God—either our redemption must come from God or we must remain unredeemed. But it is historic, experienced fact that our redemption *has* come through a Man: Jesus Christ and him crucified. In Luther's words: 'this Man is God; this God is Man.'[1] Thus the distinctive genius of Christian theology is disclosed in a seeming contradiction; a rationally impossible combination of deity and humanity in one Person. In the action and passion of this Person deity calls saying: 'Come unto Me all ye that labour and are heavy laden...and ye shall find rest unto your souls.' And in the action and passion of this same Person humanity answers saying: 'Lo I come; in the volume of the book it is written of me, to do thy will, O God.' To put this seeming contradiction in another way: in Phil. ii. 5–11 St Paul, a Hebrew of the Hebrews who has become a Christian, strains Hebraic monotheism almost to the breaking-point as he puts Christ on an equality with God and worships him: and in the word *God-Man* which he has newly coined out of the crucible of experience Origen, the Christian Platonist philosopher who has become a great biblical scholar, strains to the breaking-point the fundamental axiom of Hellenism; namely, that the divine and the human are necessarily and eternally disparate.

In short, here we see Hebraism and Hellenism modifying their respective ways of understanding God and Man, in the light of what God has done in the Man, Christ Jesus. This theological modification was a long and painful process, dominating the first five centuries of the Christian era. At Nicaea the Church proclaimed that the Son, who took flesh and became man, was eternally consubstantial with the Father. At Chalcedon it proclaimed the mode of that Incarnation: the eternal Son, the second person of the

[1] *WA*, VI, 512.

Trinity, took man's 'nature' upon himself in Jesus Christ: two natures, not two individuals, were and are conjoined in the one person, the properties of each being preserved in the union, and the human nature being impersonal. This Two-Natures Christology is the definitive and orthodox Christology of the Church catholic, the *specifica differentia* of the historic faith.

But what are we to think of Christology? Is it the vain attempt to apprehend reflectively that which necessarily transcends all reflective apprehension? If so, we shall agree with the oft-quoted sentence in the first edition of a famous Reformation treatise,[1] that the knowledge of Christ is not to be equated with christological speculation. Indeed, we may boldly adapt Matt. xvi. 17, saying: 'Blessed art thou, Philip Melanchthon, for Nicaea and Chalcedon did not reveal it unto thee, but the Father which is in heaven.' Melanchthon knew that saving knowledge of the Redeemer is revealed only to faith, and that such faith is *fiducia* before it is *assensus*: it is commitment and trust and devotion to him that loved us, rather than the recitation of the correct Chalcedonian (or Leontian) formula about him.

Yet the christological problem is always with us and it will not be ignored; some men have to serve God with the mind, even here. As Melanchthon became older therefore (or, as the cloven hoof of Protestant scholasticism began to show itself beneath his preacher's gown) he quietly withdrew the famous sentence from later editions of the *Loci*. We may surely regret that he did, for we cannot have too much of such evangelical testimony. Indeed, we may treasure the refreshing story of the divine at the oecumenical

---

[1] 'To know Christ is not to speculate about the mode of his incarnation, but to know his saving benefits' (*Loci communes* of 1521; the Introduction).

conference on faith and order at Edinburgh who atten-
ded a session devoted to the classic faith of Christendom,
where Brunner was arguing with the impenitent liberals
and the Eastern Orthodox were being annoyed by the
controversial methods of the (late) Bishop of Gloucester.
On emerging from the session our brother was heard to say
to a fellow-delegate: 'What *is* this Nicene Creed? I'd like
to see a copy.'

That story will be refreshing to any students of patristic
theology, who have spent time and strength on the savage
logomachies, the dreary, hair-splitting, christological
battles of the fourth and fifth centuries, and have come
near to that mood of exasperation which would dismiss the
whole matter as a clutter of mythological verbiage. Look,
for example, at the issue between the traditions of Alexandria and Antioch in the drafting committee during that
final week at Chalcedon,—'of two natures' (ἐκ δύο φύσεων)
or 'in two natures' (ἐν δύο φύσεσιν). Is the man whose
Christian faith and life are deeply rooted in the Scriptures
to be blamed for finding such abstract metaphysical
terminology as irrelevant as it is artificial?

Certainly not, so long as he and we remember the great
technical achievement of the Cappadocian, Antiochene
and Alexandrian fathers as they grappled with the
inescapable christological paradox in terms of the only
intellectual categories available to them. Are our own
categories any better? Are they any more successful in
compassing that ineffable mystery of Christ's person which
is implied and confessed by the Gospels and the Epistles?
The subtle definitions of the fathers, so far from being
irrelevant, are highly instructive: as dogmatic apprehensions of evangelical truth they belong to the data historically transmitted to us across the centuries and the conti-

nents. The important thing to establish is that they are not necessary to salvation. To say, as the *Quicunque* does, that unless we confess its orthodoxy we shall perish everlastingly, is error far greater than any truth which its brilliant paradoxes conserve. The most meticulous confession of orthodoxy can be the height of religious unbelief; and if ever it be used to unchurch those who are content to believe simply in Christ and Him crucified, it becomes perilously akin to the sin against the Holy Ghost.

But these symbols given to the world at Nicaea and Chalcedon may well play a relevant and necessary role in the movement towards reunion. The very paradox which they embody is a public announcement (στηλογραφία)[1] by means of which subsequent heretical aberrations may be automatically, so to speak, detected and judged. And, as a paradox is a unity of opposites, all aberrations here have always been attempts to dissolve the paradox in the interest of one or other of its two 'opposites'; they have aimed at the virtual elimination of one or other of the two 'natures'.

Let us assume this Two-Natures Christology, against which damaging criticisms have been brought during the last hundred years, if only to understand better the heretical aberrations from it. And let us assume (as we must, since we are not Nestorians) that Christ was not two personalities, but one. Where, then, was the seat or form of the one personality? In which 'nature'? This was and is the crucial question. The answer of orthodox Christology was: 'in his divine or logos nature.' But how, then, could he be verily and completely human (*perfectus homo*)? How could his experience be like ours, as the Epistle to the Hebrews (iv. 15; ii. 17–18) insists that it was? How could his victory over sin be the pledge of like victory for us

---

[1] στηλογραφιά κατὰ πάσης αἱρεσέως (Athanasius, *Ad Afros*, xi).

through him? This is the intractable difficulty which attaches to the genius and structure of patristic orthodoxy. Its thought carefully confesses an incarnate Word in two natures, but too often its aberrant working assumption is One Divine Nature which absorbs and virtually eliminates what is vitally distinctive of human nature. Greek theology is often criticized as being *at heart* monophysite (i.e. having one 'nature') in spite of its formal repudiation of Apollinarian and monophysite heresies; and if the Logos was the seat of personality in the man Jesus, the criticism can hardly be avoided.

The history of doctrine illustrates the difficulty. For all his brilliant subtlety, Cyril of Alexandria betrays his real inclination when he explains the limitation of our Lord's knowledge, as recorded in the Gospels. In Mark xiii. 32 Jesus disclaims knowledge of the time of his coming again: 'of that day and that hour knoweth no man, no, not the angels which are in heaven, neither the Son, but the Father'. Cyril, like all the Greeks, is embarrassed by this: at any rate he explains it away by saying that Christ pretends not to know for the benefit of his hearers, in accordance with his manhood.[1] Before 428, at any rate, Cyril's christology sails as close to the cliffs of Docetism (i.e. the teaching that the humanity of Jesus is apparent rather than real) as it could possibly do without becoming completely shipwrecked on the docetist rocks.

If this is the way in which the Two-Natures Christology tends to work out in the Greek East, what of the Latin West? Is there any real difference of emphasis in the West,

---

[1] σκήπτεται χρησίμως τὸ μὴ εἰδέναι καθ' ὁ ἄνθρωπος (*Adv. Anthrop.* xiv). See also Dr W. Telfer's review of Prof. J. Liébaert's 'La doctrine christologique de S. Cyrille d'Alexandrie avant la querelle nestorienne' (*J.T.S.* Oct. 1952). 'What is remarkable is Cyril's complete disregard for the dangers of Apollinarianism.'

as is often alleged? It is true that though the West, like the East, accepts the Chalcedonian doctrine of an impersonal human nature, the underlying tendency of Latin Christology as influenced by St Augustine is to recognize a real and unambiguously complete personality in the man Christ Jesus. Yet it is sometimes forgotten that even St Augustine's famous phrase *homo dominicus* ('the Man who is Lord') may not be taken quite at its face value since its author later retracted it. Further, there is that notorious tenth chapter of the *De Trinitate*, written by the Western father St Hilary of Poitiers, which explains that the hunger, thirst, weariness, pain and ignorance of future events undoubtedly ascribed to Christ in the Gospel story, were not real for Him in the way that they are for us. Hilary is like Cyril in saying that such statements represented concessions, not to His necessities but to our habits. But why does Hilary go out of his way to say anything so perversely contrary to the plain evidence of the Gospels? The answer seems to be that he is obsessed with the truth that God is impassible; that the Divine as such cannot suffer. And as it was the eternal Logos of God who became the controlling and formative agency, the acting Subject, for the Two Natures in Christ (the human nature being impersonal), Hilary is piously reluctant to allow the Redeemer's humanity to be really subject to our human limitations. Speaking of Gethsemane and the Cross, Hilary actually says that Christ could not *fear* death, since his purpose was to die only for a moment. But human emotions such as fear are very largely due to limited knowledge; in any case, such limitation is of the very essence of manhood, and the Gospel record plainly attributes it to Christ. The Incarnation would be unreal on any other terms. Nevertheless, from its very presuppositions

335

classic Christology, especially in the eastern orthodox world, was unable to face such facts. The desperate expedients of a Hilary in the West or of a Cyril in the East to evade the full psychological realism of the Gospel story reduce to absurdity the philosophical assumptions which led to those expedients. The difficulty was inherent and inevitable since the fundamental presupposition of all Greek theology was not the dynamic, biblical conception of God as Spirit but the abstract philosophical conception of God as Absolute Being, and of human nature as radically un-divine. Christology is thus almost given over to unreality; for that is what docetism means.

Just as this is a real issue for the Latin West as well as for the Greek East, it is also real for Protestantism. Anyone familiar with Luther's eucharistic theology knows how close the Reformer's christology is to that of Alexandria. The christology of the Lutheran Church strongly emphasizes the *majesty* of Christ's humanity: the Reformed confessions, on the other hand, are closer to Antioch in emphasizing its *reality*.[1] The issue between Brenz and Cheminitz in the sixteenth century was the issue between Thomasius and Dorner in the nineteenth. And in our day Brunner actually argues in *The Mediator* that Jesus Christ could not have had a human personality because human personality as such is necessarily sinful.

In short, Apollinarianism (and its variants) was officially condemned after its well-meaning author had done the Church the service of blurting it out and making its

---

[1] See H. J. Schoeps, *Von himmlischen Fleisch Christi* (reviewed by Prof. T. W. Manson, *J.T.S.* Oct. 1952). The notion, not uncommon in the Greek East of the fourth and fifth centuries, that the flesh of Christ was heavenly and uncreated (cf. the thought of some Apollinarians, and Eutyches) reappears in the 'Spirituals' and 'Anabaptists' who were Luther's contemporaries (Schwenckfeld, Hoffmann, Menno Simons, for example).

implicit heresy explicit; nevertheless it has had wide-spread ramifications throughout Christian history. It has been the characteristic heresy of an over-zealous orthodoxy. The truth of the mystery of the Incarnation is as much undermined by pious and unscriptural heresies which would destroy Christ's humanity as by the equally un-scriptural heresies which would destroy His divinity.

This brings us to the second main distortion of the christological paradox; but it is so familiar that it needs little description. The Ebionites did for this heresy what Apollinaris did for the other. They seem to have been a very early group of Christians whose real affinities were with Judaism rather than with Christianity, and for whom Jesus Christ, albeit miraculously born, was unambiguously and exclusively human. On its presuppositions, this group obviously needed and had no christology. It has never been typical of Christendom as a whole, of course. But, again, it did blurt out and make explicit something which very many modern men have implicitly accepted as the truth about Jesus Christ, even though they have not worn socinian or unitarian labels. For large numbers of Christians of all confessions in the modern world the acceptance of the classic christological paradox—the confession of the divine as well as the human 'natures' in Christ—has been a formality rather than a conviction; it has been nominal rather than real. Indeed, this 'humanitarian' christology, along with its correlative, an exemplarist soteriology, has been widespread throughout Europe and the English-speaking world for well over a century.

There, then, are three main christological positions or attitudes, two of which have been more widely adopted by Christian people than we may like to admit: the orthodox, the monophysite and the ebionite: or, to use a useful though improper analogy—centre, right and left. What bearing have these types of christology on ecclesiology? How do they correspond to those different doctrines of the Church which it will be the task of the oecumenical movement to reconcile or resolve if it is to come to anything effective?

Monophysite conceptions of the Church regard it as a purely divine society[1] with a priesthood making the most exalted pretensions, exercising enormous powers and administering miraculous means of grace.

At the other extreme from the central or classic position is the 'ebionite' view of the Church, which virtually eliminates the dimension of the supernatural and the eternal from much of its ongoing life, and reduces its worship to the matter-of-fact level of a public meeting. It is almost a purely human society, providing religious services for those who want them and suitable social amenities for fostering fellowship among its members. On this view there is little essential difference between many a flourishing Community Church, Central Hall or 'Institutional Church', and the admirable and useful Y.M.C.A. in the next street.

But neither of these ecclesiological 'aberrations' are truly Christian, even though one might prefer the first to the second for its sense of the supernatural and for the depth and richness of its sacramental life: and the second to the first for the warmth of its human fellowship and its precious vindication of the simplicities of the gospel which sacramental and sacerdotal solemnities have been known to obscure.

The central, classic or orthodox view—already discernible in the Epistle to the Ephesians—is genuinely sacra-

---

[1] See above, pp. 169–70, 185, 196–7.

mental. It regards the Church as both divine and human. As a wonderful and sacred mystery, it is a Body animated by the divine life of the risen Redeemer and finding in the Word and the Sacraments the organs of his life-giving Spirit: but it is none the less a human society, made up of sinful and fallible people such as ourselves, the earthen vessel by means of which the treasure of Christ's grace is manifested and mediated to the world. It is this double aspect of the Church—divine and human, invisible and visible, universal and particular, heavenly and earthly—which makes it the extension of the Incarnation in time, and the fundamental sacrament.

The fundamental sacrament. What is a sacrament? The Catechism included in the Book of Common Prayer has given to the English-speaking world a classic definition: 'an outward and visible sign of an inward and spiritual grace'. The sign is no *mere* sign, of course; it conveys what it signifies and, *in some sense*, it *is* what it signifies. The very words 'in some sense' illustrate the limitation and inadequacy of words; for 'in some sense' means 'in the sacramental sense', where words are transcended. The sign (*signum*) does what words fail to do; it is a *signum efficax*, a symbol which makes the reality signified effectively real. What is the relation, then, between *signum* and *res*? To equate them, or to make then synonymous would be to 'overthrow the nature of a sacrament': and this is the dangerous tendency in all forms of monophysitism.

Three such tendencies disclose themselves within Catholicism itself. In answering the question which is crucial for the oecumenical movement—namely, how is divine grace mediated to us men?—Catholicism is reluctant to allow that the treasure of redeeming grace is given to us in really earthen vessels. The outward and visible—the human, finite and fallible—vehicles of that grace must be somehow transmuted or transsubstantiated. Even the orthodox christology of Catholicism illustrates this, since the Chalcedonian definition (itself a compromise) concedes to the Alexandrians that the human nature in Christ is impersonal: that is, it is not what man knows as human nature, nor what he means by it: the human in Christ must be received by us only through and in his divine nature. Again, as christology conditions and controls ecclesiology, for Roman and Greek Catholicism the Church, too, is deemed to be transformed and sanctified by its divine character. In spite of its finitude, fallibility, and sin—'the inevitable expression of its historical relativity' in this fallen world-order[1]—the Church, too, is 'impersonal' or 'in-human'. To quote Dryden again,[2] the Church is deemed to be the milk-white hind

> ...immortal and unchanged,
> Without unspotted, innocent within,
> She feared no danger, for she knew no sin.

This is dangerously docetist and unreal, to say the least. Again, the Roman doctrine of the eucharistic sacrifice is monophysite in the same way; for the material of the sacrament, bread and wine, is 'filled with divine grace and so transsubstantiated'.[3] Tillich argues that the true sacramentalism 'asserts the reality of supernatural grace *through* the natural; through a form or vehicle *which remains in itself what it is*' (italics mine). Nothing less than the divine is given to us, but it is *through* the full, empirical humanity of Christ the Redeemer; it is *through* the historic weakness and fallibility of the visible Church; it is *through* the finite

[1] Paul Tillich, *The Protestant Era* (University of Chicago Press, 1948), pp. 211–12.
[2] See above, p. 170. [3] Tillich, *op. cit.*

material of baker's bread and vintner's wine. 'The divine', says Tillich, 'appears through these finite realities as their transcendent meaning.'

The genius of orthodox christology, ecclesiology and eucharistic theology (as distinct from monophysite aberrations) is sacramental. Indeed, the Church itself, as the Body of Christ, is the fundamental sacrament. Origen's famous simile of iron, the human element, made to glow by the fire of the divine Logos, is more in harmony with the witness of the New Testament, and with its Hebraic psychology, than is the venerable Chalcedonian formula, even though that formula did maintain the precious truth of the divine incarnation in the man Christ Jesus. Its greatest value for succeeding generations was that it did leave the irresolvable divine-human paradox as such: in intention, at least, it did not overthrow the nature of this supreme sacrament—a truly and fully human life as the outward and visible sign of the eternal God.

4. ONE, HOLY, CATHOLIC AND APOSTOLIC

As the fundamental sacrament, the Church should have some outward and visible character. The profound words of John Oman, quoted on an earlier page with reference to ecclesiastical systems and confessional orthodoxies, define the mood rather than the goal of our oecumenical aspiration. Vague generalities will not help us to move out of our present impasse. Reunion necessarily means some general movement out of schism into a visible and ordered unity, if the words One Body are to mean anything that matters. With the classic credal attributes of the Church as our guide—One, Holy, Catholic and Apostolic—what will such a movement involve?

The Church is One. This means that the Church should have some outwardly manifested unity. Agreement to differ must be genuinely safeguarded, or external unity would merely be the prelude to new schism. But there is a large, positive agreement on the fundamental truths and doctrines of the Christian faith, and this surely provides a broad and firm basis on which to build anew. Pulling down our barns to build greater (Luke xii. 18) has its dangers, but rebuilding will mean some genuine reconstruction. The oecumenical movement will be convincing only when each separated communion is prepared to give up some cherished feature of its own architecture, in the interests of the great design of architectonic unity. To come down to illustrative brass tacks, this means that the writer of this book must be prepared to accept some form of episcopacy, however much this may offend his inherited suspicions of the claims made in its name. This is the immediate and searching demand which the general situation makes upon him: he must leave it to the great episcopalian churches to make a similar recognition that the gathered company of believers must have a constitutive and permanent function within the great Church of the future, such as it has not had in the past.

The Church is Holy. It must, therefore, be a living institution, with some power to insist—in humility and with unfeigned charity—that its membership be not nominal, but believingly personal and real: that its members be actively concerned with the obligations of their discipleship in Christ. All Churches (the writer submits this with great respect) are obsessed with numbers; the numbers of their adherents; as though magnitude were the criterion of spiritual substance. Excommunication has had so ugly a history that modern Christendom has almost ceased to require any searching condition or test of discipleship. And its instinct here is sound enough, since human rules and tests are always as dangerous as they are ultimately impracticable. But though history is eloquent of a thousand difficulties here, the one holy Church of the Christian creed must be able—somehow and in the last resort—to define its terms of admission more exactingly, if only to prevent itself from lapsing into varying forms of religiosity which are incontestably sub-Christian, if not non-Christian.

The Church is Catholic. This means that a reunited Christendom must be able to include all that is of value (a question-begging word, admittedly) in the tradition of the great Christian communions of history, while at the same time correcting the deficiencies due to their past isolation from one another. Unless we are all prepared to take the initiative—without tarrying for any—in admitting and declaring our own deficiencies, the reunion of the Churches is likely to be postponed to the Greek Kalends.

Lastly, the one holy catholic Church is and must remain Apostolic. It is not free to witness to and to live by the mere sentiments of the hour. It is allowed of God to be put in trust with the Gospel. The essential Gospel is what it has been from the beginning, the κήρυγμα, proclaimed in the Words, the Action, the Passion and the Victory of Christ, as handed on to us from his first disciples. Further, it must celebrate the Gospel Sacraments which he instituted; those appointed channels by means of which the redeeming grace of God is verily (*realiter et efficaciter*) conveyed to needy men. Doctrinal differences as to the exact mode whereby the grace of the Gospel operates in the sacraments cannot, of course, be dismissed as a matter for mere academic discussion: no great issues which divide serious people can be. But the essential significance of the sacramental approach to religious truth is that the 'what' is always more important than the 'how'. There is something to be learned from the uncommon sense of that shrewd child of this world, the Tudor Queen Elizabeth, who saw the unity of sixteenth-century Protestantism being wrecked on the rocks of divisive eucharistic controversy, and who is alleged to have written

> He was the Word, who spake it;
> He took the Bread and brake it;
> And what his Word doth make it,
> That I believe, and take it.

This English pragmatism has much to teach us.

In skating so speedily over the thin ice of many a dogmatic controversy, the writer knows that he has raised many questions and answered none. But it may be that the old questions demand a new attitude rather than new answers. The questions must be raised and faced, against the background of that Protestant tradition which it has been the purpose of this essay to interpret and criticize. They must be faced in the light and under the judgement of history: history with all its grievous mistakes, and all its glorious vindications of evangelical truth.

BIBLIOGRAPHY

The literature is vast. A conspectus of much of it is given in
Handbuch der Kirchengeschichte. By G. KRÜGER and others (1923–31):
Vol. III. *Reformation und Gegenreformation*. By H. HERMELINK
(1931); Vol. IV. *Die Neuzeit*. By H. STEPHAN and H. LEUBE (1931).
Lehrbuch der Dogmengeschichte. By R. SEEBERG (1920–33); Vol. III.
Die Dogmengeschichte des Mittelalters (1930); Vol. IV (1). *Die Lehre
Luthers* (1933); Vol. IV (2). *Die Fortbildung der reformatorischen
Lehre und die gegenreformatorische Lehre* (1920).

A comprehensive and useful list of materials in English is given in
The Reformation of the Sixteenth Century by R. H. BAINTON (1952), itself
an excellent introduction to the whole subject. The list which follows
has been selected for the general reader rather than for the specialist.

GENERAL

CURTIS, A. W. Article on 'Confessions' in *Encyclopaedia of Religion and
Ethics* (1908–21).
HEIM, K. *Das Wesen des evangelischen Christentums* (1929), translated
as *Spirit and Truth* by E. P. Dickie (1935).
VON HÜGEL, F. *Essays and Addresses*, especially chs. VIII–X (1921).
KIDD, B. J. *Documents Illustrative of the Continental Reformation* (1911).
LINDSAY, T. M. *A History of the Reformation*, 2 vols. (1906–7).
MACKINNON, J. *The Origins of the Reformation* (1939).
PAUCK, W. *The Heritage of the Reformation* (1950).
TILLICH, P. *The Protestant Era*, especially chs. XI–XV (1948).

LUTHER

The Weimar Edition of Luther's Works (89 volumes, 1883 ff.). Details
of this and other editions are given in Hermelink, *op. cit.* pp. 71–2.
JACOBS, H. E. (ed.). *Works of Martin Luther*, 6 vols. (1915–32).
WACE, H. and BUCHHEIM, C. A. *Luther's Primary Works* (1896).
STROHL, H. *La Substance de l'Evangile selon Luther: Témoignages choisis,
traduits et annotés* (1934).
BAINTON, R. H. *Here I Stand: A Life of Martin Luther* (1950).
BÖHMER, H. *Luther im Lichte der neueren Forschung* (5th ed. 1917),
translated as *Luther in the Light of Recent Research* (1930).

345

CARLSON, E. M. *The Reinterpretation of Luther* (1948).
HILDEBRANDT, F. *Melanchthon, Alien or Ally?* (1946).
HOLL, K. *Gesammelte Aufsätze.* I. *Luther* (1927).
KRAMM, H. H. *The Theology of Martin Luther* (1947).
MACKINNON, J. *Luther and the Reformation*, 4 vols. (1925–30).
NYGREN, A. *Agape and Eros* (English trans., 1937).
REU, M. *Thirty-five years of Luther Research* (1917).
RUPP, E. G. *Luther's Progress to the Diet of Worms* (1951).
RUPP, E. G. *The Righteousness of God* (1953).
WATSON, P. S. *Let God be God* (1947).
WERNLE, P. *Der evangelische Glaube.* I. *Luther* (1918).

CALVIN

Opera Calvini. Edited by W. BAUM, E. CUNITZ and E. REUSS (*Corpus Reformatorum*, vols. XXIX–LXXXVII, 1863–1900).
English translation of Calvin's Works, published by the Calvin Translation Society (1844 f.).
BARTH, P. and NIESEL, W. *Joannis Calvini Opera Selecta* (1926–36).
CHOISY, E. *La Théocratie à Genève au temps de Calvin* (1898).
DOUMERGUE E. *Jean Calvin: Les Hommes et les choses de son temps*, 7 vols. (1899–1927). Especially vol. IV, *La Pensée religieuse de Calvin* (1910); and vol. V, *La Pensée ecclésiastique et la pensée politique de Calvin* (1917).
HENDERSON, G. D. *Presbyterianism* (1954).
IMBART DE LA TOUR, P. *Les Origines de la Réforme.* Especially vol. IV, *Calvin et l'Institution chrétienne* (1935).
Jubilee Essays by E. DOUMERGUE, A. LANG, H. BAVINCK and B. B. WARFIELD, *Calvin and the Reformation* (1909).
MACKINNON, J. *Calvin and the Reformation* (1936).
McNEILL, J. T. *The History and Character of Calvinism* (1954).
MAXWELL, W. D. *An Outline of Christian Worship* (1936).
PERCY, LORD E. *John Knox* (1937).
WALKER, W. *John Calvin* (1906).
WARFIELD, B. B. *Calvin and Calvinism* (1931).
WERNLE, P. *Der evangelische Glaube.* III. *Calvin* (1919).

THE SECT-TYPE

Mennonite Quarterly Review, XXIV (January 1950).
BAINTON, R. H. *The Travail of Religious Liberty* (1951).
BURRAGE, C. *The Early English Dissenters* (1912).

DAVIES, H. *The English Free Churches* (1952).
JONES, R. M. *Studies in Mystical Religion* (1909).
JONES, R. M. *Spiritual Reformers of the Sixteenth and Seventeenth Centuries* (1914).
JORDAN, W. K. *The Development of Religious Toleration in England*, 4 vols. (1932–40).
MANNING, B. L. *The Making of Modern English Religion* (1929).
MANNING, B. L. *Essays in Orthodox Dissent* (1939).
MANNING, B. L. *The Hymns of Watts and Wesley* (1942).
MATTHEWS, A. G. *Calamy Revised* (1934).
MATTHEWS, A. G. *Walker Revised* (1948).
MOFFATT, J. *The Golden Book of John Owen* (1904).
PAYNE, E. A. *The Fellowship of Believers* (1952).
POWICKE, F. J. *Robert Browne* (1910).
POWICKE, F. J. *John Robinson* (1920).
TAYLER, J. J. *A Retrospect of Religious Life in England* (1876).
TROELTSCH, E. *The Social Teaching of the Christian Churches*, 2 vols. (1931). A translation of *Die Soziallehren...* (1911).

MODERN ISSUES

BAINTON, R. H. *Sebastian Castellio and the Toleration Controversy* (1931).
BURY, J. B. *A History of the Papacy in the Nineteenth Century* (1930).
CADOUX, C. J. *Catholicism and Christianity* (1928).
HEILER, F. *Der Katholizismus* (1923).
MICKLEM, N. *The Pope's Men* (1953).
WOOD, H. G. *Religious Liberty To-Day* (1949).

EHRENSTRÖM, N. *Christian Faith and the Modern State* (1937).
HOBHOUSE, W. *The Church and the World in Idea and in History* (1910).
HEADLAM, A. C. and DUNKERLEY, R. (eds.). *The Ministry and the Sacraments* (1937).
'T HOOFT, W. A. V. and OLDHAM, J. H. *The Church and its Function in Society* (1937).

MANSON, T. W. *The Church's Ministry* (1948).
OMAN, J. *The Church and the Divine Order* (1911).
ROBINSON, W. *The Shattered Cross: The Many Churches and the One Church* (1945).
ROUSE, R. and NEILL, S. (eds.). *A History of the Ecumenical Movement, 1517 to 1948* (1954).

INDEX